ABSTRACTS

OF

WILLS

BLADEN COUNTY, NORTH CAROLINA

(1734-1900)

ABSTRACTED, COMPILED AND MIMEOGRAPHED

BY

WANDA S. CAMPBELL

ELIZABETHTOWN, NORTH CAROLINA

This volume was reproduced from
An 1962 edition located in the
Publisher's private library,
Greenville, South Carolina

Please direct all correspondence and orders to:

www.southernhistoricalpress.com
or
SOUTHERN HISTORICAL PRESS, Inc.
PO BOX 1267
375 West Broad Street
Greenville, SC   29601
southernhistoricalpress@gmail.com

Originally published: Elizabethtown, NC. 1962
Reprinted by: Southern Historical Press, Inc.
Greenville, SC
ISBN #0-89308-940-0
All rights Reserved.
Printed in the United States of America

FOREWORD

THE COMPILATION OF THESE WILLS HAS BEEN A HOBBY FOR MANY YEARS. MY LOVE OF BLADEN COUNTY, HER HISTORY AND HER PEOPLE, HAS MOTIVATED THIS BOOK.

SINCE ITS FORMATION IN 1734, SO MUCH OF THE DOCUMENTED HISTORY OF THE COUNTY CONTAINED IN THE OFFICIAL RECORDS HAS BEEN DESTROYED IN THE TWO COURTHOUSE FIRES WHICH HAVE TAKEN PLACE. ACCORDING TO A PLAQUE ON THE WALL OF THE REGISTER OF DEEDS VAULT ALL THE RECORDS WERE DESTROYED IN THE 1765 FIRE. PART OF THE RECORDS WERE AGAIN DESTROYED IN THE FIRE OF 1893.

ALL OF THE BLADEN COUNTY WILLS FROM THE EXTRACTS OF GRIMES' "ABSTRACTS OF NORTH CAROLINA WILLS" 1663-1760 ARE INCLUDED HEREIN. THE OTHER ABSTRACTS HAVE BEEN MADE FROM THE WILLS CONTAINED IN BOOKS 1 AND 2 IN THE OFFICE OF THE CLERK OF THE SUPERIOR COURT AND A FEW WHICH ARE RECORDED IN MISCELLANEOUS DEED BOOKS. I BELIEVE THIS WAS BECAUSE OF RE-RECORDING ORIGINALS, WHEN AVAILABLE, AND RE-COPYING AFTER THE COURTHOUSE FIRES. OFTEN THERE IS NO DATE ON THE WILL AND MORE OFTEN NO DATE OF PROBATE. THE FIRST DATE LISTED IS THAT SHOWN AS THE DATE THE WILL WAS MADE.

IT IS MY SINCERE DESIRE THAT THESE ABSTRACTS WILL CREATE A GREATER INTEREST IN THE HISTORY OF BLADEN COUNTY AND HER PEOPLE.

ELIZABETHTOWN, N. C.
JULY 1962

WANDA S. (MRS. CARL C. CAMPBELL)

EXTRACTS FROM

GRIMES' ABSTRACTS OF NORTH CAROLINA WILLS,

1690 - 1760

NOTE: ONLY WILLS LISTED AS BLADEN COUNTY ARE INCLUDED.

ADAMS, ROGER   AUGUST 2, 1739. AUGUST 6, 1739
     WIFE AND EXECUTRIX: FRANCES. OTHER LEGATEES: LUCY
AND JOHN GREEN, GABRIEL JOHNSTON, SAMUEL WOODWARD, JAMES
INNES, JAMES MURRAY. WITNESSES: THOMAS HART, ROBERT
KNOWLS, JAMES MENZIES. PROVEN BEFORE GABRIEL JOHNSTON.

BARTRAM, ELIZABETH   DECEMBER 27, 1771. AUGUST COURT,
                                              1772
     (WIFE OF WM. BARTRAM) DAUGHTERS: SARAH BROWN,
WIFE OF THOMAS BROWN, MARY ROBESON, WIFE OF THOMAS ROBESON.
EXECUTORS: THOMAS BROWN (SON-IN-LAW), AND SARAH BROWN
(DAUGHTER). WITNESSES: JNO. JONES, HENRIETTA JONES,
MARY LYON. CLERK: MATURIN COLVILL.

BENBOW, GERSHON   JANUARY 12, 1750.
     SONS: POWELL, RICHARD AND EVANS. DAUGHTER:
SUSANNAH. EXECUTORS: POWELL BENBOW (SON) AND CHARLES
BENBOW (BROTHER). WITNESSES: ABRAM SANDERS, RICHARD
MAY, JOHN JONES.

BLANING, HUGH   MAY 10, 1751, MARCH COURT 1752.
     WIFE AND EXECUTRIX: ELIZABETH. WIFE'S CHILDREN:
WILLIAM AND ELIZABETH HALL. SISTER: SARAH STAR.
EXECUTOR: MATTHEW ROWAN. WITNESSES: ROBERT DOWIE,
THOS. HALL. CLERK: THOS. ROBESON.

CALDWELL, ROBERT   MARCH 24, 1749. JUNE 20, 1750
     WIFE AND TWO SONS MENTIONED, BUT NOT NAMED.
BROTHER: JOSHUA CALDWELL. FRIEND: WILLIAM NEALE.
EXECUTORS: JOSHUA CALWELL (BROTHER), JOSEPH CLARK.
WITNESSES: GERSHON BENBOW, JOHN LEARY, SAMUEL NEALE.
CLERK: THOS. ROBESON.

CARVER, JAMES   MAY 7, 1738. JUNE 7, 1739
WIFE AND EXECUTRIX: ELIZABETH: SONS AND EXECUTORS: JAMES (LAND ON NORTH SIDE OF THE NORTH WEST RIVER), SAMUEL. DAUGHTERS: MARY BENBOW, ANN CARVER. WITNESSES: RICHARD HELLIER, ANN HELLIER. WILL PROVEN BEFORE GAB. JOHNSTON.

CARVER, JAMES   FEBRUARY 27, 1753. JUNE COURT, 1753
WIFE & EXECUTRIX: ELIZABETH. SON: JOB. DAUGHTER: ELIZABETH CARVER. BROTHER AND EXECUTOR: SAMUEL CARVER. WITNESSES: RICHARD MALLINGTON, PATRICK MCKONKEY, GEORGE WILLIS. CLERK: THOS. ROBESON. THE TESTATOR DEVISES TWO ACRES OF LAND "WHERE THE MEETING HOUSE NOW STANDS," "TO OUR SOCIETY OF PEOPLE CALLED QUAKERS."

CARVER, SAMUEL   APRIL 23, 1758. JULY COURT, 1758
WIFE AND EXECUTRIX: ARCADIA. SONS: SAMUEL, JAMES. DAUGHTERS: SARAH AND MARY CARVER. BROTHER: WILLIAM MAULTSBY. WITNESSES: SAML. MILHOUS, CHARLES BENBOW, RICHARD MALLINGTON. CLERK: C. BURGWIN.

CLARK, JAMES, SENR.   APRIL 26, 1757. ON COW BRANCH UPON DROWNING CREEK. THIS IS MORE A DEED OF ASSIGNMENT THAN A WILL AND ASSIGNS ALL RIGHT, TITLE AND INTEREST OF JAMES CLARK OF "THE PLANTATION I NOW LIVE UPON" TO JOHN STACK. WITNESSES: WILLIAM BARTRAM, JOHN MITCHELL.

DAVIS, DAVID   DECEMBER 9, 1740. SEPTEMBER COURT, 1741.
SISTER: RACHEL DAVIS (PLANTATION PURCHASED OF GABRIEL WAYNE). EXECUTOR: WILLIAM BARTRAM. WITNESSES: JONOTHAN EVANS, THOS. WALKER, THOMAS JONES. CLERK: JOHN CLAYTON.

DAVIS, THOMAS   OCTOBER 2, 1761. MAY COURT 1769.
DAUGHTER-IN-LAW: KATHERINE GREADY. DAUGHTER: MARY GREADY. BROTHER: WILLIAM DAVIS. EXECUTORS: WILLIAM DAVIS AND JOHN LUCAS. WITNESSES: JNO. TURNER, RALPH MILLER, THOS. NEWTON. CODICIL TO WILL APPOINTS ANN DAVIS (WIFE) AND THOMAS OWEN, EXECUTORS IN PLACE OF WILLIAM DAVIS AND JOHN LUCAS. WITNESSES TO CODICIL: THOS. HALL, JOHN ROOT, RALPH MILLER. CLERK: ARTHUR HOWE.

DOWAY, ROBERT　　　　JANUARY 30, 1756. JANUARY COURT, 1758.

WIFE: CATHERINE. SONS: JAMES AND ROBERT. DAUGHTER: ELIZABETH. WITNESSES: JOHN STACK, HENRY LEWIS, JAMES WHITE. CLERK: J. BURGWIN.

EAGAN, JAMES　　　　OCTOBER 30, 1737. MARCH COURT, 1738.

"CAPE FARE, IN BLADEN PRECINCT". WIFE AND DAUGHTER: MENTIONED BUT NOT NAMED. EXECUTOR: WILLIAM CARY. WITNESSES: THOMAS LOCK, WILLIAM BARTRAM, ARTHUR DANIEL. CLERK: RICHARD HETEIER.

EDWARDS, CATHERINE　　MAY 2, 1755. OCTOBER COURT, 1755.

SON AND EXECUTOR: ROBERT. DAUGHTER: ANN SUTTON. GRANDSONS: JOHN, SAMUEL AND ISAAC HOLLINGSWORTH. EXECUTOR: VALENTINE HOLLINGSWORTH. WITNESSES: JAMES PROTHRO, JEREMIAH PROTHRO, ANN D. LAURENCY. CLERK: EDWARD NUGENT.

GREEN, JOHN　　　　APRIL 28, 1749. JUNE COURT, 1749.

WIFE: MENTIONED, BUT NOT NAMED. SONS: JAMES, ROBERT, JOHN. DAUGHTER: SARAH. EXECUTORS: JAMES GRANGE AND JAMES CARR. WITNESSES: JOHN ELISS, JOHN STUBBS, JAMES JONES, DAVID MONLEY. CLERK: THOS. ROBESON.

HALL, WILLIAM　　　FEBRUARY 6, 1764. APRIL 21, 1765.

WIFE AND EXECUTRIX: ELIZABETH. WITNESSES: A. GREEN, JAMES HENDERSON, MARY GREEN. PROVEN BEFORE WM. TRYON AT WILMINGTON.

HAMILTON, JOHN　　　OCTOBER 22, 1764. FEBRUARY COURT, 1765.

WIFE AND EXECUTRIX: ESTHER. SON: JAMES. OTHER LEGATEE: ESABEL HAMILTON. EXECUTOR: WM. CREE. WITNESSES: JOHN KENNEY, LEVI MOORE. JUSTICES: GEORGE BROWN, JOHN SMITH, JOHN TURNER, GEORGE GIBBS, JOSEPH CLARK. CLERK: MATURIN COLVILL.

HOG, RICHARD　　　JUNE 18, 1768. SEPTEMBER 21, 1769.

SISTER: ELIZABETH HOG OF TISHERAW, IN THE PARISH OF INVERESK IN NORTH BRITTAIN. EXECUTORS: ROBERT

4

JOHNSTON, ROBERT AND JOHN HOGG. WITNESSES: WILLIAM BARTRAM, THOMAS BAYLY, LILLAH JOHNSTON. PROVEN BEFORE WM. TRYON.

HOUGHTON, THOMAS   JANUARY COURT, 1743.
    WIFE AND EXECUTRIX: ELIZABETH. DAUGHTER: MARY HOUGHTON. BROTHERS AND EXECUTORS: JOSHUA AND WILLIAM HOUGHTON. WITNESSES: DAVID BUTLER, MARY BUTLER. CLERK: RICH'D MCCLURE.

HUMPHREY, JOSEPH   OCTOBER 14, 1752. DECEMBER COURT 1752.
    COUSIN: SARAH ROBERTS. NEPHEW: JOSEPH HUMPHREY. FRIEND: EVAN ELLIS. TO CARVERS CREEK MEETING IS GIVEN THREE POUNDS. EXECUTORS:: JONOTHAN EVANS AND ISAAC JONES. WITNESSES: ALEXANDER MCCONKEY, THOMAS SPEIRS. CLERK: THOS. ROBESON

JONES, ARTHUR   OCTOBER 21, 1750. DECEMBER COURT, 1750.
    SONS: LEWIS, SIPHRES. DAUGHTER: ANN JONES. EXECUTORS: GERSHON BENBOW, GRIFFITH JONES. WITNESSES: CYPRIAN SHIPHERD, SAMUEL PIKE. CLERK: THOS. ROBESON

JONES, EDWARD   OCTOBER 8, 1751. SEPTEMBER COURT 1752.
    WIFE: SUSANNA. SON AND EXECUTOR: ISAAC. DAUGHTERS: HANNAH LOCK, JANE ENECKS. GRANDSONS: ISAAC AND WILLIAM ENECKS. GRANDDAOGHTER: ANN ENECKS. TO CARVERS CREEK MEETING IS GIVEN TEN POUNDS. WITNESSES: JOHN SMITH, WM. SIBBLY, JOHN GRAY. JUSTICES: BENJAMIN FITZRANDOLPH, HENRY SIMMOND, JONATHAN EVENS. CLERK: THOS. ROBESON.

JORDAN, DEBORAH   SEPTEMBER 4, 1769. FEBRUARY 14, 1770
    BROTHERS: ITHAMAR AND JOHN SINGLETARY. DAUGHTER: MARGARET GIBSON. NIECE: DEBROAH SINGLETARY (DAUGHTER OF ITHAMAR). EXECUTORS: JOHN SINGLETARY (BROTHER) AND WALTER GIBSON (SON-IN-LAW). WITNESSES: JOHN RUSS, EPH'M. MULFORD, JOSEPH POWERS. WILL PROVEN BEFORE WM. TRYON.

LENNON, JOHN   OCTOBER 13, 1757. OCTOBER COURT, 1757.

  PARISH OF ST. MARTIN'S. WIFE AND EXECUTRIX: ANN. SONS: JOHN, ("THIS LAND I NOW LIVE ON"), DENIS (LAND ON WACCAMAW SWAMP), EPHRIAM. DAUGHTER: PHILLIS ELLICE. EXECUTOR AND SON-IN-LAW: EVEN. WITNESSES: SAM'L BAKER, WM. MCREE, MARY MACKKEY. CLERK: JNO. BURGWIN.

LOCK, BENJAMIN   APRIL 25, 1756. JANUARY COURT, 1757.

  WIFE: MIRIAM. SON: JOHN. EXECUTORS: NEIL BEARD (FATHER) AND JOHN LOCK, (BROTHER). WITNESSES: THOMAS THEMS, DANIEL BEARD, ELIZABETH LOCK. CLERK: THOS. ROBESON.

LOCK, THOMAS   AUGUST 29, 1739. DECEMBER 19, 1739.

  WIFE AND EXECUTRIX: SUSANNAH. SONS: BENJAMIN, DAVID AND LEONARD. JOSEPH (LAND ON NORTHWEST RIVER). DAUGHTERS: ELIZABETH BARTRAM, MARY LOCK. WITNESSES: THOMAS WIER, PETER WALLSON, WILLIS HUGHES. PROVEN BEFORE GAB. JOHNSTON AT BROMPTON.

LYON, JAMES   APRIL 27, 1752. JUNE COURT, 1752.
  WIFE AND EXECUTRIX: ZILLAH. SON: GEORGE. DAUGHTERS: ANN, ELIZABETH, MARY. EXECUTORS: MATT. ROWAN, JOHN LYON. WITNESSES: THOS. ROBESON, RICH'D. MULLINGTON, ROBERT WILSON. CLERK: THOS. ROBESON.

McCLALLAND, ANDREW MARCH 21, 1752.

  GRANDCHILDREN: THOMAS, JANE, ANDREW AND JAMES McCLALLAND. EXECUTOR: ANDREW McCLALLAND (SON-IN-LAW). WITNESSES: GEORGE BROWN, BENJA. MOOR, BENJ. FITZRANDOLPH. CLERK: THOS. ROBESON.

McKEITHAN, DUGALD JANUARY 1, 1750-1751. MARCH COURT, 1750.

  WIFE: MARY. FATHER: DONALD McKEITHAN. BROTHER: JAMES McKEITHAN. COUSINS: JOHN McKEITHAN, JAMES McKEITHAN. SISTERS: NANCY McLAUCHLIN, SARAH McKEITHAN. SON-IN-LAW: ROBERT HILLYARD. NIECE: MARY McKEITHAN. WITNESSES: HECT. McNEILL, ALEXR. McALESTER, ANGUS SHAW. CLERK: THOS. ROBESON.

MacLEARAN, ARCHIBALD   OCTOBER 26, 1751.   DECEMBER COURT,
1751.
     WIFE AND EXECUTRIX: FLORENCE.   SONS: JOHN AND
ARCHIBALD.   EXECUTOR: DUNCAN MCLEARAN.   WITNESSES:
DUSHEE SHAW, ARCHIBALD MACDONALD, DUNCAN MACFEE.   CLERK:
THOMAS ROBESON.

MacNAUGHTEN, RANALD   OCTOBER 5, 1752.   DECEMBER 19,
1752.
     WIFE: ISABELL.   SONS: NEILL AND CHARLES.   DAUGHTER:
MARY.   EXECUTORS: DUNCAN AND NEILL MACCOULASKIE.
WITNESSES: ANGUISH SHAW, JOHN OPTAN, JOHN CAMPBELL.
JUSTICES OF BLADEN COUNTY COURT: GRIFFITH JONES AND
BENJAMIN FITZRANDOLPH.   CLERK: THOS. ROBESON.

MAULTSBY, JOHN   OCTOBER 5, 1749.   JULY 29, 1757.
     WIFE AND EXECUTRIX: MARY.   SONS: JOHN AND WILLIAM.
DAUGHTERS: HANNAH ROOTS, MARY AND SARAH.   WITNESSES:
ROBT. FORSHA, JOHN JONES, WILLIAM HARRISON.   CLERK:
THOS. ROBESON.   JUSTICES OF THE PEACE: CALEB HOWEL,
E. CARTLIDGE.

MOORHEAD, JAMES   APRIL 4, 1759.   JULY COURT, 1759.
     WIFE AND EXECUTRIX: SARAH.   SONS: WILLIAM AND
JAMES.   DAUGHTERS: JANE AND SARAH.   EXECUTOR: ALEXAN-
DER MCCONKEY.   WITNESSES: PETER CATES, LAWRENCE BYRNE,
MARY ARINTON.   CLERK: J. BURGWIN.

NESSFEILD, JOHN   MARCH 27, 1764.   APRIL 20, 1764.
     WIFE AND EXECUTRIX: ANN.   OTHER LEGATEES: THOMAS
WHITE AND WIFE, ANN.   EXECUTOR: JOHN ROBESON OF WILMING-
TON.   WITNESSES: HU. WADDELL, JAMES BAILEY, EDW. BRYAN.
PROVEN BEFORE ARTHUR DOBBS.   TESTATOR PROVIDES FOR SALE
OF ALL HIS ESTATE, PROCEEDS TO BE INVESTED IN YOUNG
FEMALE SLAVES FOR USE OF WIFE AND CHILDREN.

NEWTON, THOMAS   SEPTEMBER 7, 1765.
     WIFE AND EXECUTRIX: MARY.   SON: JOHN.   DAUGHTER:
JANE.   EXECUTOR: CORNELIUS HARNETT.   WITNESSES: WILL'M.
BARTRAM, JACOB MEZIES.

NORTON, WILLIAM   DECEMBER 1, 1746.   SEPTEMBER
COURT, 1751.
     SONS: WILLIAM, DANIEL, JACOB, THOMAS.   DAUGHTER:
ELIZABETH.   EXECUTORS: JACOB AND THOMAS NORTON.
WITNESSES: WM. LEWIS, JOHN MITCHELL, JOSIAH LEWIS,
CLERK, THOS. ROBESON.

PORTER, SAMUEL   SEPTEMBER 30, 1757. OCTOBER
                                            COURT, 1757.
     SONS: JAMES, JOHN, HUGH AND SAMUEL. EXECUTORS:
PETER LORD AND WILLIAM MCREE. WITNESSES: MATTHEW BYRNE,
NATHL PLATT, JOHN LOCK. CLERK: J. BURGWIN.

RAYFORD, MATTHEW   JULY 21, 1752. APRIL COURT, 1758.
     WIFE AND EXECUTRIX: MOURNING. SONS: MATTHEW,
ROBERT, WILLIAM AND PHILIP. DAUGHTERS: MARY, ANNE,
MOURNING, REBECKAH, GRACE AND DRUSILLA. EXECUTOR:
ISAAC BUSH. WITNESSES: MARGARET ARMSTRONG, FRANK ARM-
STRONG, AND THOMAS JONES. CLERK OF COURT OF CUMBERLAND
COUNTY: JAMES SIMPSON.

ROURK, EDMOND   MAY 15, 1769. DECEMBER 16, 1769.
     "PARISH OF ST. MARTIANS IN THE COUNTY OF BLADEN."
WIFE: DOROTHY. SON AND EXECUTOR: SAMUEL. DAUGHTER:
MARY ADDISON. OTHER LEGATEES: HENRY MCCOY. WITNESSES:
MARY ADDISON, DAVID MORLEY. PROVEN BEFORE WILLIAM TRYON.

SIMMONDS. HENRY   JANUARY 9, 1758. JANUARY COURT,
                                              1758.
     BROTHERS: WILLIAM SIMMONDS, BENINJR MOORE. SISTERS:
ANN MOORE, JUDITH DAVIS. OTHER LEGATEE: EDMUND FOG-
ARTY. EXECUTOR: BENINJR. MOORE, WILLIAM SIMMONDS, THOS.
HALL. WITNESSES: MARY SMITH, JOHN GRANGE, SAM'L.
WATTERS. CLERK: J. BURGWIN.

THOMAS, FRANCIS   JUNE 8, 1756. OCTOBER COURT,
                                              1756.
     WIFE AND EXECUTRIX: JOAN. SON: GEORGE. WITNESS-
ES: THOS. HALL, LUCY HALL, THOMAS SMITH. CLERK: J.
BURGWIN.

THOMAS, THOMAS   MARCH 6, 1758. APRIL COURT, 1758.
     WIFE AND EXECUTRIX: PRUDENCE. SONS: SAMUEL,
JOSEPH, CORNELIUS, THOMAS (LAND IN CRAVEN ON FLAT SWAMP),
JOHN AND AMOS. DAUGHTERS: PHEBE, MARTHA AND ELIZABETH
THOMAS, PRISCILLA DUNN, WITNESSES: JOSIAH EVANS,
JONOTHAN EVANS. CLERK: J. BURGWIN.

TYLER, MOSES   JUNE 25, 1762. AUGUST 9, 1762.
     WIFE AND EXECUTRIX: SARAH. SONS: NEEDHAM, OWEN,
MOSES. DAUGHTERS: PENELEBY, ELISABETH, CHRISTIAN AND
LUCRETIA TYLER. EXECUTOR: JOS. HOWARD. WITNESSES:

ROBERT STEWART, ITHAMAR SINGLETARY, JOHN FLOYD. PROVED
BEFORE ARTHUR DOBBS.

WILKINSON, PHILLIP   FEBRUARY 24, 1757. JULY COURT,
                                            1758.
     WIFE AND EXECUTRIX: MARTHA. SONS: THOMAS (LAND ON
WILKESON'S CREEK), RICHARD AND JOHN WILLIAM. DAUGHTERS:
ELIZABETH, MARY AND MARGARET WILLIAMS. WITNESSES:
BENJAMIN SLUYTER, THOMAS PLATT, ALEXANDER MCCONKEY.
CLERK: J. BURGWIN.

WORTH, JOHN   AUGUST 1, 1743. SEPTEMBER COURT,
                                            1743.
     FATHER: JOHN WORTH OF NEW JERSEY. SISTER: ELIZA-
BETH. COUSIN AND EXECUTOR: JOSEPH CLARK OF NEW HANOVER
COUNTY. WITNESSES: THOMAS WAMAN, E. VERNON, JOHN
WILLIAMSON. CLERK: JOHN CLAYTON.

ABSTRACTS OF

BLADEN COUNTY WILLS

ADAIR, JAMES   SEPTEMBER 21, 1778
    DAUGHTERS: SARANNA MCTYER, ELIZABETH HOLESON CADE,
AGNES GIBSON. GRANDSONS: STEPHEN, JAMES & WASHINGTON
CADE, ADAIR MCTYER, WILLIAM MCTYER, ELIZABETH, CLARK,
RATRAIN ADAIR. OTHER LEGATEES: ROBERT ADAIR (IN IRE-
LAND), JAMES BOX, ALEXANDER JOHNSTON, JOHN GIBSON. "I
DO DESIRE NONE OF MY ESTATE MAY BE SOLD BY ORDER OF COURT
WHEN GOODS COME AS CHEAP AS THEY HAVE IN THE YEAR 1774."
EXECUTRIX: DAUGHTER, SARANNA MCTYER. WITNESSES: ARCH'D
MCKISSACK, BENILLA BULLARD.

ALLEN, EPHRAIM W.   NOVEMBER 1, 1855. FEBRUARY TERM,
                                              1868.
    WIFE: ANN. SONS & EXECUTORS: HUGH & HENRY ALLEN.
DAUGHTERS: MARGARET BRYAN, NANCY EVERS, MOLEY ROBERTS,
JANE BRYAN, GRANDDAUGHTER: HELEN SOPHIA BRISSON. OTHER
LEGATEE: AARON EVERS. WITNESSES: C. MONROE, THOMAS J.
SERIVIN, DUNCAN KELLY. CLERK: D. BLUE. DEPUTY CLERK:
L. J. HALL.

ALLEN, HENRY   MAY 1, 1890. JUNE 2, 1890.
    WIFE: EDNA. SON: HENRY NATHAN. EXECUTOR: A. M.
MCNEILL. WITNESSES: NATHAN JONES, W. F. DEVANE. CLERK:
GEO. F. MELVIN.

ALLEN, JOHN   FEBRUARY 23, 1875. FEBRUARY 4,
                                              1884.
    WIFE & EXECUTRIX: E. P. ALLEN. SONS: SIMPSON,
JOHN. (OTHER CHILDREN NOT NAMED) WITNESSES: DAVID
ALLEN, E. M. ROBESON. CLERK: G. F. MELVIN.

ALLEN, JOSEPH   DECEMBER 28, 1847. MAY TERM,
                                              1864.
    WIFE: ANN. SONS: JOSEPH B., CHARLES W., WILLIAM
R., DAVID LEWIS, COLEMAN. DAUGHTERS: (NOT NAMED).
EXECUTORS: NATHAN BRYAN, DAVID LEWIS. WITNESSES:
G. D. ROBESON, DANIEL WILLIS. CLERK: D. BLUE

ANDERS, JOHN, JR.   (NUNCUPATIVE WILL) DIED SEPTEMBER
                                                    8, 1796.
    FATHER & FAMILY (NOT NAMED. WITNESSES: LARRY
SUTTON, BAILEY SUTTON, WILLIAM ANDRES.

ANDERS, SIMON & MARIN MAY 4, 1897.
    CATHERINE SCOTT, GUARDIAN OF OUR CHILDREN. WITNESS-
ES: W. K. ANDERS, TIBBY MURPHY. CLERK: W. J. SUTTON.

ANDRES, B.   FEBRUARY 21, 1804. DAUGHTER:
ANNE JEAN WHITE. SONS: HAYES GRAHAM WHITE, WILLIAM
HAYES BEATTY (MY ELDEST SON)., JAMES BENBURY WHITE.
EXECUTOR: WILLIAM WATTS JONES. WITNESS: CHARLES CARNS.

ANDRES, EDWIN FRANKLIN OCTOBER 17, 1844. CODICIL:
    BROTHER & EXECUTOR: W. S.ANDRES   JANUARY 2, 1845.
(MY PLANTATION "RAMAH"). SISTERS: ELIZA, MARY, SOPHIA,
LUCY, SALLY, AUNT: MRS. ANN BROWN. EXECUTOR :
JOSIAH MAULTSBY. WITNESSES: JOHN KING, C. R. COUNCIL

ANDRES, ELIZA B.   JULY 12, 1887. OCTOBER 12, 1887.
    SISTERS: SOPHIA ANDRES, MARY TROY. NEPHEWS: A. A.
TROY, T. A. JONES. NIECE: E. S. JONES. COUNSEL, J. A.
MAULTSBY OF WHITEVILLE. EXECUTRIX: SISTER, SOPHIA
ANDRES. WITNESSES: J. S. DEVANE, J. D. DEVANE. CLERK:
GEO. F. MELVIN.

ANDRES, SAMUEL B.   MARCH 26, 1837. CODICILS: JULY
    15, 1838. MARCH 24, 1840. WIFE: FLORA ANN. SONS:
WILLIAM SAMUEL & EDWIN FRANKLIN. (MY TWO PLANTATIONS,
RAMAH AND PORTER'S NECK). DAUGHTERS: MARY, ELIZA,
SOPHIA, LUCY AND SALLIE. (GIVES SON WILLIAM "THE EN-
CYCLOPEDIA AMERICAN" AND "THE WHOLE OF MY MEDICAL BOOKS").
"MARRIAGE AGREEMENT BETWEEN WIFE BEFORE MARRIAGE IN
JUNE 1836, WILL SHOW SHE NOT TO EXPECT TO RECEIVE ANY
PART OF MY PROPERTY." AUNT: ANN BROWN. OTHER LEGATEE:
LUCY BROWN, DAUGHTER OF GEORGE W. BROWN. EXECUTORS:
GOVERNOR JOHN OWEN AND ISAAC WRIGHT. WITNESSES: THOS.
H. BYRNE, A. DOWNIE, JOHN B. BROWN.

ANDRES, SOPHIA   SEPT. 14, 1897. OCTOBER 8, 1897.
    NEPHEWS: ALEXANDER A. TROY, THOMAS A. JONES.
NIECE: LIZZIE S. DEVANE. EXECUTOR: THOMAS A. JONES.
WITNESSES: LEE SMITH, T. HARVEY GILLESPIE, ANNA GUION

STITH. CLERK: W. J. SUTTON

ANDRES, WILLIAM S. *NOVEMBER 1, 1847. AUG. TERM 1849.*
"MY PLANTATION KNOWN AS PORTERS NECK OR STRAWBERRY HILL." "I GIVE ALL MY SLAVES THEIR FREEDOM, CONDITION OF THEIR REMOVAL TO COLONY OF LIBERIA IN AFRICA, AND I HEREBY BEQUEATH TO THEM THE SUM OF FIVE HUNDRED DOLLARS TO AID THE COLONIZATION SOCIETY IN REMOVING THEM AS SPEEDILY AS POSSIBLE TO SAID COLONY." COUSIN: WILLIAM ANDRES CUMMING OF GREENSBORO, N. C. SISTERS: (NOT NAMED). OTHER LEGATEES: MRS. ANN J. CUMMINGS OF ELIZABETHTOWN. EXECUTOR: ROBERT E. TROY, ESQ. WITNESSES: WM. ELWELL, CHARLES R. COUNCIL. CLERK: H. H. ROBINSON

ANDREWS, JAMES M. *FEBRUARY 4, 1850.*
WIFE: ELIZABETH. SON: JAMES WASHINGTON ANDREWS. DAUGHTERS: MARGARET ELIZABETH MERIDETH, ELIZA KELLY ANDREWS, CATHERINE JANE BANNERMAN, HANNAH ANN ANDREWS. EXECUTOR: COLIN SHAW. WITNESSES: J. T. LEACH, WALTER R. MOORE.

ANDREWS, JOHN *MARCH 8, 1850*
EXECUTORS & SONS: WILLIAM W., PATRICK S. DAUGHTERS: ANN C., HANNAH J., ELIZABETH, MARY. GRANDDAUGHTERS: MARY E. JOHNSON, SARAH A. JOHNSON. WITNESSES: G. W. BANNERMAN, TIMOTHY PRIDGEN.

ASHFORD, STREET *JANUARY 3, 1816*
WIFE: ANN. DAUGHTERS: ANN & HUSBAND, JOHN MCGILL, LENORA KING & HUSBAND, GEORGE KING. GRANDSON: ASHFORD BRYAN MCGILL. EXECUTOR: JOHN MCGILL. WITNESSES: ANN BAKER, ANN WILLIAMSON.

ATKINSON, WILLIE *NOV. TERM 1857.*
WIFE: SUSANNA. DAUGHTERS: MARY SIKES, WIFE OF LUKE SIKES. (KINCHEN K. COUNCIL, TRUSTEE OF MY DAUGHTER MARY, LANDS KNOWN AS THE SALTER LAND) ANN SUTTON, JANE HOLTON, WIFE OF JAMES HOLTON (LANDS IN COLUMBUS COUNTY), SON AND EXECUTOR: WILIE ALFORD ATKINSON (LANDS ON SINGLETARY LAKE AND COLLY LANDS KNOWN AS THE HAYNES). GRANDSONS: JOSIAH PRIDGEN AND HENRY MITCHELL SIKES, SONS OF MARY AND LUKE SIKES. GRANDDAUGHTERS: CATHERINE ANN COUNCIL, MARY ELIZA MELVIN, ANN SIKES (CHILDREN OF LUKE AND MARY SIKES). GREAT GRANDDAUGHTER: EMILY JANE CURRIE. WITNESSES: NEILL GRAHAM, JOHN J. MELVIN. CLERK: F. F. CUMMING.

AVERITT, DEMPSEY, SR. SEPTEMBER 14, 1848. NOV. TERM 1848.
WIFE: DORCAS. SONS & EXECUTORS: WILLIAM AVERITT,
ROBERT A. AVERITT, FRIEND & EXECUTOR: RAIFORD FISHER.
WITNESSES: WM. C. THAGGARD, JOHN AVERITT. CLERK: H. H.
ROBINSON.

AVERY, MARY   JANUARY 18, 1875. JUNE 27, 1877.
SONS & EXECUTORS: JOHN A. BURNEY, FRANKLIN BURNEY,
JAMES BURNEY. DAUGHTERS: SALLIE, WIFE OF C. MARTIN,
ELLEN, WIFE OF JAMES EVANS, MARY E., WIFE OF AMOS BAKER.
FATHER: JOSEPH WILSON. OTHER LEGATEES: JOSEPH S. BURNEY,
WASTON BURNEY. WITNESSES: ALEX W. KINLAW, JOHN PRICE
(OR RICE). JUDGE OF PROBATE: E. SINGLETARY.

BACON, EDWIN WANE   6 DECEMBER 1893. 15 JANUARY 1894.
FRIEND: ANN JANE MELVIN, WIFE OF DAVID B. MELVIN.
SISTER: SARAH B. DORTCH OF DURHAM, N. C. OTHER LEGATEE:
WILLIAM T. BACON OF DURHAM, N. C. EXECUTOR: JAMES B.
YOUNG. WITNESSES: CHARLES T. DAVIS, T. J. JOHNSON.
CLERK: GEO. F. MELVIN.

BAILEY, THOMAS   AUGUST 11, 1767.
WIFE & EXECUTRIX: HESTER. SON: THOMAS. EXECUTOR:
JOSEPH FORDS. WITNESSES: JACOB PITTMAN, JOSEPH FORT.

BALDWIN, JOHN, SR.   NOVEMBER 5, 1791.
SONS & EXECUTORS: JOHN, CHARLES, WILLIAM.
DAUGHTERS: SARAH, BETSEY, ANNA, NANCY. WITNESSES:
MOSES RICHARDSON, JOSEPH M. CARLISLE, J. LEWIS.

BALDWIN (BAULDWIN), WILLIAM SEPTEMBER 21, 1801.
WIFE & EXECUTRIX: PENELOPE. DAUGHTERS: ELIZABETH,
ESTHER, PENELOPE. SONS & EXECUTORS: CHARLES, DAVID
& WILLIAM. WITNESSES: WILLIAM BAULDWIN, JONOTHAN BRYAN,
CHARLES BALDWIN.

BALLENTINE, GEORGE W. JULY 3, 1862. FEB. TERM 1866.
"SERVING AT PRESENT TIME IN THE ARMY AS CORPORAL
IN CAPT. TAIT'S COMPANY OF ARTILLERY, STATIONED AT FORT
ST. PHILIP, BRUNSWICK COUNTY, STATE OF N. C." MOTHER:
CATHERINE BALLENTINE. OTHER LEGATEE: MALCOM MCLEOD,
SR. EXECUTOR: HUGH C. MCCOLLOM. WITNESSES: GEORGE
TAIT, D. J. CLARK. CLERK: D. BLUE

BARFIELD, RICHARD   MAY 13, 1785
     WIFE & EXECUTRIX: ANN. SONS: ELISHA, WILLIS,
SHADRACK, BODERICK. DAUGHTERS: UNITY EDWARDS, URIDIA
HARRELL, MARY FLOWERS. EXECUTOR: SON, ELISHA BARFIELD.
WITNESSES: JESSE JERNIGAN, JAMES INMAN.

BARNHILL, A. J.   DECEMBER 7, 1882. MARCH 24, 1883.
     WIFE & EXECUTRIX: MARGARET. SON: JOHN R. BARNHILL.
WITNESSES: A. J. BORDEAUX, N. H. BARNHILL. JUDGE OF
PROBATE: G. F. MELVIN.

BARNHILL, CATHARINE ANN_ JULY 19, 1878. AUGUST 5, 1878.
     FRENCHES CREEK TOWNSHIP. SON: COLUMBUS ANDERS.
SISTER: ELIZABETH L. LARKINS. OTHER LEGATEES: MARGARET
SHERMAN, WILLIE SHERMAN (SON OF MARGARET), BETHIA ROBE-
SON KELLY, REV. J. W. FAISON, ANN M. BOSWELL, PRISILLA
BOSWELL, ELLEN BOSWELL, LEWIS C. BOSWELL, ANN SOPHIA
GLISSON. EXECUTOR: FRANKLIN J. ANDERS. WITNESSES:
FREDERICK THOMPSON, LEWIS F. BOSWELL, JAMES SHOARD.
JUDGE OF PROBATE: EVANDER SINGLETARY.

BEARD, CATHARINE L.   DECEMBER 5, 1874. MARCH 16, 1875.
     SISTERS: ELIZA S. MELVIN, MARGARET M. MELVIN, ANN
C. WEST. BROTHER: JAMES S. BEARD. EXECUTOR: WILLIAM
S. MELVIN. WITNESSES: DAVID MILES MELVIN, R. A. MELVIN.
JUDGE OF PROBATE: EVANDER SINGLETARY.

BEARD, ELIZABETH   MAY 2, 1853. CODICIL: APRIL 16,
     1872. SEPTEMBER 4, 1872. DAUGHTERS: KATHERINE,
MARGARET, ELIZA MELVIN, ANN C. WEST. SON: JAMES S.
BEARD. EXECUTOR: WILLIAM S. MELVIN. WITNESSES: OWEN
SMITH, JAMES MELVIN, D. M. MELVIN, R. A. MELVIN. CLERK:
D. BLUE.

BEARD JOHN: JULY 6, 1835
     WIFE AND CHILDREN MENTIONED, BUT NOT NAMED. EXECU-
TORS: JOHN STOKES PEARSON. WITNESSES: JOHN BRYAN
AND RICHARD SIKES.

BEARD, NEILL (PLANTER) FEBRUARY 17, 1772.
     WIFE, CATHERINE. SONS: JAMES, JOHN, DANIEL.
DAUGHTER: CATHERINE MOORE. EXECUTORS: SONS, JOHN &
JAMES BEARD. WITNESSES: ANDREW GRAHAM, JOHN MCLAIN.

BEASLEY, ROBERT   OCTOBER 26, 1808
     WIFE: NOT NAMED. SONS: RICHARD, JOHN, HENRY.
DAUGHTER: MARY. EXECUTOR: JOHN BALDWIN, SR.
WITNESSES: HENRY SWINDELL, LEVI JONES.

BEATTY, JOHN   JULY 22, 1774.
     WIFE: MARGARET. DAUGHTERS: MARGARET, MARY
BINMAN, FLORA HALLS, CRESSE BRYANT. WITNESSES: CATHER-
INE OWEN, JANE BRYAN, SAMUEL CURRY.

BEATTY, JOHN D.   MARCH 15, 1849. MAY TERM 1849.
     WIFE & EXECUTRIX: JANE. DAUGHTERS: POLLY, ELLA,
MARGARET, MARIA, ANNABELLA. SONS: WILLIAM, LUCIEN, HAYS,
G. H. BEATTY. GRANDSON: JOHN BEATTY REID. FATHER &
EXECUTOR: WILLIAM H. BEATTY. WITNESSES: PATRICK L.
CROMARTIE, LUTHER CROMARTIE. CLERK: H. H. ROBINSON.
(SON-IN-LAW & EX.: DAVID REID. EXECUTOR: HAYS W. BEATTY)
BEATTY, LUCIEN T.   FEBRUARY 11, 1899. APRIL 10, 1899.
     WIFE: ANNA W. DAUGHTERS: MARGARET HUNTER BEATTY,
MARY ANNA BEATTY. SON: HENRY. (GRAVELY HILL HOMESTEAD
FROM W. H. G. BEATTY). EXECUTORS: W. H. SPRUNT OF
WILMINGTON, N. C., N. MCL. BEATTY OF KLONDIKE, N. C.
WITNESSES: W. I. SHAW, N. M. BEATTY. CLERK: A. M.
MCNEILL.

BEATTY, WILLIAM HENRY MAY 16, 1849. AUG. TERM 1853.
     PLEASANT RETREAT IN BLADEN COUNTY. GRANDCHILDREN:
WILLIAM H. BEATTY, DOUGLAS BEATTY, CHILDREN OF MY
DECEASED SON WILLIAM G., HENRY, SON OF MY DECEASED SON,
HENRY BENBURY BEATTY. MARGARET HOLMES & LUCIEN HOLMES,
CHILDREN OF MY DECEASED DAUGHTER, MARGARET ANN HOLMES.
WILLIAM, JOHN, ELIZA & ANNABELLA, CHILDREN OF MY DE-
CEASED DAUGHTER, ANNABELLA PEARSON. PETER MALLETT,
"MY BEST FLUTE". DAUGHTERS: MARGARET ANN HOLMES (DEC-
EASED), SOPHIA S. MALLETT (DECEASED). DAUGHTER-IN-LAW:
JANE S. H. BEATTY, WIDOW OF MY LATE SON, JOHN D. BEATTY.
SON-IN-LAW: JOHN S. PEARSON, HUSBAND OF ANNABELLA
PEARSON. SONS: HAYS WHITE BEATTY (MY PLANTATION PLEAS-
ANT RETREAT), HENRY B. BEATTY. OTHER LEGATEES: HUGH Y.
WADDELL, SON OF THE LATE HUGH WADDELL, "MY VIOLIN, THE
SAME HAVING BEEN THE PROPERTY OF HUGH WADDELL, SR."
"TOLL BRIDGE KNOWN AS BEATTY'S BRIDGE." EXECUTORS:
SON, HAYS WHITE BEATTY, GRANDSON, WILLIAM H. BEATTY, SON
OF MY DECEASED SON, WILLIAM G. BEATTY AND CHARLES B.

MALLETT, SON OF MY DECEASED DAUGHTER, SOPHIA S. MALLETT.
WITNESSES: CALVIN J. DICKSON, GEORGE W. BANNERMAN,
WILLIAM A. WRIGHT. CLERK: J. I. MCREE.

BENBOW, CHARLES   JANUARY 25, 1774
      SONS: BENJAMIN, THOMAS. DAUGHTERS: ANN, MARY,
SARAH, SOPHIA ELIZABETH CLAYTON, MARY. EXECUTORS:
SONS, BENJAMIN & THOMAS, & DAUGHTERS, ANN & SARAH.
WITNESSES: THOS. BROWN, BENONE CLAYTON, JOSE MYRILD.
"JUSTIFIED AS EXECUTORS BY MAKING AFFIRMATION, THOS.
& BEN BENBOW."

BENSON, DAVID   FEBRUARY 19, 1831. "N. B."
      MARCH 15, 1834. WIFE: NANCY. SONS: AARON, ARCHI-
BALD, WILLIAM WASHINGTON (YOUNGEST SON). DAUGHTERS:
MARY JANE, HELANDER ANN, CAROLINE. WITNESSES: JACOB
WALLACE, JOHN A. MARTIN, EDWARD J. BERNARD.

BIZZELL, A. F.   NOV. 12, 1866. JUNE 10, 1896.
      (CERTIFIED COPY FROM RICHMOND COUNTY, N. C.) WIFE:
SALLY. CHILDREN NOT NAMED. EXECUTORS: JOHN A. MCBRYDE,
M. H. MCBRYDE. WITNESSES: WALTER H. NEAL, JAS. C.
THOMAS.

BLACKWELL, ELIZABETH   MARCH 28, 1864. MAY TERM 1864.
      SONS: STEPHEN, W. J., OWEN, P. K., J. W. GRAND-
DAUGHTER: JINEY BLACKWELL. SISTER: JULIA ANN SIKES.
WITNESSES: ROBERT P. MELVIN, MARTHA BENSON. CLERK:
D. BLUE.

BLUE, CATHERINE   SEPTEMBER 20, 1862. MAY TERM 1863.
      SON & EXECUTOR: JOHN F. BLUE. DAUGHTER: MARGARET
CLARK, WIFE OF ARCH'D B. CLARK. GRANDCHILDREN: JOHN,
DANIEL, DUGALD B., CATHERINE & ELIZABETH ANN MURPHY.
WITNESSES: J. L. ALLEN, A. J. THAGGARD. CLERK: D. BLUE.

BOON, SAMUEL   MARCH 5, 1890. OCTOBER 27, 1891.
      WIFE: MARGARET. SONS: JOSHUA, JEREMIAH, ISAIAH,
NOAH. DAUGHTER: JANE ROGIER (OTHERS NOT NAMED).
WITNESSES: A. MCDONALD, W. F. MCDONALD. EXECUTOR:
SON, JOSHUA BOON. CLERK: GEO. F. MELVIN.

BORDESS (BRODESS), PETER JANUARY 8, 1777.
      WIFE & EXECUTRIX: (NOT NAMED). BROTHER: WILLIAM
BRODESS OF PHILADELPHIA, PENN. WITNESSES: EPHRIAM

MULFORD, JOHN RUSS, MARGARET ROSE.

BOSWELL, L. F.   JULY 27, 1887. SEPTEMBER 3, 1888.
     WIFE: (NOT NAMED). SON & EXECUTOR: CASS.
DAUGHTERS: NANCY, PRICILER, ELER HUFFMAN. OTHER LEGATEES:
WILLIAM B. SMITH, LONIMAS & SUSAN SMITH, WILLIAM LEWIS
BOSWELL & HIS SISTERS. WITNESSES: WILLIAM H. BARNHILL,
D. M. BARNHILL. CLERK: GEO. F. MELVIN.

BOWIN, GOODEN   JULY 11, 1793. LONDON, NOV. 7,
     1799. WILMINGTON, MAY 19, 1800. "OF MOUNT PLEAS-
ANT NEAR WILMINGTON, CAPE FEAR, N. C., NOW OF ST. PANTRUS,
THE COUNTY OF MIDDLESEX IN THE KINGDOM OF ENGLAND".
LEGATEES: JUDITH, NOW OF MOUNT PLEASANT. MY NATURAL
CHILDREN: WILLIAM FORBES MCBEAN & JAMES MCBEAN, WHICH
I HAD BY SAID JUDITH. EXECUTOR: JOHN YOUNGER. GOODEN E.
BOWEN.

BRADLEY, ANN   JULY 26, 1809.
     SISTER: MARGARET DRAUGHAN. NEPHEWS: WILLIAM J.
COWAN, MILLER DRAUGHAN. NIECE: ANN DRAUGHAN. OTHER
LEGATEES: JANE & MARGARET MCALLISTER OF CUMBERLAND
COUNTY.

BRADLEY, JAMES   FEBRUARY 19, 1804.
     WIFE & EXECUTRIX: ANNA. OTHER LEGATEES: JOHN
BRADLEY COWAN, ANN ELIZABETH COWAN, WILLIAM JAMES COWAN,
JANE DRAUGHAN, DAUGHTER OF ROBERT DRAUGHAN OF CUMBERLAND
COUNTY, JAMES H. DRAUGHAN, SON OF ROBERT DRAUGHAN, JOSHUA
POTTS, MARGARET DRAUGHAN WIFE OF ROBERT DRAUGHAN, FORMER-
LY MARGARET COWAN, NANCY DRAUGHAN WIFE OF CHARLES DRAUGH-
AN, FORMERLY NANCY BRADLEY. BROTHERS & SISTERS (NOT
NAMED). "IN HALIFAX COUNTY, VA. FATHER LEFT BILL OF
SALE FOR SUNDRY NEGROES." EXECUTORS: DAVID LLOYD,
JAMES H. DRAUGHAN. HANDWRITING PROVED BY H. WADDELL,
THOMAS SMITH.

BRADLEY, JAMES, SR.   JANUARY 31, 1807.
     WIFE: MARGARET. DAUGHTER: PATSEY BRADLEY. GRAND-
DAUGHTER: MARY MAYNARD. SON & EXECUTOR: JAMES BRADLEY.
WITNESSES: MAGRET DRAUGHON, MARY DRAUGHON.

BRADLEY, MARGARET   MAY 4, 1816.
     DAUGHTER: PATSEY MORGAN. GRANDDAUGHTERS: MARGAR-
ET ANN MORGAN, MARY SIMPSON. GRANDSON: JOHN BRADLEY

MORGAN. EXECUTORS: WILLIAM JOHNSON, MARGARET DRAUGHAN,
DAVID LLOYD. WITNESSES: SETH DUE, JOHN SINGLETARY.

BRIGHT, ROBERT   JANUARY 22, 1829.
     WIFE & EXECUTRIX: ROXANNA. SON: WILLIAM HENRY
BRIGHT. DAUGHTER: ROXANNE BRIGHT WIFE OF JOHN BRIGHT.
ROBERT SIMPSON SON OF MY WIFE'S DAUGHTER. TRUSTEES: JOHN
B. BROWN, JOHN OWEN, DAVID GILLESPIE. EXECUTOR: JOHN
B. BROWN, JOHN OWEN. WITNESS: EDWARD J. BERNARD.

BRIGHT, SIMON   FEBRUARY 18, 1797.
     WIFE: MARY. SONS: SIMON, RICHARD, BENJAMIN,
ROBERT, JAMES. DAUGHTERS: ELRICHAK, CHRISTIAN. OTHER
LEGATEES: JOHN SHAW, WILLIAM SIBET AND WIFE MARY,
EDWARD DAVIS AND WIFE ELIZABETH. EXECUTORS: (SON)
ROBERT BRIGHT, JOHN BROWN, THOMAS BROWN. WITNESSES:
THOMAS BROWN, NEILL MCNAUGHTON.

BROWN, BETTIE   MAY 18, 1887. MARCH 12, 1887
     BROWN MARSH. LEGATEES: BILL BROWN, EMILY ARMSTRONG,
CAROLINE BROWN, ANNA BROWN, PENNY BROWN, ELIZA BROWN,
SAMUEL BROWN, FORNEY BROWN, JAMES IVER BROWN. WITNESSES:
W. M. KELLY, F. M. MASON. CLERK: G. F. MELVIN.

BROWN, GEORGE   MARCH 20, 1782.
     WIFE: ELIZABETH. SONS: GEORGE, RICHARD, THOMAS,
JOHN. DAUGHTERS: MARY, PEGGY WHITE BROWN, UPHEMIA
OLIPHANT. COUSIN: MARY RUSS. EXECUTORS: THOMAS BROWN,
JOHN BROWN, RICHARD BROWN. WITNESSES: DAVID RUSS,
SIMON SMITH, BENJ. HUMPHREY.

BROWN, JOHN   OCTOBER 28, 1812
     WIFE & EXECUTRIX: LUCY (SISTER OF WILLIAM JONES,
DEC'D.). BROTHERS: THOMAS, GEORGE, RICHARD. SISTERS:
EUPHAMY OLIPHANT, MARGARET WHITE STEPHENS, MARY ANDERS.
NIECE: MARY MILLER, DAUGHTER OF THOMAS BROWN. NEPHEW:
JOHN BRIGHT BROWN. OTHER LEGATEE: JOHN JONES RUSS.
EXECUTORS: JAMES MARSHALL, W. H. BEATTY, ESQ. WITNESSES:
DAVID LLOYD, DAVID GILLESPIE, J. LEWIS.

BROWN, JOHN B. (PLANTER) FEB. 12, 1835. CODICIL - MARCH
     30, 1839. FEB. TERM 1848. "I DESIRE TO LEAVE THIS
TESTIMONY TO MY CHILDREN THAT I DIE IN FIRM BELIEF THAT
GOD FOR CHRIST'S SAKE HAS PARDONED MY SINS, THAT NONE OF
MY WORKS OTHERWISE WOULD ENTITLE ME TO HEAVEN. I DESIRE

THAT THEY MAY NEVER REST UNTIL THEY HAVE THE SAME WITNESS AND STRIVE TO MEET ME IN HEAVEN." WIFE & EXECUTRIX: REBECCA. CHILDREN: ELIZA LLOYD, LUCY B. BROWN, JOHN B. BROWN, EDWARD A. BROWN, THOMAS O. BROWN, HANNAH M. BROWN, WILLIAM H. BROWN, REBECCA BROWN. WITNESSES: EDWARD J. BERNARD, THOMAS C. MILLER, H. H. ROBINSON. CLERK: H. H. ROBINSON.

BROWN, LUCY ANN   MAY 21, 1863. SEPTEMBER 26, 1871.
*   LOWNDES COUNTY, MISSISSIPPI) COUSINS: MISS MATTNA BROWN, JOHN BRIGHT BROWN, ASA BROWN, MARY LYMAN BROWN, WESLY PURDY, ELIZA PURDY, MISS ELLEN GUION, MISS SARAH B. NORMAN, LITTLE MARY & CHARLIE, CHILDREN OF DR. H. ROBINSON, MARY KING, SALTER LLOYD, MORTIMER BROWN. OTHER LEGATEES: REV. J. O. STEDMAN, CHARLES EAGER SON OF MRS. LAURA EAGER, REV. GEORGE SHAFFER. AUNT: MRS. A. M. PURDIE FOR BENEFIT OF THE PURDIE CHURCH IN N. C., REV. J. A. LYON, NETTIE NEELEY DAUGHTER OF REV. P. P. NEELEY. EXECUTORS: THOMAS CHRISTIAN, DR. H. ROBINSON OF N. C. WITNESSES: LAURA E. EAGER, HENRIETTA BANKS, A. C. CHRISTIAN. CLERK: D. BLUE.*

BROWN, MRS. MARY E.   27 FEBRUARY 1884. 7 DECEMBER 1898.
*   MY LATE HUSBAND, THOMAS O. BROWN. SISTERS: S. J. S. HALL, GODINA W. BROWN WIFE OF W. H. BROWN. EXECUTORS & TRUSTEES: THOMAS G. HALL, WILLIAM WATTERS. WITNESSES: C. V. HINES, ANGUS MCFADYEN, C. C. LYON. CLERK: A. M. MCNEILL.*

BROWN, THOMAS   OCTOBER 30, 1813. CODICIL.
*   NOVEMBER 22, 1814. WIFE & EXECUTRIX: LUCY. SONS & EXECUTORS: THOMAS, JOHN B. DAUGHTERS: MARY MILLER, WIFE OF ALEXANDER C. MILLER, LUCY ANN OWEN WIFE OF JOHN OWEN. SISTER: MISS MARGARET WHITE BROWN. PLANTATIONS: ASHWOOD, SEDGEFIELD ON THE SOUND, OAKLAND, PURCHASED FROM COL. ASHE, DRUNKEN RUN, WALKERS BLUFF, "BARTRAMS LAKE". OTHER LEGATEES: WILLIAM WATTS JONES, JOHN R. LONDON, JOHN D. TOOMER. (LANDS KNOWN AS DONAHOES BLUFF). WITNESSES: ROBERT COCHRAN, EDWARD B. DUDLEY, JOHN WOOSTER. JOHN SMITH, J. GILLESPIE.*

BRYAN, CAROLINE   JANUARY 13, 1862. FEB. TERM 1862.
*   HUSBAND & EXECUTOR: JAMES H. BRYAN. BROTHERS: MALLETT SIKES, RUSION SIKES, AMOS SIKES, LUCIUS SIKES. SISTERS: SARAH E. SIKES, HARRIET MOORE. WITNESSES:*

G. W. ELLIS, S. Q. CAIN. CLERK: D. BLUE.

BRYAN, GEORGE W.   SEPTEMBER 13, 1856. NOV. TERM L856.
     (TO BE BURIED IN FAMILY BURYING GROUND ON BAKERS
CREEK). PROPERTY WHICH CAME FROM MY GUARDIAN, JOHN G.
MCDUGALD. I BECAME OF AGE ON 4TH JULY 1856. WIFE: MARY
ANN. DAUGHTER: AN INFANT, NOT YET NAMED. SISTERS &
BROTHERS (NOT NAMED). EXECUTORS: DUNCAN KELLY, JOHN A.
RICHARDSON. WITNESSES: D. M. BUIE, JOHN P. LYTLE.
CLERK: F. F. CUMMING.

BRYAN, JOHN   JUNE 25, 1774.
     WIFE & EXECUTRIX: JANE. SONS: JOHN, PHILMORE,
JAMES. DAUGHTER: ANN. EXECUTOR: THOMAS OWEN. WITNESS-
ES: JOHN OWEN, WILLIAM BRYAN.

BRYAN, NATHAN   JANUARY 17, 1876. JANUARY 15,
     1884. WIFE: MARGARET. OTHER LEGATEES: WILLIAM
H. BRYAN, SARAH ANN SINGLETARY. WITNESSES: N. CARROLL,
JAS. F. GILLESPIE. CLERK: G. F. MELVIN.

BRYAN, NEEDHAM   JULY 2, 1894. AUGUST 6, 1894.
     WIFE (NOT NAMED). GRANDSONS: LLOYD BRYAN, HENRY
BRYAN. DAUGHTERS: HELLEN SCRIVEN, SALLIE BURNEY,
MARGARET HANCOCK, MOLEY GUYTON & R. H. BRYAN. SON:
JOSEPH M. BRYAN (CECEASED). EXECUTOR: A. M. MCNEILL.
WITNESSES: GILMORE EDWARDS, E. T. HESTER. CLERK:
GEO. F. MELVIN.

BRYAN, THOMAS (PLANTER) FEBRUARY 25, 1766. MAY COURT,
     1767. WIFE (NOT NAMED). SONS: STEPHEN, WILLIAM,
PHILEMON, JOHN, EDWARD, THOMAS. DAUGHTERS: SARAH
SIMSON, ELIZABETH O., AMY BALDWIN. EXECUTOR: EDWARD
BRYAN. WITNESSES: JACOB MUNTS. CLERK: MATUREN COLVILL.

BRYAN, THOMAS   JANUARY 23, 1786.
     SISTER: KORENHOFER, (OTHER SISTERS NOT NAMED).
EXECUTORS: WILLIAM BRYAN, JAMES BRADLEY, JOHN WHITE.
WITNESSES: JAMES WARD, JOHN PATRICK.

BRYANT, WILLIAM   SEPTEMBER 1854. AUGUST TERM 1855.
     WIFE (NOT NAMED). DAUGHTERS: ELIZA, ELIZABETH
ANN, LUCY, ZELPHIA, REBECCA JANE. SONS: ROBERT H.,
LEVI, DAVID, J. J. EXECUTOR: JOHN SMITH. WITNESSES:
NATHAN JONES, ROBERT MELVIN. FEB. TERM 1856: THE

EXECUTOR, JOHN SMITH, DECLINED TO SERVE, WILLIAM BRYANT
APPOINTED ADMR. WITH JAMES HALL AND WILLIAM T. FISHER AS
SURETIES ON HIS BOND. CLERK: F. F. CUMMING.

BUIE, NEIL   MAY 11, 1880. JUNE 7, 1880.
        SONS: DANIEL, ALBERT, MONROE. DAUGHTERS: CELIA,
FLORA, FRANCES. EXECUTOR: JOHN A. EDWARDS. WITNESSES:
L. J. CARROLL, D. C. CLARK. JUDGE OF PROBATE: EVANDER
SINGLETARY.

BURNEY, JOHN N. (FARMER) MAY 25, 1882. FEBRUARY 21, 1884.
        WIFE: M. R. J. BURNEY. SONS: DANIEL J., DAVID T.,
ANDREW F., JOHN R., CHARLES I., FRANCIS F. DAUGHTERS:
LUCY, SARAH, JANE ESTHER, ELIZABETH HART. EXECUTOR: SON,
DAVID T. BURNEY. WITNESSES: A. K. CROMARTIE, J. M.
JOHNSTON. CLERK: GEO. F. MELVIN.

BURNEY, WILLIAM   JUNE 13, 1783.
        WIFE: ELIZABETH. SONS: JAMES, WILLIAM, ARTHUR,
SAMUEL. BROTHER & EXECUTOR: SIMON BURNEY. OTHER LEGATEE:
MARY TAYLOR. EXECUTOR: DUNCAN KING. WITNESSES: JEREMIAH
BIGFORD, MARY WHITE.

BUSH, WILLIAM J. C.   FEBRUARY 7, 1885. DECEMBER 28,
        1886. WIFE (NOT NAMED). SONS: NEILL G., THOMAS
S., OLIVER L., OSBORNE B. DAUGHTER: MARY. WITNESSES:
J. S. DEVANE, J. B. PORTER. CLERK: G. F. MELVIN.

BUTLER, JOHN   OCTOBER 2, 1875.
        WIFE, ELIZABETH G. SONS: JAMES A., JOHN T., CHARLES
T., GEORGE E., ROBERT Q., THOMAS V. DAUGHTERS: MARY ANN
WIFE OF DANIEL JOHNSTON, ELIZABETH G. FORMERLY WIFE OF
AMOS HIGH, NEPSEY W. WIFE OF DANIEL WHITE, MARTH ANN BUTLER,
SALLIE F. BUTLER, ISABEL BUTLER. EXECUTORS: ELIAS D.
JOHNSON, ROBERT M. SESSOMS. WITNESSES: GEORGE W. JONES,
JOE HESTER. CLERK: G. F. MELVIN.

BYRNE, ALEXANDER   JUNE 25, 1787.
        BROTHER & EXECUTOR: MATTHEW BYRNE. SISTER: MARY
WILLKINGS. NEPHEW: WILLIAM WILKINGS. WITNESSES: BAR-
TRAM ROBESON, JONOTHAN ROBESON, ROBERT JOHNSON.

BYRNE, JOHN M.   APRIL 20, 1858. MAY TERM 1858.
        BROTHERS: A. J. BYRNE, (MY PLANTATION ON CAPE
FEAR RIVER LYING BETWEEN THE LANDS OF JAMES ROBESON AND

MATTHEW BYRNE AND HOUSE AT MAYSVILLE). SISTER: MRS. ANN
MARIA ROBESON. EXECUTOR: MATTHEW BYRNE. WITNESSES:
ANGUS MUNN, DONALD MCDONALD. CLERK: A. K. CROMARTIE.

BYRNE, MARY   JUNE 19, 1848. MAY TERM 1853.
    DAUGHTERS: ANN MARIAH ROBESON, MARY J. BYRNE. SONS:
MATTHEW, JOHN M. (EXECUTOR). WITNESSES: A. J. BYRNE,
THOS. J. ROBESON. CLERK: J. I. MCREE.

BYRNE, MATTHEW   DECEMBER 12, 1837.
    WIFE: MARY. SONS: JAMES A., ALEX J., RICHARD L.,
THOMAS H., JOHN M., MATTHEW. DAUGHTERS: SARAH ANDRES
(NOW DECEASED, HER CHILDREN'S PROPERTY IN POSSESSION OF
SAM'L. ANDERS), SOPHIA CARVER, ANNA MARIE ROBESON, MOLSEY
M. BYRNE. EXECUTORS: SONS, JAMES. ALEXR., RICHARD &
THOMAS BYRNE. WITNESS: B. ROBESON.

CAIN, EDWARD J., SR.   24 OCTOBER 1893. 6 APRIL 1896.
    BROTHER & EXECUTOR: ISAAC J. CAIN. NIECE: FLORA
H. B. CAIN. NEPHEW: AMOS S. CAIN. OTHER LEGATEE: MARY
E. SIKES. WITNESSES: OWAN REGISTER, A. A. REGISTER.
CLERK: W. J. SUTTON.

CAIN, JAMES SR.   JULY 8, 1826.
    SONS: JAMES, WILLIAM, SAMUEL, JONOTHAN. DAUGHTERS:
ANN PIERCE, SARAH DUNHAM, MAG, ELIZABETH, MARY, MARTHA
MCMILLAN. GRANDSON: RICHARD CAIN. EXECUTORS: SAMUEL
ROBESON, JAMES CAIN (SON). WITNESSES: THOMAS SCRIVIN,
JONATHAN ALLEN, DANIEL MOORE.

CAIN, JAMES H.   APRIL 23, 1847. AUG. TERM 1847.
    WIFE: MARY E. SONS: SAMUEL F., JOHN R., JAMES K.
P. DAUGHTERS: HARRIETT M., ELLEN E., ANN JANE, SUSAN
CAROLINA. EXECUTOR: JOHN SMITH. WITNESSES: DARIUS B.
AYRES, ISAIAH TOLAR. CLERK: H. H. ROBINSON. .

CAIN, JOSEPH (PLANTER) DECEMBER 29, 1798.
    HALF BROTHERS: JOHN CAIN, JAMES CAIN. NEPHEW:
JOSEPH CAIN (SON OF SAMUEL CAIN. OTHER LEGATEES: GEORGE
WILLIS, SR., ANN ROBESON WIFE OF JONATHAN ROBESON AND
DAUGHTER OF SAMUEL & SUSAN CAIN, SAMUEL ROBESON SON OF ANN
& JONATHAN ROBESON, MARY STEDMAN, ELIZABETH LOCK WIFE OF
BENJAMIN LOCK, SARAH HERRING WIFE OF RICHARD HERRING,
JAMES & JOHN OWEN, JAMES MOREHEAD, THOMAS OWEN, JEAN SCRIV-
EN, JONATHAN ROBESON, JAMES WALKER (A FREE BLACK BOY),
WIFE TO THOMAS SCRIVEN

ROGER (NEGRO) "THUS ENDS THE WILL IN THE ORIGINAL WILL BOOK."

CAIN, SAMUEL (SHERIFF OF BLADEN COUNTY.) AUG. 17, 1830.
WIFE: NANCY. SON: JAMES. DAUGHTERS: SUSANNA CAIN, MARGARET DOWLESS, ANNA DOWLESS. EXECUTORS: ROBERT MELVIN, AMOS CAIN.

CAIN,SAMUEL   AUGUST 17, 1857. NOV. 20, 1871.
WIFE & EXECUTRIX: MALSEY. BROTHERS: WILLIAM,JOHN, PETER. SISTERS: ELIZABETH CAIN, SARAH BURDOX, KATHARINE DAVIS. WITNESSES: AMOS SMITH, OWEN SMITH, O. J. GARDNER, R. B. CAIN. CLERK: D. BLUE.

CAIN, WILLIAM (PLANTER) FEB. 10, 1781.
WIFE: OLIVE. SONS: JOSEPH, SAMUEL, JOHN, JAMES. GRANDSON: SAMUEL CAIN, SON OF SAMUEL & LUCY CAIN. SON-IN-LAW: GEO. WILLIS. (LANDS KNOWN AS "CAINS CAMPS"). EXECUTORS: SAMUEL & JOHN CAIN (SONS). WITNESSES: RICHARD SINGLETARY, JNO.CAIN, SAM'L. CAIN.

CAMEL, SAMUEL, SR.   1853. MAY TERM 1853.
WIFE: FANNY (EUPHEMIA). DAUGHTERS: ALANDER YOUNG, RHODA SPAULDING, DRUCILLA GOODEN, DELPHA LACEWELL, NANCY MITCHELL, CAROLINE JACOBS. SONS: SAMUEL, HUGH. WITNESSES: CALVIN JONES, A. SPAULDING. ADMRS. C.T.A.: EUPHEMIA CAMPBELL, A. SPAULDING. SURETIES: W. I. SESSIONS, MOSES FREEMAN.

CAMPBELL, ARCHIBALD   MAY 1, 1844. MAY TERM 1856.
WIFE: FLORA. SON & EXECUTOR: JAMES K. DAUGHTERS: MARY CURRY WIFE OF ANGUS CURRY, FLORA BUIE WIFE OF DAN'L. N. BUIE, EUPHEMIA CAMPBELL (SINGLE WOMAN). GRANDDAUGHTER: MARGERY BRUCE. WITNESSES: NEILL KELLY, DUNCAN KELLY. (EXECUTOR DIED PREVIOUS TO THE DEATH OF THE TESTATOR. LETTERS OF ADM. ISSUED TO H. H. ROBINSON UPON HIS ENTERING INTO A BOND OF SEVEN THOUSAND DOLLARS WITH D. CROMARTIE & D. KELLY AS SURETIES. CLERK: F. F. CUMMING.

CAMPBELL, CHRISTIAN   JANUARY 19, 1819.
SON & EXECUTOR: JOHN HARGROVES. DAUGHTER: MARION CAMPBELL. WITNESSES: JOHN DARROCH, ARCHIBALD MCKEITHAN.

CAMPBELL, JAMES   JUNE 11, 1842
     WIFE: ISABELLA. SONS: ANGUS, JOHN. DAUGHTERS:
CATHERINE GOODEN WIFE OF DAN'L. GOODEN, MARY SHAW WIFE OF
ARCH'D. SHAW, ELIZA JANE SWINDALL WIFE OF OWEN SWINDALL,
ISABELLA ANN CAMPBELL. FRIEND DANIEL N. CAMPBELL APPOINT-
ED GUARDIAN OF ISABELLA ANN CAMPBELL WHO IS 13 YEARS OLD.
EXECUTORS: JAMES K. CAMPBELL, DANIEL D. CAMPBELL.
WITNESSES: A. TAYLOR, JAS. K. CAMPBELL.

CAMPBELL, MARGARET   APRIL 18, 1862. NOV. TERM 1862.
     BROTHERS: JOHN SHAW, ARCHIBALD SHAW, WILLIAM SHAW,
ALEXANDER SHAW. SISTERS: CHRISTIAN SHAW, ELIZABETH
CAMPBELL, MARY DOVE, ANNA WHITE. EXECUTOR: ALEXANDER
SHAW (BROTHER). WITNESSES: NEILL McGILL, NEILL A.
McGILL. CLERK: D. BLUE.

CARTER, SARAH HAUSE   JUNE 23, 1868. OCTOBER 8, 1875.
     SON & EXECUTOR: HAUSE J. CARTER. GRANDSON: JERE-
MIAH MELDON PETERSON. GRANDDAUGHTER: MARY NEILL PETER-
SON. DAUGHTER: MARY M. PETERSON WIFE OF WILLIAM PETER-
SON. WITNESSES: A. K. CROMARTIE, JAMES JOHNSON. PRO-
BATE JUDGE: EVANDER SINGLETARY.

CARVER, JAMES   DECEMBER 6, 1778.
     FRIENDS: GRACE SIMMONDS, MARY SIMMONDS, DAUGHTERS
OF GRACE SIMMONDS (LANDS ON CARVERS CREEK), JOSIAH EVANS,
SARAH NIXON, THOMAS LUCAS SON OF FRANCIS LUCAS. COUSIN:
JOB CARVER. EXECUTORS: FRANCIS LUCAS, GEORGE LUCAS.
WITNESSES: JEREMIAH DAFFERN, THOMAS LUCAS, LUCY STREETY.

CASHWELL, JOHN SR.   JUNE 21, 1823.
     WIFE: MARGARET. NEPHEWS: JOHN, SON OF JAMES CASH--
WELL, THOMAS CASHWELL. "TO WILL & SINA, TWO OLD NEGROES
I GIVE THEIR FREEDOM." WITNESSES: ELANZER BARNES, ROBT.
FURMIDGE.

CASHWELL, JOHN SR.   JANUARY 14, 1848. APRIL 25, 1882.
     WIFE: SALLEY. SONS: JAMES, THOMAS LEE. EXECUTORS:
NEVEL CASHWELL, JR., REUBEN FISHER. WITNESSES: ELIJAH
FISHER, SIVIL FISHER. ALEX McA. COUNCIL. PROBATE JUDGE:
G. F. MELVIN.

CHANCY, NEILL   OCTOBER 25, 1881. FEBRUARY 6,
     1882. WIFE: ELIZABETH. SON: CHARLES. DAUGHTERS:
ELIZABETH, FANEY, PENELOPE WIFE OF W. H. CHANCY. (JANE

WIFE OF CHARLES.) WITNESSES: G. R. JONES, R. E. DEESE,
A. J. BALDWIN. JOHN D. THOMAS. JUDGE OF PROBATE: N. A.
STEDMAN, JR.

CHESHIRE, RICHARD   OCTOBER 21, 1842
    WIFE: PURDIENCE. DAUGHTERS: ALICE SINGLETARY,
CATHERINE CHESHIRE, MOLSEY ALLEN. SONS: BRYAN, NICHOLAS.
EXECUTORS: NATHAN BRYAN, DURRUM LEWIS. WITNESSES:
DANIEL WILLIS, ELEANOR LYON.

CHILD, JAMES   JANUARY 28, 1855. MAY TERM 1855.
    LEGATEE: DAVID MOTE (LAND IN TOWN OF ELIZABETH,
WHERE I LIVE). EXECUTOR: JOHN A. McDOWELL. WITNESSES:
JOHN P. LYTLE, JOHN A. RICHARDSON. CLERK: F. F. CUMMING.

CLARDY, JAMES   NOVEMBER 8, 1793.
    WIFE & SONS (NOT NAMED) GRANDDAUGHTER: PENELOPE
SHAW. EXECUTORS: BRITIAN HARGROVE, WILLIAM BRYAN, SAMUEL
& JAMES SHIPMAN. WITNESSES: MOSES PITTMAN, WILLIAM
BIGFORD, ABRAHAM BEASLEY.

CLARK, BENJAMIN   NOVEMBER 7, 1783
    WIFE & EXECUTRIX: MARY. DAUGHTER: ELIZABETH.
SONS: LUKE, WILLIAM, THOMAS. EXECUTORS: WILLIAM CLARK,
SAMUEL CAIN. WITNESSES: ROBERT COUNCIL, DANIEL BEARD,
JOHN ROBESON.

CLARK, DANIEL   APRIL 26, 1854.
    WIFE: FLORA (LAND ON LITTLE PINE LOG INCLUDING THE
MANSION & HOUSE PLANTATION). SONS: DUGALD, NEILL,
DUNCAN N. DAUGHTERS: CATHERINE BUIE, NANCY SMITH,
ISABEL, CHRISTIAN, MARY, EMELINE. EXECUTORS: JOHN G.
McDOUGALD, DUNCAN N. CLARK. WITNESSES: K. K. COUNCIL,
A. H. PERRY.

CLARK, DAVID   JUNE 16, 1798. CODICIL: JUNE
    26, 1798. NEPHEW: SILAS CLARK FRAYSHER. (LANDS
WHEREON THOMAS MITCHELL LIVES). WITNESSES: GEORGE
ROBESON, ELIZABETH ROBESON.

CLARK, DUGALD   OCTOBER 4, 1807.
    SONS: DUNCAN, ANGUS, NEILL, WILLIAM. DAUGHTERS:
NANCY, ELIZABETH, EUPHAMY. EXECUTOR: NEILL CLARK,
ESQ. (SON). WITNESSES: HUGH McDOUGALD, ANGUS CURRIE,
ARCH'D. PRUSH. CLERK: J. S. PURDIE.

CLARK, DUNCAN   14 JUNE 1845. DEC. TERM 1850.
     (NEW HANOVER COUNTY). WIFE & EXECUTRIX: MARY.
DAUGHTERS: MARY ANN HINES, ELIZA WATSON, MARGARET PRIEST,
SARAH WILLIAMS, MOLEY, CATHERIN ANN. SONS: DAVID, JAMES,
DUNCAN, JOHN, BENJAMIN. EXECUTORS: BENJAMIN LILES, JOHN
H. CLARK. WITNESSES: JAMES T. MILLER, L. H. MARSTELLA.

CLARK, JOHN WASHINGTON AUGUST 5, 1887. NOVEMBER 22, 1887.
     (RESIDENCE - PHOEBUS PLANTATION). WIFE & EXECUTRIX:
CATHERINE AMELIA. SONS: ERIC C., J. MARVIN, WILLIE A.,
JEROME B., JAMES H. DAUGHTER: JANIE WASHINGTON CLARK.
WITNESSES: A. L. BLUE, D. T. BURNEY. CLERK: GEO. F.
MELVIN.

COHOON, JOHN (PLANTER) DECEMBER 25, 1781.
     WIFE: JEAN. SONS: ROWLAND, DARBY, MICAJAH, WILLIAM.
DAUGHTERS: ELIZABETH, DEBORA. OTHER LEGATEES: PENELOPE
CLARK. EXECUTORS: WILLIAM COHOON (SON), JOHN CLARK.
WITNESSES: BRITIAN JONES, DAVID MIMS, MICAJAH COHOON.

COLEMAN, MOSES   MAY 25, 1799.
     WIFE & EXECUTRIX: LURAINE. SONS: JOHN, THEOPHILUS,
AMOS, PHILLIP, MOSES, DEMPSEY, HENRY. DAUGHTERS: LUCRETIA,
CHARITY, POLLY. EXECUTORS: JOHN & THEOPILUS COLEMAN
(SONS). WITNESSES: JOHN YATES, RICHARD FAULK.

COLLUM, DENNIS   FEBRUARY 23, 1780.
     WIFE: (NOT NAMED). SON: RICHARD COLLUM. DAUGHTER:
MARGARET COLLUM. EXECUTORS: FRANCIS COLLUM, WILLIAM
WHITE. WITNESSES: JAMES ISHAM, JOHN HARRISON.

COLLUM, RICHARD (PLANTER) JULY 7, 1791.
     WIFE & EXECUTRIX: ELIZABETH. EXECUTORS: WILLIAM
JAMES WATSON, WILLIAM BRYAN. WITNESSES: FANNIE ANNIS
WELCH, JOEL MESHAW.

COLLUM, SION   AUGUST 30, 1875. SEPTEMBER 7,
     1875. DAUGHTER-IN-LAW: MARY JANE COLLUM WIFE OF
ARCHIBALD COLLUM. GRANDSON & EXECUTOR: SION JAMES COLLUM
(SON OF ARCHIBALD). WITNESSES: JOHN M. BENSON, ANDREW
H. PERRY. JUDGE OF PROBATE: E. SINGLETARY.

COLVILL, MATURIN   FEBRUARY 10, 1776.
     "MY NATURAL SON", HENRY COLVILL. FATHER: REVEREND
ALEXANDER COLVILL OF DRUMMERS COUNTY, TOWN AND KINGDOM OF

IRELAND. EXECUTORS: HENRY GRAHAM, ESQ., WILLIAM MCREE,
ESQ., MR. JOHN WHITE, SR. WITNESSES: JOHN WHITE, DAVID
RUSS, JOSEPH MUMPHREY.

COLVIN, CHARLES   APRIL 1, 1868. AUGUST 9, 1869.
     COUSIN: MARY JANE COUNCIL. EXECUTOR: JOHN G.
COUNCIL. WITNESSES: D. B. MELVIN, CHARLES T. DAVIS.
JUDGE OF PROBATE: H. P. CROWELL.

COOPER, BENJAMIN   MARCH 11, 1784.
     SISTER: ELIZABETH LOCK. COUSINS: BENJAMIN, JOSEPH
& WILLIAM COOPER, SONS OF JOSEPH COOPER, DECEASED. OTHER
LEGATEE: LEONARD LOCK, EXECUTOR: JOHN LOCK. WITNESSES:
BENJAMIN LANNELL, THOMAS LOCK, JOSEPH LOCK.
COOPER, JOSEPH   MARCH 12, 1779.
     WIFE & EXECUTRIX: MARY. SONS: WILLIAM, BENJAMIN,
JOSEPH. DAUGHTERS: ELIZABETH, AGNES, TOBITHA. BROTHER
& EXECUTOR: BENJAMIN COOPER. WITNESSES: JAMES MCDANIEL,
WILLIAM SIMS, WILLIAM MCDANIEL.

CORBETT, JAMES R.   JULY 2, 1885. CODICIL-OCT. 1, 1887.
     SEPTEMBER 6, 1892. DAUGHTERS: MARTHA J. KEITH WIFE
OF B. F. KEITH, SR., HELEN EVANS, MARY E. BLAND, CAROLINE
THOMPSON. OTHER LEGATEE: FOREIGN MISSION BOARD. EXECU-
TOR: DANIEL P. BLAND (SON-IN-LAW). WITNESSES: J. F.
CROOM, G. W. CORBETT. CLERK: GEORGE F. MELVIN.

COUNCIL, ARTHUR   MAY 10, 1819
     MOTHER & EXECUTRIX: MARY COUNCIL. OTHER LEGATEES:
THOMAS CYRUS COUNCIL SMITH, WILLIAM JAMES GAUSE. WITNESSES:
J. WILSON, J. A. ROBESON, T. A. ROBESON.

COUNCIL, KINCHIN K.   APRIL 17, 1879. MAY 31, 1887.
     WIFE: CATHARINE ANN. CHILDREN: ARTHUR L., KINCHIN
B., CATY, SABRY, JAMES, CECIL K., JOHN P., ADDA SUTTON,
MARY F. SIKES, RACHEL E. NYE, LOU, SALLY BRINKLEY. OTHER
LEGATEE: J. D. RUSS. EXECUTOR: JAMES COUNCIL (SON).
WITNESSES TO HANDWRITING: B. FITZRANDOLPH, H. K. WILKIN-
SON, W. H. SYKES. CLERK: G. F. MELVIN.

COUNCIL,MARY   NOVEMBER 24, 1822.
     DAUGHTERS: ANN SMITH, MARIA PURDIE, MARGARET JANE .
NIECES: MARY GAUSE, HANY GAUSE, ANN GAUSE. NEPHEW:
SAMUEL GAUSE. NIECE: MARY SMITH (DAUGHTER OF MARGARET JANE).
EXECUTORS: THOMAS SMITH, J. W. GAUSE. WITNESSES: W. L.
MILLER, T. J. ROBESON, J. A. ROBESON.

COUNCIL, TYMAN   MAY 26, 1882. AUGUST 4, 1885.
    WIFE: CAROLINE. SONS: TYMAN, JR., SHEPHERD, ALEX.
DAUGHTERS: LILLIAN, LOUISA, ELIZABETH. EXECUTOR: TYMAN
ROBESON. WITNESSES: ALEX MCDONALD, ASBERY RIGGAN.
CLERK: G. F. MELVIN.

COWAN, JOHN   MAY 17, 1807.
    SONS: WILLIAM JAMES & JOHN BRADLY COWAN. (MOUNT JOY
LANDS). DAUGHTER: AMELIA COWAN. EXECUTORS: JAMES
BRADLEY, DAVID LLOYD. WITNESSES: GEORGE WEIR, RICHARD
GARVIN.

COWAN, WILLIAM J.   APRIL 14, 1855. FEBRUARY TERM 1864.
    (FORMERLY A RESIDENT OF BLADEN COUNTY, NORTH CAROLINA,
BUT AT THIS TIME OF WASHINGTON, DISTRICT OF COLUMBIA)
STEPSON & EXECUTOR: JAMES W. LESESNE. WITNESSES:
DURRUM LEWIS, ELIJAH KNOX. CLERK: D. BLUE.

CRAWFORD, MARGARET   APRIL 23, 1768.

    SONS: ROBERT WEIR, NED SHAW. DAUGHTERS: MARGARET
WEIR, MARY SHAW. GRANDDAUGHTERS: CATHERINE SHAW, MARY
CRAWFORD, MARGARET WEIR. GRANDSONS: SANDERS, NEILL &
DUNCAN SHAW, GEORGE WEIR. EXECUTORS: ROBERT WEIR,
MARGARET WEIR. WITNESSES: JOHN DRANTON, JOHN WHITE.

CROMARTIE, A.   NOVEMBER 4, 1838. CODICIL:
    JANUARY 11, 1839. WIFE: ELIZABETH. SONS: DANIEL
WASHINGTON, PATRICK LAFAYETTE, WILLIAM, GEORGE, ALEXANDER,
JOHN, JAMES, DUNCAN. DAUGHTERS: ELIZABETH ANN SELLERS,
MARIAN N. "PLANTATION ON THE CAPE FEAR RIVER ABOUT 1
MILE ABOVE ELIZABETH FERRY". EXECUTOR: GEORGE CROMARTIE
(SON). WITNESSES: ALEX'R MCDOUGALD, JOHN Q. CROMARTIE,
SUGAR SUTTON.

CROMARTIE, CALVIN   APRIL 25, 1849. AUG. TERM 1849.
    MOTHER: (NOT NAMED). BROTHERS: JAMES WILLIAM,
LUTHER, JOHN QUINCY, FRANKLIN TAYLOR. OTHER LEGATEE:
JULIA ROBINSON, DAUGHTER OF GEORGE & ELEANOR ROBINSON.
EXECUTOR: JAMES WILLIAMS CROMARTIE (BROTHER). WITNESSES:
DANIEL N. MCMILLAN, WILLIAM J. CROMARTIE. CLERK: H. H.
ROBINSON.

CROMARTIE, GEORGE   MAY 10, 1880. SEPTEMBER 3, 1887.
    JUNE 15, 1892. WIFE & EXECUTRIX: SARAH A. SON:
A. K. DAUGHTERS: ANN, ELIZA A. GRAHAM. WITNESSES:
ARCHIBALD MCFADYEN, JOHN M. BENSON, LUTHER A. BLUE. CLERK:
GEO. F. MELVIN.

CROMARTIE, JAMES   MARCH 13, 1845. FEB. TERM 1846.
    WIFE & EXECUTRIX: CATHERINE. SONS: JAMES WILLIAM
(EXECUTOR), FRANKLIN TAYLOR, LUTHER, JOHN QUINCY, CALVIN.
WITNESSES: DANIEL N. MCMILLAN, DANIEL W. CROMARTIE, JAMES
B. MELVIN.

CROMARTIE, JOHN   MAY 20, 1850.
    WIFE (NOT NAMED). SON: W. J. DAUGHTERS: ELIZABETH
KIRBY, JANE MURPHY, MARY C. FENNEL, ANN BROBSTON, HARRIET
A. SLOAN, ELLEN CROMARTIE. (THE REMAINDER OF WILL NOT
RECORDED)

CROMARTIE, PATRICK LAFAYETTE   26 AUGUST 1896. 1 NOV.
    1896. WIFE: ELEANOR J. SONS: HENRY A., P. SIDNEY,
HOWARD, CHARLEY D. DAUGHTERS: CORA J. GRAHAM, MAGGIE F.
CROMARTIE, KATE N. LOOPS, DELLA MAY CAROMARTIE, STELLA
CROMARTIE, ELIZABETH E. PARKER. EXECUTORS: GEO. A. GRAHAM.
WITNESSES: GEO. S. CROMARTIE, R. S. GILLESPIE. CLERK:
W. J. SUTTON.

CROMARTIE, RHENNY (RUHAMAK)   DECEMBER 25, 1813
    (WIFE OF WILLIAM CROMARTIE, DECEASED) SONS: JOHN,
PETER. DAUGHTERS: HANNAH, ANN, JEAN JOHNSON. EXECUTOR:
JAMES CROMARTIE. WITNESSES: ELIZABETH MCMILLAN, PETER
CROMARTIE, WILLIAM WILLIAMS, J. MCKAY.

CROMARTIE, WILLIAM   OCTOBER 11, 1806.
    WIFE (NOT NAMED) DAUGHTERS: THANKFUL, ELIZABETH,
MARY, CATHERINE, MARGARET, HANNAH, ANN, JEAN. SONS:
JAMES, ALEXANDER, JOHN, PETER. GRANDDAUGHTER: MARGARET
DAUGHTER OF JAMES. EXECUTORS: JAMES & JOHN CROMARTIE
(SONS). WITNESSES: ROBERT MCMILLAN, JENNETT MCMILLAN,
JOHN CROMARTIE.

CULBRAITH, ARCHIBALD   JANUARY 18, 1844.
    WIFE: MARY. GRANDDAUGHTERS: JANNETTA CULBRAITH,
HARRIET CULBRAITH. SON & EXECUTOR: JOB CULBRAITH
WITNESSES: DAVID JOHNSON, RAFORD HALL, JOHN MCGEE, JOB
CULBRAITH. EXECUTOR: JOHN MCGEE

CULBRETH, JOHN J.   12 OCTOBER 1893. 13 JANUARY 1894.
    WIFE: CATHERINE. SON: McK. DAUGHTERS: ANNA M.
FAIRCLOTH, MARY M. EDGE. EXECUTOR: ISAAC J. CAIN.
WITNESSES: JAMES M. JESSUP, OWEN REGISTER. CLERK:
GEO. F. MELVIN.

CUMMING, F. F.   AUGUST 15, 1887. JUNE 13, 1890.
    WIFE & EXECUTRIX: ANN OLIVIA. WITNESSES: C. C. LYON,
L. M. SMITH. CLERK: GEORGE F. MELVIN.

CUMMING, FRANCIS E. SEPT. 12, 1890. JUNE 29, 1891.
    LEGATEE & EXECUTRIX: ANN O. CUMMING WIDOW OF F. F.
CUMMING. WITNESSES: R. A. LYTLE, L. M. SMITH. CLERK:
GEO. F. MELVIN.

CURRIE, DANIEL   10 SEPTEMBER 1892. 27 MARCH 1899.
    WIFE: F. ANN. OTHER LEGATEES: NOVELA D. CURRIE,
D. M. CURRIE, M. G. SUTTON AND HER HEIRS. WITNESSES:
C. C. LYON, L. M. SMITH. CLERK: A. M. McNEILL.

DANIEL, OVERTON   (NO DATE)
    WIFE & EXECUTRIX: ANNA. STEP-DAUGHTER: MARY WILES.
SON: JOHN. DAUGHTER: ANNA. EXECUTORS PETER W. GONTIER,
HENRY LUCAS. WITNESSES: ELISHA MORSE, S. JOSEPHRYS.

DAVIS, EDMOND   NOVEMBER 1, 1839.
    WIFE: ZILPHA. SONS: EDWARD, GABRIEL, THOMAS.
DAUGHTER: ELIZABETH DAVIS. OTHER LEGATEES: MARY SIKES,
WILLIAM DAVIS, PETER DAVIS. EXECUTOR: JAMES MELVIN, SR.
WITNESSES: JOHN McGEE, WILEY HALL.

DAVIS, EDWARD   JANUARY 20, 1780.
    WIFE: MARGARET. SONS: EDWARD GREENWOOD, WILLIAM,
JOHN BURGWIN. DAUGHTERS: MARY & MARGARET DAVIS, JEAN
BLOCKER. GRANDSON: EDWARD DAVIS BLOCKER. EXECUTORS:
JOHN BURGWIN, ESQ., MR. BENJ'M STONE, EDWARD GREENWOOD
DAVIS (SON). WITNESSES: WILLIAM McREE, JOSIAH HENDON,
MARGARET McREE.

DAVIS, HENRY   SEPTEMBER 28, 1832.
    WIFE: MARY. SON & EXECUTOR: ELIAS. WITNESSES:
WILLIS SINGLETARY & JOHN HESTER.

DAVIS, ISABELLA   OCTOBER 10. 1824.
    NIECES: MARGARET W. CAMPBELL, MARY J. CAMPBELL,

ELIZABETH BALLENTINE, ISABELLA BALLENTINE (DAUGHTERS OF
MY NIECE SARAH BALLENTINE, DECEASED). EXECUTORS: G. J.
WHITE, ALEXANDER McDOWELL. WITNESSES: JOSEPH R. KEMP,
SARAH ANN HENDON.

DAVIS, JAMES   JUNE 4, 1871. OCTOBER 5, 1886.
     WIFE: MARY JANE. SONS: JAMES McKAY, JOHN RICHARDSON.
DAUGHTERS: SARAH JANE, MARGARET HARRIS, ELIZA, SUSY,
MOLLY. GRANDSON: G. W. DAVIS. EXECUTOR: J. W. CROMAR-
TIE. WITNESSES: H. R. FRANCIS, THOS. A. JESSUP. CLERK:
G. F. MELVIN.

DAVIS, MICAJAH, SR.   APRIL 1827.
     WIFE: NANCY. SON: MICAJAH. DAUGHTER: MARY
WITNESS: DANIEL McDUFFIE, JR.

DAVIS, TURNER   JANUARY 25, 1794.
     WIFE & EXECUTRIX: SUSANNAH. SONS: JOSHUA, JOHN,
THOMAS. DAUGHTERS: SARAH, ANN, ELIZABETH. GRANDSON:
THOMAS DAVIS, SON OF JOSHUA. BROTHER: HESEKIAH DAVIS.
EXECUTOR: RICHARD SALTER. WITNESSES: WILLIAM RILLEY,
JAMES RUSS.

DAVIS, WILLIAM   JULY 8, 1790.
     DAUGHTERS: ANN, SARAH. SONS: WILLIAM, HEXAH, JOHN.
BROTHER & EXECUTOR: H. DAVIS. EXECUTOR: THOMAS SMITH.
WITNESSES: RALPH MILLER, TURNER DAVIS, JOSHUA DAVIS.

DAVIS, WILLIAM   DECEMBER 31, 1858. CODICIL - FEB.
     21, 1859. DAUGHTERS: ANNIE JANE, ANNA MARIA, PHOEBE
ELIZABETH, SARAH ELVIRA. SONS: THOMAS, WILLIAM, CHARLES
T. EXECUTOR: CHARLES T. DAVIS (SON). WITNESSES:
JOHN S. RICHARDSON, EDWARD B. RICHARDSON, W. C. DUNHAM,
MALCOM LAMON, OWEN SMITH.

DAVIS, WILLIAM SR.   SEPTEMBER 24, 1817.
     WIFE & EXECUTRIX: ISABELLA. EXECUTOR: PATRICK
KELLY. WITNESSES: J. J. CUMMING, DAVID T. MELVIN, ROBERT
LYTLE.

DEACON, MARY   SEPTEMBER 7, 1770. AUGUST TERM.
     LEGATEES: HENRY TOOMER, JOHN & ANTHONY TOOMER (SONS
OF HENRY), MARY OWENS, CATHERINE OWENS, SUALLA SANDERS,
MARY NURTONS. EXECUTORS: JOHN OWENS, THOMAS OWENS.
WITNESSES: THOMAS SINGLETARY, OWEN BRADY. CLERK: MATURIN
COLVILL.

DERRY, LONDON   MAY 16, 1818
    SONS: LONDON, BEN. GRANDDAUGHTER: MILLY. FRIEND &
EXECUTOR: JOSIAH LEWIS (SON OF AARON LEWIS, ESQ.)
WITNESSES: JAMES KELLY, SR., A'D KELLY.

DEVANE, JOHN   SEPTEMBER 14, 1783. JUNE TERM 1806.
    WIFE: (NOT NAMED) SONS: THOMAS, JOHN, JAMES, WILLIAM,
GEORGE. DAUGHTERS: TOBITHA, ANN, MARGARET, REBECCA.
EXECUTORS: THOMAS DEVANE, SR., TIMOTHY BLOODWORTH, JAMES
BLOODWORTH. WITNESSES: JOHN PORTERVINE, JOHN HERRING,
SAMUEL PORTERVINE. CLERK: J. S. PURDIE.

DEWEY, EUPHEMIA   OCTOBER 11, 1796. CODICIL: MARCH
    29, 1797. "....IT IS MY WILL AND DESIRE THAT MY NE-
GROES NOW IN STATE OF SLAVERY SHOULD BE EMANCIPATED AND
SET FREE." THOMAS BROWN, SENIOR AND JOSHUA GRANGER
WRIGHT TO SEE THAT NEGROES BE EMANCIPATED AND LIBERATED
FROM PRESENT STATE OF SLAVERY. LEGATEES: PLANTATION TO
SLAVES, MRS. SARAH CARTHEY, MRS. AGNES ELKINS, THOMAS BROWN,
JUNIOR SON OF WILLIAM BROWN, DEC'D., MARGARET WHITE BROWN,
MRS. ANN GAUTIER, ABAGAIL MULFORD, THOMAS BROWN, SR., SON
OF GEORGE BROWN, DEC'D., LUCY BROWN, WIFE OF THOMAS BROWN,
MARY BROWN, DAUGHTER OF THOMAS BROWN, SR., MARY ANDRES,
WIFE OF SAM'S ANDRES, THOMAS BROWN, SON OF THOMAS BROWN,
SR., JOHN BRIGHT BROWN, WILLIAM AND THOMAS JONES, SONS OF
DAVID JONES, DEC'D., MRS. SUSANNAH WRIGHT, ELIZABETH
WHITE, DAUGHTER OF WILLIAM WHITE, CHILDREN OF THE LATE
WILLIAM EVENS OF WILMINGTON, JOHN HASLER CARTHEY, SON OF
DAVID & SARAH CARTHEY, EUPHEMIA OLIPHANT, JAMES BROWN,
RICHARD BROWN, JOHN BROWN, CHILDREN OF GEORGE BROWN,
JR. EXECUTORS: JOSHUA GRANGER WRIGHT, THOMAS BROWN,
SR. WITNESSES: JAMES WHITE, MARY WHITE. CODICIL: "IF
FREEDOM OF NEGROES CANNOT BE PUT INTO EFFECT, THEY TO BE
PROPERTY OF MRS. SARAH CARTHEY." WITNESSES: ELISHA
MERGE, SAM'L. ANDERS, ROSANNAH BRIGHT.

DICKSON, CALVIN J.   OCTOBER 15, 1860. MAY TERM 1862.
    (LANDS ON BLACK RIVER WITH THE FERRY KNOWN AS BEATTY'S
BRIDGE FERRY) WIFE: CATHERINE. DAUGHTERS: LUCY JANE
DAVIS, SUSAN E. DICKSON, CATHERINE F. DICKSON. SONS:
JAMES W., JOSEPH, ROBERT, JOHN, PICKETT. "IT IS MY WISH
THAT NO STEPFATHER SHALL HAVE THE CONTROL OF MY CHILDREN
OR THEIR PROPERTY." (MY INTEREST IN THE ESTATE OF THE
LATE GEORGE FENNELL) EXECUTOR: PATRICK MURPHY. WITNESS-
ES: H. W. BEATTY, J. W. DICKSON. CLERK: D. BLUE.

DICKSON, S. F.   18 August 1896. 19 July 1898.
     LEGATEE: SALLIE D. SINGLETARY. (MY EXECUTOR TO MOVE
MY WIFE'S BODY FROM WHERE SHE IS TO PURDIES CHURCH, WHERE
I WISH TO BE BURIED) EXECUTOR: CASSIUS WADE LYON.
WITNESSES: JNO. I. MCMILLAN, DAVID WILLIS. CLERK:
W. J. SUTTON.

DOVE, ESTHER   FEBRUARY 10, 1799.
     NEPHEW: JAMES EVANS AND HIS SISTER ESTHER KNOWLES.
NIECE: JANE WHITE. EXECUTORS: JOHN WHITE, JAMES BRADLEY.
WITNESSES: JAMES BRADLEY, DAVID RUSS.

DOWEY, JAMES   MAY 28, 1811.
     WIFE: MARY. SON & EXECUTOR: ROBERT DOWEY. DAUGHT-
ER: NANCY MCKAY. EXECUTOR: DAVID LLOYD. WITNESSES:
WILLIAM SIMPSON, JAMES SIMPSON.

DOWEY, JAMES   JANUARY 11, 1842.
     WIFE: ELIZABETH ANN. BROTHER: ROBERT DOWEY.
(MOTHER NOT NAMED) EXECUTOR: DAVID LEWIS. WITNESSES:
D. B. GILLESPIE, ALEXR MCDUGALD.

DOWNING, GEORGE   NOVEMBER 4, 1837.
     WIFE: MARY ANN. SONS: GEORGE W., JOHN J.,
VALENTINE. DAUGHTERS: SARAH, MARY ANN, MARY JANE.
EXECUTOR: VALENTINE (SON). WITNESSES: EVAN DOWNING,
JOSEPH DOWNING.

DUNHAM, JAMES S.   AUGUST 8, 1879.
     SONS: W. C., J. R., G. B. DAUGHTER: S. E. ROBESON.
GRANDCHILDREN: JAMES A. & ALLICE DUNHAM. WITNESSES:
JOHN S. DUNHAM, C. T. MELVIN.

DUNHAM, WILLIAM J.   JANUARY 21, 1861. MAY TERM 1861.
     WIFE: SILVIAH. SON & EXECUTOR: WILLIAM H. BROTHERS:
JOHN S., JAMES S. (EXECUTOR) OTHER CHILDREN NOT NAMED.
WITNESSES: EDMD. B. RICHARDSON, JOSEPH S. DUNN, JR.,
J. R. DUNHAM. CLERK: D. BLUE.

DUNHAM, WILLIAM R.   APRIL 17, 1823. CODICIL: JAN. 1.
     1827. WIFE & EXECUTRIX: SARAH. SON: JONATHAN S.,
WILLIAM J., JOHN S., SAMUEL, THOMAS. DAUGHTER: SARAH
ALLEN WIFE OF DAVID ALLEN, ELIZABETH. EXECUTORS: DAVID
ALLEN, WILLIAM J. DUNHAM. WITNESSES: WILLIAM DAVIS, WILL
ROBESON, SAMUEL N. RICHARDSON.

DUPRER, AMELIA   JANUARY 8, 1796.
    NIECE: SUSANNAH MOORE. OTHER LEGATEES: MARY
POWELL, ESTHER POWELL, ZYLPHIA POWELL, JOHN GIBBS, SOPHIA
GIBBS, MR. MORRISON. EXECUTOR: JOHN GIBBS. WITNESSES:
DUNCAN KING, ROBERT GIBBS.

EDGE, ALLEN   JANUARY 3, 1866. MARCH 23, 1874.
    WIFE: SOPHIA. SON & EXECUTOR: JOHN W. EDGE.
GRANDSON: ALEXANDER MATHEW EDGE. WITNESSES: OWEN SMITH,
MARGARET A. EDGE, LUCY A. EDGE. CLERK: EVANDER SINGLE-
TARY.

EDGE, ELIZA M.   SEPTEMBER 8, 1875. SEPTEMBER 21,
    1881. SISTER: DRUSILLA J. EDGE. EXECUTOR: CHARLES
L. EDGE. WITNESSES: M. K. CULBRETH, RACHEL CULBRETH.
JUDGE OF PROBATE: N. A. STEDMAN, JR.

EDWARDS, ALLEN   SEPTEMBER 18, 1876. SEPTEMBER 5,
    1881. WIFE: RHODA ANN. SONS: HAYNES, GILMORE, CAL-
VIN, WRIGHT, ROBERT J. DAUGHTERS: MARGARET DOVE, ELIZA
SINGLETARY. EXECUTORS: HAYNES & GILMORE EDWARDS (SONS).
WITNESSES: JAMES CASHWELL, NEVEL CASHWELL. JUDGE OF
PROBATE: N. A. STEDMAN, JR.

EDWARDS, CHARLES   JANUARY 6, 1811.
    WIFE & EXECUTRIX: LYDIA. SONS: JAMES, CHARLES, JOHN.
DAUGHTERS: ELIZABETH, SUSANNAH, LIZZIE. OTHER LEGATEES:
MARY REEVES AND HER DAUGHTER, SARAH. EXECUTORS: JAMES
KING, JAMES EDWARDS. WITNESSES: SOLOMON KING, BETSY
EDWARDS.

EDWARDS, ROBERT J.   3 OCTOBER 1895. 2 DECEMBER 1895.
    WIFE: HARRIETT B. DAUGHTERS: ELLA J., SALLIE L.,
SALLIE C., ANNA F. (LANDS KNOWN AS ALLEN EDWARDS PLACE
AND GEORGE MELVIN LANDS) EXECUTOR: LENNON P. SINGLETARY.
WITNESSES: A. E. PAIT, MONROE HESTER. CLERK: W. J.
SUTTON.

EDWARDS, STEPHEN   AUGUST 29, 1883. AUGUST 1, 1884.
    WIFE: MARY. SONS: TRAVIS, ALFRED, RALSEY. DAUGH-
TERS: KEZIAH WHITE WIDOW OF ARCHIBALD WHITE, SUSY, APPA,
SOPHIA, MARY COMFORT WILSON WIFE OF J. D. WILSON, CELIA
F., NANCY J. SINGLETARY. EXECUTORS: ALFRED & RALSEY
EDWARDS (SONS). WITNESSES: GEORGE W. JONES, JOHN PAIT.
CLERK: G. F. MELVIN.

ELLIS, EVAN
    WIFE: PHILLIS. SONS: JOHN EVAN, WILLIAM, REYE
"RUSS". DAUGHTERS: ANN PORTER, JANNETT. GRANDDAUGHTER:
SUSANNAH PORTER. BROTHER & EXECUTOR: WILLIAM ELLIS.
OTHER LEGATEE & EXECUTOR: SAMUEL PORTER. WITNESSES:
JOHN LENNON, G. J. McREE.

ELLIS, JOHN   OCTOBER 23, 1795.
    WIFE & EXECUTRIX: LUCY. (CHILDREN NOT NAMED)
EXECUTOR: WILLIAM GREEN. WITNESSES: DANIEL SHIPMAN,
CALEB GREEN, RICHARD HOLMES.

ELLIS, JOHN   JANUARY 6, 1818.
    SON: JAMES SAMUEL. DAUGHTER: ELIZABETH. EXECUTORS:
JOHN McKAY, JOHN OWEN, JAMES SAMUEL ELLIS. WITNESSES:
J. J. CUMMING, J. STREATY, R. HARVEY.

EVERS, JAMES (PLANTER) JUNE 23, 1854. FEB. TERM 1862.
    WIFE: ZYLPHIA. SONS: WILLIAM JAMES, DAVID.
DAUGHTER: ZYLPHIA. SON-IN-LAW: HENRY ALLEN. (OTHER
CHILDREN NOT NAMED. EXECUTORS: JOHN A. McDOWELL, HEMAN
H. ROBINSON. WITNESSES: J. W. LESESNE, THOMAS J. NORMAN.
CLERK: D. BLUE

FISHER, RAIFORD   JUNE 24, 1873. NOV. 21, 1873.
    WIFE (NOT NAMED). SONS & EXECUTORS: HAYWOOD, JOHN.
WITNESSES: M. W. FISHER, MAURICE HALL, SUSAN A. THAGGARD.
JUDGE OF PROBATE: EVANDER SINGLETARY.

FITZRANDOLPH, BENJAMIN APRIL 23, 1818.
    SON: EDWARD. DAUGHTERS: RUTH, GAINOR. GRANDSONS:
BENJAMIN FITZRANDOLPH, EDWARD LAWRENCE McREE, BENJAMIN
RANDOLPH WHITE. SON-IN-LAW: JAMES McREE. EXECUTORS:
EDWARD FITZRANDOLPH, MALCOM McNEILL, GEORGE KNOWLES.
WITNESSES: THO. WHITE, SAM'L McLELLAND, ALEX McDOWELL.

FITZRANDOLPH, BENJAMIN APRIL 10. 1841. JUNE 7, 1841.
    WIFE: SARAH. DAUGHTERS (NOT NAMED). WIFE TO"MAKE
ONE RAFT EVERY YEAR IF SHE WISHES SO TO DO." EXECUTORS:
GEORGE CROMARTIE, BENJAMIN FITZRANDOLPH, JR. WITNESSES:
ALEX McDOWELL, ELEANOR LYON.

FLINN, DANIEL   MARCH 7, 1785.
    WIFE: MARY. SONS: DANIEL, JAMES. DAUGHTER & EX-
ECUTRIX: ELIZABETH FLINN. OTHER LEGATEES: DANIEL FLINN,
JR. SON OF JOHN FLINN, DANIEL FLINN, SR., CHARITY, MARY,

CATHERINE. EXECUTOR: DANIEL FLINN (SON). WITNESSES: JOHN DUBOSE, JOHN YOUNG.

FLOWERS, DAVID F.   29 OCTOBER 1889. 21 AUGUST 1899.
    SONS: JAMES G., FRED J. GRANDSONS: DAVID F.
NICHOLSON, JAMES L. NICHOLSON. OTHER LEGATEES: MARY A.
TROY, SALLIE F. TROY, SARAH E. FLOWERS. WITNESSES: G. D.
PERRY, D. A. LAMONT. CLERK: A. M. McNEILL.

FLOWERS: IGNATIOUS   OCTOBER 25, 1793.
    SONS: GOOLSBURY, URIAH, IGNATIOUS, RICHARD.
DAUGHTERS: SARAH, SUSANNAH, EMMA, NANCY, MILLY, ALICE,
MORGAN. EXECUTORS: URIAH & IGNATIOUS FLOWERS (SONS).
WITNESS: RETERON STRONG.

FORT, JOHN   JULY 22, 1852. MAY TERM 1853.
    WIFE: JULIA ANN. DAUGHTERS: EDNEY FAIRCLOTH WIFE OF
SOLOMON FAIRCLOTH, JANNET MELVIN WIFE OF WILLIAM MELVIN.
GUARDIANS FOR DAUGHTERS: ELIJAH FISHER & THOMAS FORT.
GRANDDAUGHTERS: ELIZABETH SIMPSON, JENETY HOLLINGSWORTH,
MARY JANE HOLLINGSWORTH. DAUGHTER: JEMIMA FISHER. SON
& EXECUTOR: THOMAS FORT. GRANDSONS: GRAY FORT, THOMAS
M. FORT. OTHER LEGATEE: TAMER McDANIEL. EXECUTOR:
ELIJAH FISHER. WITNESSES: DANIEL D. BEARD, W. F. BEARD.
CLERK: J. I. McREE.

FRANCES, HUBERT R.   AUGUST 25, 1887. JANUARY 4, 1890.
    WIFE: NANCY E. DAUGHTER: HELEN M. WHITEHEAD.
EXECUTORS: J. H. TATOM, SYLVESTER BOARDEAUX. WITNESSES:
GEO. O. PARKER, A. L. TATOM. CLERK: G. F. MELVIN.

GARVAN, ANN   JANUARY 27, 1836.
    SON: WILLIAM WILLIAMS. DAUGHTER: ELIZABETH ANN
THOMAS WIFE OF GEORGE THOMAS. GRANDSON: DAVID LLOYD
THOMAS, SON OF GEORGE THOMAS (PLANTATION ON COLLY SWAMP).
GRANDDAUGHTERS: JANE FLOYD THOMAS, ELIZABETH ANN THOMAS
AND ELIZABETH MARY THOMAS. (PLANTATION KNOWN AS BELVAT
PLANTATION AND LANDS ADJOINING WADDELL'S FERRY) FRIENDS
& EXECUTORS: JOHN L. McKAY, THOMAS C. SMITH. WITNESSES:
JAMES CHILD AND W. J. COWAN.

GARVAN, RICHARD   APRIL 3, 1827.
    WIFE & EXECUTRIX: ANN. SISTER: SARAH MULFORD.
OTHER LEGATEE: CHARLES LEE GARVAN. EXECUTOR: PATRICK
KELLY. WITNESSES: WM. JOHNSTON, DAVID LLOYD.

GATES, JANE   JANUARY 7, 1799.
    SON & EXECUTOR: EDWARD GATES. OTHER LEGATEES: MAR-
GARET GATES DAUGHTER OF PETER GATES, DEC'D., ELIZABETH
GATES DAUGHTER OF JEAN SCRIVEN, MARY GATES, WIDOW OF PETER
GATES, JOHN GATES. WITNESSES: WILLIAM GLOVER, F. MILLER.

GATES, PETER   DECEMBER 3, 1789.
    WIFE: MARY. (CHILDREN NOT NAMED) BROTHER & EXECU-
TOR: EDWARD GATES. WITNESSES: BENJAMIN LANSDELL, WILLIAM
GODFREY.

GAUSE, NEEDHAM   JANUARY 17, 1792.
    WIFE & EXECUTRIX: ELIZABETH. SISTERS: ELIZABETH
GAUSE, MARY (BLOOMER OR BELLUM). BROTHER & EXECUTRIX:
SAMUEL GAUSE. FATHER & EXECUTOR: WILLIAM GAUSE. WITNESS-
ES: WILLIAM GAUSE, SAMUEL GAUSE, JOHN GAUSE.

GAUTIER, JR.   AUGUST 4, 1800.
    SISTER: MRS. ANN HART. BROTHERS: T. N. GAUTIER,
P. W. GAUTIER. COUSIN: WILLIAM RICHARDSON. NEPHEW:
JOSEPH R. GAUTIER, JR. OTHER LEGATEES: NANCY SHERIDAN
"MY EMANCIPATED BLACK WOMAN, MY PLANTATION AT THE MARSH."
LOUIS SHERIDAN, CHILD OF NANCY, THOMAS SHERIDAN.
EXECUTOR: JOHN ELLIS.

GIBBS, GEORGE   MAY 26, 1778.
    WIFE & EXECUTRIX: MARGARET. SONS: JOHN, GEORGE,
ROBERT, JOSEPH. BROTHER: JOHN GIBBS. EXECUTORS: HENRY
TOURNER, RICHARD QUINCE, JOHN BURGOIN, JOHN ANCROM.
WITNESSES: JOHN TOURNER, BENJAMIN LAMBERTSON, WILLIAM
STANFORD, JAMES LOVEL.

GIBBS, JOHN   AUGUST COURT 1771.
    WIFE: AMELIA. NEPHEWS: JOHN GIBBS SON OF GEORGE
GIBBS, JOHN PATRICK SON OF MY SISTER BETTY LARKINS.
BROTHER & EXECUTOR: GEORGE GIBBS. EXECUTORS: JOHN
BURGOIN, ALEXANDER DUNCAN. WITNESSES: STEP'N STINTON,
EDWARD CHIN, JAS. ROE. JAS. BAILEY WITNESS AS TO HANDWRIT-
ING OF STEP'N STINTON & EDWARD CHIN, ONE OF WHICH IS DEAD
& THE OTHER OUT OF THE PROVINCE. CLERK: MATURIN COLVILL.

GILLESPIE, DAVID   22 JULY 1820.
    WIFE & EXECUTRIX: SARAH. CHILDREN NOT NAMED.
TRUSTEES: ISAAC WRIGHT, JAMES OWEN, JOHN OWEN, THOMAS
BROWN, JOHN B. BROWN.

GILLESPIE, JAMES   MAY 27, 1847. AUG. TERM, 1847.
     WIFE & EXECUTRIX: SUSAN: "IT IS MY WILL AND DESIRE
THAT MY WIFE, PROVIDED SHE CANNOT LOCATE HERSELF MORE
AGREEABLY ELSEWHERE, WILL RENT A HOUSE AT FLORAL COLLEGE
IN ROBESON COUNTY FOR THE PURPOSE OF EDUCATING MORE CON-
VENIENTLY THE YOUNGER CHILDREN." SON: JAMES: BROTHERS
& EXECUTORS: JOSEPH GILLESPIE, RICHARD GILLESPIE.
WITNESSES: THOMAS S. D. McDOWELL, NEILL GRAHAM, C. G.
WRIGHT. CLERK: H. H. ROBINSON.

GILLESPIE, RICHARD T. APRIL 27, 1878. FEBRUARY 14, 1879.
     WIFE & EXECUTRIX: ELIZABETH. SON: JAMES. DAUGHTERS:
REBECCA ELIZABETH PEPPER, MARY G. PARKER, CAROLINE WHITE.
GRANDCHILDREN: MARY ELIZABETH PARKER, ROBERT HUMPHREY
PARKER, CHILDREN OF SALLIE JANE PARKER, DEC'D.
WITNESSES: WILLIAM H. WHITE, R. H. LYON, F. F. CUMMING.
JUDGE OF PROBATE: E. SINGLETARY.

GLASS, LEVY (PLANTER) JANUARY 27, 1779.
     WIFE & EXECUTRIX: MARY. SONS: SOLOMON, LITTLETON,
LEVY, THOMAS. DAUGHTERS: MARY, RITTA, BECKY. (PLAN-
TATION CALLED "LUMBER BRIDGE") EXECUTOR: DAVID SINGLE-
TARY WHITE. WITNESSES: PHILLIP PORD, HUGH BROWN.

GRAY, ABRAM   JUNE 19, 1793.
     SONS: JESSE, CORNELIUS. DAUGHTER: MORAN McLEAUD.
SON-IN-LAW: FRANCES LAWSON. EXECUTORS: WM. J. WATSON,
JAMES MOOREHEAD. WITNESSES: PENELOPE BAKER, JOSEPH D.
CAMP, JAS. MOOREHEAD.

GREEN, MARY (OF BRUNSWICK COUNTY) 26 JULY, 1792.
     BROTHER: JAMES GREEN (LANDS NEAR ROCKFISH IN BLADEN
COUNTY). SISTER: ANNA TURNER. NIECE: SARAH TURNER.
NEPHEW: THOMAS TURNER (MY RIDING HORSE, "FEARS NOT").
OTHER LEGATEE: MRS. AMEY TURNER, MRS. GRACE FAULK, MRS.
SARAH SMITH, MRS. JANE SMITH, MARY GREEN LEWIS, JOSIAH
LEWIS. EXECUTORS: PETER WILLIAM GAUTIER OF BRUNSWICK
COUNTY, MR. JOHN JONES OF BRUNSWICK COUNTY, N. C.
WITNESSES: DONALD BAIN, SAMUEL RUSSELL, ALEX'R. KING.

GRIMES, JAMES   MAY 28, 1860. NOV. TERM 1866.
     WIFE: SARAH ANN. (WIFE'S 4 CHILDREN: JOHN, ELIZA-
BETH, COLUMBIA, VICTORIA) SONS: MOSES W., JAMES C.,
DANIEL J., FRANKLIN, DAVID. DAUGHTER: ELIZA ROWELL.
GRANDSON: SAMUEL SWENDAL. EXECUTOR & SON: DAVID J.

GRIMES. WITNESSES: DANIEL EVANS, DURRAN LEWIS. CLERK:
D. BLUE. DEPUTY CLERK: J. A. RICHARDSON.

GUION, ELLEN P. (OF OWEN HILL FARM) 20 DECEMBER 1881.
24 APRIL 1897. ADOPTED DAUGHTER & EXECUTRIX: ANNA
GUION STITH. WITNESSES: ALMIRIA THERESIA MOORE, THOS.
C. MOORE. CLERK: W. J. SUTTON.

HALL, JONATHAN (PLANTER) JANUARY 22, 1837.
WIFE: PACHYAUE. (CHILDREN MENTIONED BUT NOT NAMED)
EXECUTORS: JAMES HALL, LOVE MCDANIEL. WITNESSES: JOHN
HAILES, SAMUEL HAILES.

HARRISON, JOHN   JANUARY 5, 1785. MAY TERM 1785.
WIFE: MARGARET. SONS: WILLIAM SINGLETARY (EXECUTOR),
EDWARD HARRISON. DAUGHTERS: SUSAN, ANN, MARGARET, ELIZA-
BETH. OTHER LEGATEE: JOSEPH BUTLER. WITNESSES TO
NUNCUPATIVE WILL: WILLIAM CHESHIRE, RICHARD CHESHIRE.
CLERK: JOHN WHITE.

HARVEY, PRISCILLA   DECEMBER 26, 1855. AUGUST TERM 1861.
NEPHEW: SIMEON NORMAN. OTHER LEGATEES: METHODIST
CHURCH SOUTH, THOMAS J. NORMAN, DUNCAN CROMARTIE, GEN'L.
JAS. I MCKAY. EXECUTORS: THOS. J. NORMAN, D. CROMARTIE.
WITNESSES: DAVID LEWIS, GEO. CROMARTIE.

HARVEY, ROBERT (PLANTER)   DECEMBER 7, 1839. FEBRUARY
TERM 1859. WIFE: ANNA JANE. SONS: WILLIAM WHITE,
ALEXANDER L., JOHN TRAVERS. DAUGHTERS; HARRIET NEWELL,
MARGARET, ELIZA ANN. (MY GREEN OAK PLANTATION TO SON WM.
WHITE HARVEY) EXECUTORS: BENJAMIN FITZRANDOLPH & WILLIAM
WHITE HARVEY. WITNESSES: DUNCAN CROMARTIE AND B.
FITZRANDOLPH.

HARVEY, TRAVIS W.   MARCH 6, 1805. CODICIL - MAY 8,
1805. BROTHER & EXECUTOR: ROBERT HARVEY. DAUGHTERS:
ELIZA ANN, SARAH. SISTER: MARY SMITH, HER CHILDREN,
LUCY & RICHARD SMITH. WIFE'S BROTHERS: WILLIAM ROBESON,
BARTRAM ROBESON & JONATHAN ROBESON. EXECUTOR: WILLIAM
ROBESON. WITNESSES: ALEX'R. MCDOWELL, JAS. SALTER,
MUSGROVE JONES.

HARVEY, WILLIAM W. (PLANTER)   JANUARY 31, 1850.
(WIFE & CHILDREN MENTIONED, BUT NOT NAMED) EXECUTORS:
JOEL JOHNSON, HEMAN H. ROBINSON. WITNESSES: J. D. SALTER,
JOHN EDGE.

HAYNES, ELIZABETH   JANUARY 3,   .
     DAUGHTERS: MARY, ELIZABETH, ANN. (PLANTATION KNOWN AS BRUMTON) SON: JOHN HAYNES. (CHILDREN BY MY LAST HUSBAND, MR. HAYNES) BROTHERS & EXECUTORS: THOMAS AND JONATHAN SMITH. WITNESSES: ELISHA MORSE, ANN WATSON.

HAYNES, JOSHUA   OCTOBER 20, 1794. Nov. 6, 1794.
     LEGATEES: REBECCA MANLY, KITRAH MANLY. WITNESSES TO NUNCUPATIVE WILL: JOSHUA LEWIS, ROBERT SCOTT, W. BRYAN.

HAYS, SOUTHY   JULY 25, 1805.
     GRANDSONS: SOUTHY HAYS SON OF WILLIAM HAYS & SOUTHY HAYS SON OF JOHN HAYS. WITNESSES TO NUNCUPATIVE WILL: PHOEBY DUN, JOHN D. DUN, RICHARD HOLMES, J. P. CLERK: JAMES S. PURDIE.

HEGGONS, JEPTETH   FEBRUARY 17, 1768. AUG. COURT 1768.
     WIFE & EXECUTRIX: MARTHAR. DAUGHTER: ANNA. WITNESSES: JOHN SWAIN, JOSEPH CAIN, JOHN CROSS. CLERK: MATURIN COLVILL.

HENDON, JOSIAH   3 MAY 1830.
     DAUGHTERS: MARGARET WILLIAMS, LYDIA BALDWIN, MARY WHITE. GRANDCHILDREN: ALEXANDER WILLIAMS, DAVID JACKSON WILLIAMS, RICHARD WILLIAMS (CHILDREN OF MARGARET), LYDIA BALDWIN, MARY BALDWIN, MARY WHITE, ELIZABETH ANN HENDON, MARGARET ANN HENDON. TRUSTEES & EXECUTORS: BENJAMIN FITZRANDOLPH, ALEXANDER MCDOWELL, ISAAC WRIGHT. WITNESSES: DUGALD MCKEITHAN, A. L. HARVEY.

HENDON, WILLIAM (PLANTER)   AUGUST 22, 1778.
     WIFE: LYDIA. SONS & EXECUTORS: WILLIAM, JOSIAH. WITNESSES: AGATHEY POINTER, JOSEPH SINGLETARY.

HERRING, MARY   JULY 31, 1834
     SON & EXECUTOR: LUKE HERRING (PLANTATION BOUGHT FROM DURTIS DEAL CALLED THE MOORE PLANTATION). GRANDDAUGHTERS: MARY ANN HERRING, ELIZABETH. WITNESSES: WILL WILLIAMS, MOSES LEWIS, JR., THEOPHILUS TATOM.

HERRINGTON, ELIZABETH   APRIL 14, 1846. MAY TERM 1849.
     SON: JOHN B. HERRINGTON (OTHER CHILDREN MENTIONED, BUT NOT NAMED). OTHER LEGATEES: BAPTIST HOME MISSIONARY SOCIETY, JOHN CROMARTIE. EXECUTOR: ARCH'D. MURPHY. WITNESSES: D. W. CROMARTIE, JAMES W. CROMARTIE, DANIEL

N. McMillan. Clerk: H. H. Robinson.

HESTER, AARON   10 September 1885.
   Wife & Executrix: Emiline S. Witnesses: Isaac Northrop, W. T. Baldwin. Clerk: W. J. Sutton.

HESTER, ALEFAIR F.   28 March 1893. 9 August 1893.
   Sons: H. F., E. J., W. F., F. E., N. E., D. M., J. W. (4 daughters not named) Executor: E. J. Hester (son). Witnesses: Hoke Singletary, R. L. Singletary, Jas. Hester.

HESTER, DANIEL   January 26, 1880. October 6, 1884.
   Wife: Sarah. Son & Executor: Edward T. Hester. Daughters: Martha J. wife of William H. Bryan, Sarah E. wife of Gillmore Edwards, Mary F. wife of John D. Biggs. Nephew: Edward S. Lewis. Witnesses: George W. Jones, R. S. Lewis. Clerk: G. F. Melvin.

HESTER, DAVID (Farmer) 4 August 1887. 27 October 1896.
   Wife: Rachel. Sons & Executors: Daniel Edmond, David Asberry, Leonard Grant. Daughters: Not named. Witnesses: Jno. W. Cashwell, James Cashwell. Clerk: W. J. Sutton.

HESTER, THOMAS   April 27, 1839.
   Wife: Rebecca. Sons: A. Killis, Stephen. Daughters: Elizabeth Br tt, Mary Britt, Sarah Phillips, Rebecca Hardy, Comfort Hester, Margaret Britt. Granddaughters: Mary Hester, Patience Hester, Margaret Hester. Grandson: William Hester. Executor: Daniel M. Nance. Witnesses: C. Munroe, Daniel M. Nance.

HILL, ISAAC (Laborer) April 10, 1770.
   Brother: William Bartram. Nephew: Bartram Robeson. Executor & Friend: Joseph Lock. Witnesses: William Salter, William Oliphant.

HODGE, ROBERT   March 25, 1797.
   (Nuncupative will) Legatees: Moses Lewis and his wife Mary. Witnesses: John Thomas & wife Margaret Thomas, T. J. Lewis, J. P.

HOLLINGSWORTH, STEPHEN   SEPTEMBER 5, 1840.
    WIFE: MARY SONS: ALEXANDREA, AUGUSTUS. DAUGHTERS:
REBECCA J., SUSAN T., MARY MARGARET, ISABELLA. EXECUTORS:
ROBERT MELVIN, GEORGE T. BARKSDALE. WITNESSES: ARTHUR
MELVIN, JAMES THAGARD. (SOUTH RIVER MILLS TO BE REPAIRED)

HOLMES, EDWARD   APRIL 3, 1796.
    WIFE & EXECUTRIX: ANN. SON & EXECUTOR: RICHARD.
OTHER LEGATEES: NANCY BOON A MINOR UNDER TUITION OF
RICHARD HOLMES. JOHN CHICKENS SON OF REBECKA CHICKENS,
DEC'D. EXECUTORS: WILLIAM BRYAN, JOHN WINGATE, JOHN CLARK.
WITNESSES: JOHN WINGATE, JOHN SMITH, JOSEPH BALDWIN,
JESSE SMITH.

HOLMES, MOSES   JULY 27, 1804.
    WIFE & EXECUTRIX: MARY. SONS: GABRIEL & JOHN
(EXECUTOR). DAUGHTER: MARY (PLANTATION ADJOINING JENNET
SPENDLOVE'S). SON-IN-LAW & EXECUTOR: ALEXANDER KING.
WITNESSES: JAMES FLINN, JESSE BRANTLEY, JAMES WILLIAMS.

HOWARD, JOHN
    SONS: WILLIAM, PRIMUS, JAMES. DAUGHTERS: SARAH,
EMELINE (AMELIA), MARY. EXECUTORS: WILLIAM & PRIMUS
HOWARD (SONS). WITNESSES: HE.EKIAH HOWARD, NOAH STRAHAN.

HUFHAM, SOLOMON   JULY 26, 1810.
    MOTHER (NOT NAMED). SISTERS: ANN HUFHAM, FRANCIS
HUFHAM. EXECUTRIX: ANN HUFHAM (SISTER). WITNESSES:
MARGARET WATSON, BENJAMIN LOCK.

HUFMAN, HUDNAL   MARCH 15, 1790.
    WIFE & EXECUTRIX: MARTHA. SONS: JAMES, SOLOMAN.
DAUGHTER: MARY. EXECUTOR: JAMES HUFMAN (SON). WITNESSES:
BENJAMIN ELWELL, WILLIAM DAVIS RILLEY.

IKNER, GEORGE   MAY 10, 1774.
    WIFE & EXECUTRIX: DOROTHY. SONS: GEORGE, PHILLIP,
SOLOMAN. FATHER: PHILLIP IKNER. OTHER LEGATEE: WILLIAM
GODFREY. EXECUTOR: HENRY WESSON. WITNESSES: JOHN
LEGGETT, PHILZO E. GAUSE.

ISHAM, JAMES   JULY 14, 1780.
    SON: JAMES (LANDS ON ELLIS CREEK). COUSIN: ANN
ELLIS. NIECE: SUSANNA HARRISON. EXECUTORS: JOHN HARRI-
SON, SR., SAMUEL CAIN, ESQ. WITNESSES: RICHARD HARRISON,
SUSANNA HARRISON.

IVEY, CHARLES   APRIL 24. AUGUST 1, 1887.
     BROTHER: JOHN IVEY. NIECE: ELIZABETH CAROLINE
SINGLETARY WIFE OF MONROE SINGLETARY. OTHER LEGATEE:
JIMMIE ANN PAIT DAUGHTER OF ANN PAIT. EXECUTORS: MONROE
SINGLETARY, ELIZABETH CAROLINE SINGLETARY. WITNESSES:
ISAAC A. DAVIS, EVANDER SINGLETARY, G. S. EDWARDS. CLERK:
GEO. F. MELVIN.

IVEY, JOHN   APRIL 24, 1882. MAY 24, 1892.
     BROTHER: CHARLES IVEY. NIECE: ELIZABETH CAROLINE
SINGLETARY WIFE OF MONROE SINGLETARY. OTHER LEGATEE:
JINNY ANN PAIT DAUGHTER OF ANN PAIT. EXECUTORS: MONROE
SINGLETARY, ELIZABETH CAROLINE SINGLETARY. WITNESSES:
ISAAC A. DAVIS, EVANDER SINGLETARY. CLERK: GEO. F. MELVIN.

JACOBS, SHADRACH   APRIL 27, 1818. (OF COLUMBUS CO.)
     WIFE: MARY. SON: ARTHUR: DAUGHTER: PEGGY. OTHER
LEGATEE: SAMUEL CAMPBELL. WITNESSES: GEORGE RABURN,
ELIZABETH RABURN, BENJAMIN MOORE.

JERNIGAN, WHITMEL   OCTOBER 25, 1793. MARCH 18, 1804.
     BROTHER & EXECUTOR: RICHARD JERNIGAN. COUSINS:
FREDERICK JERNIGAN, NEDOM FARFAX, ELY JERNIGAN. WITNESS:
RETURN STRONG. ("THE WORK OF IGNATIOUS FLOWERS")

JESSUP, ISAAC   MARCH 30, 1852. MAY TERM 1852.
     WIFE: ELIZABETH ANN. SONS: JAS. MCD., WILLIAM S.
(DECEASED). DAUGHTER: HARRIET N. GRANDSONS: WM. H. &
ISAAC C. MELVIN (PROPERTY NOW IN POSSESSION OF ARTHUR
MELVIN). EXECUTOR: JAS. MCD. JESSUP. WITNESSES: JOSHUA
JESSUP, JAMES M. JESSUP. CLERK: J. I. MCREE.

JESSUP, JOHN   OCTOBER 28, 1786.
     WIFE & EXECUTRIX: (NOT NAMED) EXECUTORS: JONATHAN
TOMKINS, JOSIAH LEWIS, SR. WITNESSES: DUGALD BLUE, THOMAS
MELDEAN, JOSEPH DAVIS, JOHN MCLARRON.

JOHNSON, DANIEL   FEBRUARY 24, 1872. SEPTEMBER 9,
     1880. WIFE: MARGARET. OTHER LEGATEES: CATHARINE
WEST, JOSHUA JOHNSON, JAMES JOHNSON, WINSOR CHURCH.
("LANDS DEVISED TO THE SLAVES FORMERLY BELONGING TO ME, IF
THEY ASSIST & TAKE CARE OF MY BELOVED WIFE") EXECUTOR:
TAYLOR JOHNSON. WITNESSES: JOSHUA JOHNSON, ROBERT L.
BRYAN. JUDGE OF PROBATE: EVANDER SINGLETARY.

JOHNSON, JOEL   OCTOBER 23, 1856. CODICIL: NOV.
9, 1858. AUGUST TERM 1861. SONS: OWEN, R. W.,
DANIEL, KINION, EVAN. DAUGHTERS: MOLCY WEST, MARY J.
POLLOCK, ELIZA COLE, HELEN JOHNSON. GRANDDAUGHTER: MARY
E. HARVEY. GRANDSONS: ROBERT HARVEY, JOEL Y. HARVEY
(LANDS ON WEST SIDE OF TURNBULL CREEK ON JONES LAKE DRAIN).
BROTHER & EXECUTOR: DANIEL JOHNSON. WITNESSES: (HOLO-
GRAPH WILL) JOHN P. LYTLE, HUBERT R. FRANCIS, WILLIAM J.
PARKER, JOHN G. SUTTON. CLERK: D. BLUE.

JOHNSON, RICHARD   FEBRUARY 14, 1881. JULY 2, 1881.
DAUGHTER: SALLIE JOHNSON. EXECUTOR: THEODORE M.
SIKES. WITNESSES: DANIEL SMITH, TAMMESIA JEFFRIES, T. M.
SIKES. JUDGE OF PROBATE: N. A. STEDMAN, JR.

JOHNSON, SOLOMON   5 AUGUST 1831.
WIFE & EXECUTRIX: ELIZABETH JOHNSON. STEP-DAUGHTER:
ELIZABETH BLACKWELL. WITNESSES: J. MCDUFFIE, MARGARET
MCDUFFIE.

JOHNSON, WILLIAM   SEPTEMBER 9, ____
WIFE: ANN. SON & EXECUTOR: WILLIAM S. DAUGHTERS:
SARAH MONROE, MARGARET WILLIAMS. EXECUTOR: COLIN MONROE.
WITNESSES: N. BANNERMAN, G. W. BANNERMAN, P. W. BANNER-
MAN.

JOHNSTON, LELAH   MARCH 15, 1789.
DAUGHTERS: ELIZA LUCAS, MARY WHITE. SONS: GEORGE
LYON, JOHN JOHNSTON, ROBERT JOHNSTON. DAUGHTER-IN-LAW:
PRUDENCE JOHNSTON (WIFE OF ROBERT). GRANDSON: DAVID
WHITE. OTHER LEGATEES: JOHN WHITE, JEAN GATES, MARY
HARVEY, ELIZA GATES. EXECUTORS: SAMUEL CAIN, PETER
ROBESON. WITNESSES: JAMES COUNCIL, MARY COUNCIL, MARY
HARVEY.

JONES, CALVIN   FEBRUARY 14, 1885. NOV. 28, 1885.
WIFE: SARAH J. EXECUTOR: NEPHEW OF MY WIFE, JOHN
D. THOMAS. WITNESSES: S. A. SMITH, R. E. DEESE. CLERK:
G. F. MELVIN.

JONES, CHARITY   FEBRUARY 12, 1862. CODICIL -
FEB. 5, 1876. AUG. 17, 1878. BROTHERS: LEVI JONES,
REUBEN JONES, MOSES JONES. FATHER: MOSES JONES, SR.
SISTER: ELIZABETH WIFE OF KILLIS HESTER, LUCY WIFE OF GEO.
L. BROWN, RUTH WIFE OF JOHN B. WARD. NIECES: RHODA A.

JONES, MARTHA ELIZABETH WIFE OF HAYNES EDWARDS. NEPHEW
& EXECUTOR: GEORGE W. JONES. WITNESSES: C. MONROE, JOHN
M. LENNON, D. L. SINGLETARY, JAMES E. KELLY, DAVID CALLI-
HAN. JUDGE OF PROBATE: E. SINGLETARY

JONES, GRIFFITH   MARCH 21, 1757. AUG. TERM 1782.
    (OF THE PARISH OF SAINT MARTAIN & COUNTY OF BLADEN)
WIFE: NOT NAMED. DAUGHTERS: MARGARET MCREE WIFE OF WILL-
IAM MCREE, ANNA HOUSTON, MARY WHITE. SONS-IN-LAW, TRUST-
EES & EXECUTORS: WILLIAM HOUSTON, WILLIAM MCREE, JOHN
WHITE. GRANDSONS: GRIFFITH JONES WHITE, GRIFFITH HOUSTON.
SERVANT: ELIZABETH PINKINGTON. WITNESSES: ISAAC JONES,
RICHARD CRECH, PETER EVANS. WILL PROVED BY ISAAC JONES,
ESQ. CLERK: SAMUEL CAIN.

JONES, ISAAC   SEPTEMBER 10, 1783.
    SONS: EDWARD, ISAAC, MUSGROVE. GRANDDAUGHTER: JEAN
HUMPHREY. SONS-IN-LAW: BENJAMIN HUMPHREY, BENJAMIN FITZ-
RANDOLPH, JOHN LENNON, JOSIAH HENDON. (LANDS JOINING
BARTRAM'S LAKE. MY FERRY AT ELIZABETHTOWN) BROTHERS:
JOSEPH, WILLIAM & SNOWDEN SINGLETARY (THE HOUSEHOLD GOODS
I HAD WITH THEIR MOTHER BY MARRIAGE). EXECUTORS:
ISAAC & MUSGROVE JONES (SONS). WITNESSES: WILLIAM SALTER,
ROBERT HODGE, ELIZABETH FLOYD.

JONES, JONATHAN   OCTOBER 25, 1866. AUGUST 20, 1873.
    WIFE & EXECUTRIX: SARAH. SONS: JOHN F., LOVE, AMOS
L., NATHAN HENRY. DAUGHTERS: SARAH J. BORDEAUX, CHARLOTTE
M. CASHWELL, MARGARET A. WILLIS, LUCINDA JOHNSON, CLARISA
LINEAR. EXECUTORS: AMOS L. JONES & JOHN F. JONES (SONS).
WITNESSES: PETER CAIN, C. M. CAIN, JOHN AVERETT. CLERK:
EVANDER SINGLETARY.

JONES, LEVI   JANUARY 22, 1848. AUG. TERM 1849.
    WIFE: PENELOPE. DAUGHTERS: JINNEY JONES, ANN JONES,
JULIA HIGH, LUCY ANN (WIFE OF DAVID TAYLOR). SONS:
CALVIN, HENRY B., OLIVER, WILLIAM, JESSE. SON-IN-LAW:
DAVID TAYLOR. GRANDSONS: WASHINGTON L. JONES, FRANKLIN
JONES. EXECUTOR: HENRY B. JONES. WITNESSES: KINCHEN
K. COUNCIL, JOHN MCCALL. CLERK: H. H. ROBINSON.

JONES, MOSES, SR.   FEBRUARY 15, 1840. FEB. TERM 1846.
    SONS: LEVI, REUBEN (OF GEORGIA), MOSES, JR., (OF
MISSISSIPPI). DAUGHTERS: ELIZABETH HESTER, RUTH WARD,
LUCY BROWN, (NOW DEAD), CHARITY JONES. GRANDSON: GEORGE

W. JONES SON OF MOSES JONES, JR. EXECUTOR: COLIN MONROE
WITNESSES: JOHN E. LENNON, J. ELLIS. CLERK: H. H.
ROBINSON.

JONES, MUSGROVE (PLANTER) MARCH 26, 1850. NOV. TERM 1852.
    SON & EXECUTOR: DAVID (MY RIVER PLANTATION KNOWN BY
THE NAME OF PLUMMER LAND). DAUGHTER: SUSAN PLUMMER.
SONS-IN-LAW: SAMUEL CAIN, PETER CAIN, ISAAC JESSUP,
JOHN PLUMMER. GRANDDAUGHTER: MARY ELIZABETH PLUMMER,
DAUGHTER OF SUSAN & JOHN PLUMMER. EXECUTOR: ISAAC JESSUP.
WITNESSES: WM. DAVIS, DAVID SINGLETARY, CHAS. THOMAS
DAVIS. CLERK: J. I. MCREE

JONES, SARAH J.   25 APRIL 1890. 4 MAY 1896.
    NEPHEW: JOHN D. THOMAS. OTHER LEGATEE: ARCHIBALD
MONROE AND HIS WIFE MARY ANN MONORE. EXECUTOR: ARCHIBALD
MONROE. WITNESSES: JOHN W. KELLY, A. G. MCDOUGALD
CLERK: W. J. SUTTON.

JORDAN, BENJAMIN   JUNE 1, 1810.
    WIFE: NOT NAMED. SONS: JAMES, JOHN, THOMAS & RIVER
JORDAN. DAUGHTERS: NANCY MOORE, BETSY, POLLY SAUCER.
EXECUTORS: JESSE JONES, JOHN CURRIE. WITNESSES: JESSE
JONES, DAVID CURRIE.

JORDAN, RIVER   MARCH 15, 1860. NOV. TERM 1862.
    WIFE: LUCY ANN. SONS: RIVER CALVIN, THOMAS, LENON,
DAVID JAMES. DAUGHTERS: MARTHA JANE WIFE OF LUKE HIGH,
SARAH ANN (SINGLE WOMAN). EXECUTOR: LENNON JORDAN (SON).
WITNESSES: NEILL KELLY, ARCHIE MCNEILL. CLERK: D. BLUE.

KEA, JOHN   MAY 8, 1832. MAY TERM 1834.
    LEGATEES: ANDREW J. JONES SON OF WILLIAM JONES.
DAVID G. ROBESON SON OF JOHN A. ROBESON. EXECUTORS:
WILLIAM JONES & JOHN A. ROBESON. (HANDWRITING PROVEN BY
JOSEPH GILLESPIE)

KELLY, ARCHIBALD   MAY 19, 1861.
    SONS: JOHN ARCHIBALD, WILLIAM OWEN, JAMES E., DANIEL
ALEXANDER. DAUGHTERS: ELIZA ANN, CATHERINE JANE, ELCY
KELSEY MCKINNON, MARY M. WIFE OF STEPHEN B. CLARK.
WITNESSES: NEILL KELLY, JAS. C. KELLY.

KELLY, ARCHIBALD, SR. (STABLER) JUNE 12, 1813
    SONS: JAMES KELLY, SR., ARCHIBALD KELLY, JR.

DAUGHTERS: CATHERINE TAYLOR, FLORA CAMPBELL, MARY RAY.
SONS-IN-LAW: DANIEL TAYLOR, ARCHIBALD CAMPBELL, DUNCAN
RAY, DUNCAN CURRIE. EXECUTOR: JAMES KELLY, SR. (SON).
WITNESSES: JOHN TAYLOR, JR., JEAN RAY.

KELLY, JAMES SR.   JUNE 2, 1835.
     WIFE: MARY. SONS: ARCHIBALD, JOHN, NEILL, DANIEL,
DUNCAN, JAMES C. EXECUTORS: ARCHIBALD KELLY, JAMES C.
KELLY (SONS). WITNESSES: GEO. MCEWEN, GEO. MCKEE.
"P. S." OTHER HEIRS: JANE MCEWEN, CATHERINE CAMPBELL.

KELLY, JAMES E.   12 SEPTEMBER 1892. OCT. 24, 1892.
     WIFE: CAROLINE P. SONS: EARNEST A., DENNIS F.,
GEORGE W., A. J., J. N. DAUGHTERS: MARY A. KELLY, LUCY
J. ASHLEY, ELIZA L. DAVIS, ELIZABETH P. KELLY, CATHARINE
A. KELLY, E. C. KELLY. OTHER LEGATEES: J. W., W. E.,
E. L. DAVIS. EXECUTORS: A. J. KELLY, J. N. KELLY (SONS).
WITNESSES: C. W. WILLIAMS, GEORGE W. JONES. CLERK: GEO.
F. MELVIN.

KELLY, MARY   FEBRUARY 1847.
     EXECUTOR & GRAND NEPHEW: W. D. MCNEILL. OTHER LEGATEE:
MARY SWINDALL WIFE OF DAVID SWINDALL. WITNESSES: LEVI
MEARES, MARY GREEN.

KELLY, MATTHEW   APRIL 12, 1806.
     SONS & EXECUTORS: MATTHEW, JAMES. DAUGHTERS: SARAH
WINGATE, AMELIA KELLY. WITNESSES: JOHN KELLY, HUGH
JOHNSON, MULLINGTON LEWIS.

KELLY, NEILL   AUGUST 12, 1864. NOV. TERM 1864.
     WIFE: LUCY JANE (LANDS ADJOINING DR. MCKINNON).
SONS: WILLIAM A., JOHN E. (OTHER CHILDREN NOT NAMED).
EXECUTOR: A/ S. KEMP. WITNESSES: DUNCAN KELLY, R. J.
MCEWEN. (R. J. MCEWEN WHO THOUGH NOT DEAD IS NOW A SOLDIER
IN THE ARMY OF THE CONFEDERATE STATES). EXECUTOR ENTERED
INTO A BOND OF FIFTY THOUSAND DOLLARS WITH H. A. MC
DOWELL AS SECURITY. CLERK: D. BLUE.

KEMP, A. S.   FEBRUARY 6, 1877. APRIL 30, 1885.
     WIFE & EXECUTRIX: SUSAN: (CHILDREN NOT NAMED)
WITNESSES TO HANDWRITING: C. C. LYON, W. H. SYKES, F. F.
CUMMING. CLERK: G. F. MELVIN.

KEMP, JOSEPH   FEBRUARY 21, 1805.
    SONS: DAVID WHITE, WILLIAM, JOHN. DAUGHTERS: ELIZA-
BETH SALTER, MARY ELLIS WIFE OF JOHN ELLIS. GRANDSONS:
JOSEPH RICHARD KEMP, JOSEPH SALTER SON OF WILLIAM SALTER.
BROTHER: JOHN KEMP. EXECUTORS: WILLIAM ROBESON, JAMES
MOREHEAD.
WITNESSES: ROBERT LYTLE, J. KEMP.

KEMP, JOSEPH R.   AUGUST 30, 1882. MAY 8, 1883.
    CHILDREN: ELIZABETH S. BUIE, ELIZA A. KE P, EMMA I.
KEMP, JANE N. MCCALL, CHILDREN OF E. F. KEMP, DEC'D.,
JOSEPH R., FLORA C., ISAAC N., TENA H., A. J. KEMP,
MARY A.MCDONALD, JAMES I, KEMP. OTHER LEGATEE: FANNY
KEMP. WITNESSES: J. Q. NYE, RUFUS REGISTER. JUDGE OF
PROBATE: G. F. MELVIN.

KEMP, WILLIAM J.   JUNE 20, 1864. NOVEMBER TERM
    1866. BROTHER: ANDREW S. KEMP. SISTER: MARY ANN
MCDONALD. WITNESSES: THOS. M. KELLY, HUGH C. MCCOLLUM.
CLERK: D. BLUE.

KING, ALEXANDER   NOVEMBER 24, 1867. FEB. TERM 1868.
    WIFE: LYDIA. CHILDREN: CATHERINE ELIZABETH, FRANK-
LIN, SARAH K. LYTLE. FATHER: ALEXANDER KING. BROTHER &
EXECUTOR: JOHN KING. WITNESSES: S. MCNORTON, THOS. S.
EVANS. CLERK: D. BLUE.

KING, ALEXANDER, SR.   FEBRUARY 7, 1846.
    SONS: DUNCAN (LANDS ON BLENNING CREEK), WILLIAM (CRAIN
POND, ADJOINING LANDS OF GOODEN E. BOWEN), ALEXANDER,
JOHN, JAMES A., DAVID D. DAUGHTERS: MARY ROTHWELL,
CATHERINE ANN ANDERS. EXECUTORS: DUNCAN KING, JOHN
KING (SONS). WITNESSES: JAMES HOLMES, JOHN H. HOLMES,
JAMES H. FREEMAN, D. B. GILLESPIE, OVERTON DANIEL.

KING, DUNCAN   JUNE 24, 1793.
    WIFE: LYDIA. SON & EXECUTOR: ALEXANDER KING.
(OTHER CHILDREN NOT NAMED) EXECUTOR: WILLIAM WHITE.
WITNESSES: SAMUEL CARMAN, JEREMIAH BIGFORD, MARY WHITE.

KING, WILLIAM M.   JULY 5, 1883. NOV. 20, 1883.
    WIFE: MARY. SONS: WILLIAM A., MARSDEN. DAUGHTERS:
ADELINE KENNEDY, LUCY B. BRANTLY. GRANDCHILDREN: A. J.
KING, EVANDER D. KING, MARTHA L. KING, E. B. KING AND
WIFE, FRANCENIA W. KING. EXECUTOR: WILLIAM A. KING

(ELDEST SON). WITNESSES: JOHN C. DANIEL, JOHN B. LOVE, THOMAS S. EVANS. CLERK: G. F. MELVIN.

LAMB, MARY   NOVEMBER 11, 1769.
    LEGATEES: JACOB LAMB, ISAAC LAMB, THOMAS CLARK, HARDY INMAN, JOSHUA LAMB, MARY S. KEPER, THOMAS LAMB, ABSALOM LAMB, RACHEL DAVIS, PATIENCE CARTER. EXECUTORS: JACOB & ISAAC LAMB. WITNESSES: JESSE PITTMAN, NEEDHAM LAMB.

LAMON, ALEXANDER   MARCH 13, 1824.
    WIFE: MARION. SISTERS (NOT NAMED). UNCLES & EXECUTORS: DUNCAN McCALL, DOUGAL McKEITHAN. WITNESSES: DANIEL McKEITHAN, ARCH'D McCALL, NEILL McCALL.

LAMMOND, ANGUS   MARCH 18, 1815.
    WIFE: ELIZABETH. SON: ALEXANDER. DAUGHTERS: MARGARET BLUE, CATHERINE CAMPBELL, MARIAN SHAW. OTHER LEGATEE: MARY McLELLAND WIFE OF ANDREW McLELLAND. EXECUTORS: DUNCAN McCALL, DANIEL McKEITHAN. WITNESSES: J. ELLIS, J/ J. CUMMING, JAMES ELLIS.

LAMONT, DUNCAN (PLANTER) NOVEMBER 4, 1798.
    WIFE & EXECUTRIX: CHRISTIAN. DAUGHTERS: MARIAN, WIFE OF DANIEL McMILLAN, NANCY, FLORA, MARGARET, ELIZABETH. SONS: ANGUISH, DANIEL, DUNCAN. STEP-DAUGHTER: CHRISTIAN MUN. EXECUTORS: DANIEL TAYLOR, DUNCAN McCALL. WITNESSES: NEIL McCAULSKY, DUGALD CLARK, DUNCAN McCAULSKY.

LENNON, GEORGE
    (NUNCUPATIVE WILL) SPOKEN 22 DAY AUGUST 1822 IN PRESENCE OF EZEKIEL BAILEY, JR., STEPHEN PITMAN & OTHERS. CHILDREN & FAMILY MENTIONED BUT NOT NAMED.

LENNON, JOHN M.   NOVEMBER 22, 1875. FEBRUARY 7, 1876. DAUGHTERS: AMANDA FRINK, FRANCIS M. LENNON, MARY M. LENNON, LUCINDA BROWN, S. (D) T. FREEMAN. SONS: DENNIS, O. LENNON. EXECUTOR: JOSEPH E. LENNON. WITNESSES: DENNIS L. SINGLETARY, JAS. E. KELLY. PROBATE JUDGE: EVANDER SINGLETARY.

LEWIS, FRANCIS C.   AUGUST 6, 1850.
    NEPHEW: FRANCIS JAMES LEWIS, SON OF THOS. S. LEWIS. NIECES: LUCY ANN LEWIS DAUGHTER OF THOMAS S. LEWIS, MARY ELIZA LEWIS & AN INFANT (NOT NAMED), DAUGHTERS OF THOMAS S. LEWIS (LANDS ON BLACK LAKE). BROTHER: THOMAS S. LEWIS. EXECUTOR: COLIN SHAW. WITNESSES: DAVID

CALLIHAN & DURRUM LEWIS.

LEWIS, JOSIAH, SR.   MARCH 31, 1808.
     SONS: JOSHUA, AARON, RICHARD, MOSES, DURRUM.
DAUGHTERS: SILVIA, ANN, LUCY, SARAH, MARY, MARIAN.
GRANDSON & EXECUTOR: AARON LEWIS. WITNESSES: DOUGAL
McMILLAN, NEILL McMILLAN, DUNCAN McMILLAN.

LEWIS, RICHARD M., SR. FEB. 20, 1844. FALL TERM 1845.
     WIFE: MARTHA LEWIS. SONS: RICHARD M., JR., DURRUM,
EDWARD, DAVID. DAUGHTERS: LUCY ANN LESESNE, SARAH WILLIS,
(DEC'D). GRANDSON: RICHARD FRANKLIN LEWIS SON OF DAVID
LEWIS. EXECUTORS: EDWARD & DAVID LEWIS (SONS). WITNESS-
ES: ALBERT GILLESPIE, WM. DOWLESS. CLERK: WM. J. COWAN.

LEWIS, RICHARD M., SR. AUGUST 19, 1856. NOV. TERM 1856.
     WIFE: HANNAH (LANDS CONVEYED TO ME BY EPHRIAM HESTER
AND SAMUEL JOHNSON TO DANIEL HESTER'S LINE). DAUGHTER:
LUCY ANN SMITH. SONS & EXECUTORS: WILLIAM S. LEWIS,
RICHARD M. LEWIS. WITNESSES: ARCH'D KELLY, DAVID SINGLE-
TARY. CLERK: F. F. CUMMING.

LLOYD, ANNA A.   APRIL 18, 1770.
     DAUGHTER: MARY McREE. EXECUTOR & COUNSINS: WILLIAM
SMITH, JOHN SMITH. WITNESSES: ELIZABETH BAILEY, JOHN
SMITH, JAMES BAILEY.

LLOYD, NANCY   AUGUST 3, 1801.
     (WIDOW OF THE LATE DAVID LLOYD) DAUGHTER: NANCY
GARVIN WIFE OF RICHARD GARVIN. GRANDCHILDREN: WILLIAM
WILLIAMS & ELIZABETH ANN FLOYD, CHILDREN OF RICHARD
GARVIN'S WIFE BY FORMER MARRIAGE. SON-IN-LAW & EXECUTOR:
RICHARD GARVIN. EXECUTOR: PATRICK KELLY. WITNESSES:
HUGH MURPHY, JOHN McFEE. WORTHILY McMILLAN.

LOCK, DAVID   MARCH 6, 1812.
     WIFE & EXECUTRIX: SARAH. SISTER: MARY McFATTER.
EXECUTOR: DAVID LLOYD. WITNESSES: WILLIAM SIMPSON,
ELIZABETH PHOEBUS.

LOCK, ELIZABETH   SEPTEMBER 24, 1836.
     BROTHER: JAMES M. ANDERS, SR. NIECES: HANNAH
PRIDGEN WIFE OF STEPHEN PRIDGEN, ELIZABETH WIFE OF ROLEN
SUTTON, ELIZA WIFE OF ARCH'D KELLY. NEPHEWS: JOHN,
DAVID, SAMUEL, TIMOTHY & ALFRED ANDERS, STEPHEN, ARCHIBALD,

ALEXANDER & OWEN E. ANDERS, JAMES & ELISHA J. ANDERS.
OTHER LEGATEES: ANN JANE BRYAN, ENOCH & EDWARD A. HAWES.
JONES, THE SON OF NANCY JONES, MY NIECE, ANN ANDERS WIDOW
OF MY NEPHEW JAMES ANDERS, JAMES M. ANDERS, STEPHEN PRID-
GEN, JAMES MEREDITH, ELIZABETH AND MARGARET BANNERMAN
DAUGHTERS OF CHARLES BANNERMAN. FRIENDS: GEO. W. BANNER-
MAN. FRIENDS: GEO. W. BANNERMAN, WILLIAM (CAPE FEAR)
JOHNSON. EXECUTOR: JOHN D. BEATTY. WITNESSES: W.
SUTTON, TIMOTHY PRIDGEN.

LOCK, JOHN (PLANTER) NOVEMBER 8, 1787. FEB. TERM 17__.
    WIFE: ELIZABETH. SONS: JOSEPH, LEONARD, THOMAS,
JOHN. DAUGHTERS: ELIZABETH ELWELL, HANNAH, MARY, ELIZA,
SUSAN, REBECKAH. (DAUGHTER ELIZABETH'S CHILDREN: SARAH,
HANNAH, ELIZABETH). EXECUTORS: THOMAS & JOHN LOCK (SONS).
WITNESSES: JOHN STORM, JOHN MOORE, BENJAMIN ELWELL.
CLERK: SAMUEL CAIN.

LOCK, JOSEPH (PLANTER) OCTOBER 2, 1781.
    WIFE & EXECUTRIX: EUNICE. SONS: ISAAC, LEONARD.
DAUGHTER: SUSANNAH LOCK (LANDS ON SINGLETARY'S LAKE).
SON-IN-LAW: BENJAMIN ELWELL. EXECUTOR: LEONARD LOCK
(SON). WITNESSES: DAVID LOCK, BENJAMIN LOCK.

LOCK, LEONARD (PLANTER) SEPTEMBER 3, 1783.
    WIFE & EXECUTRIX: REBECCA. DAUGHTERS: REBECKAH,
ELIZABETH, SALLIE, MARY. SONS: LEONARD, JOHN, DAVID.
EXECUTOR: BENJAMIN COOPER. WITNESSES: WILLIAM PLUMMER,
ABSOLOM CAUDELL, WILLIAM CHAMPION.

LOWE, THOMAS   JANUARY 14, 1779.
    MOTHER & EXECUTRIX: AMEY HILL. SISTER-IN-LAW &
EXECUTRIX: WINIFRED LOWE. SONS: DANIEL, JOHN.
WITNESSES: ABRAHAM DAVIS, JAMES MOORE, MARY MOORE.

LUCAS, FRANCES   DECEMBER 14, 1784.
    WIFE: ELIZABETH. SONS: JOHN, HENRY. EXECUTORS:
ARCH'D MCLAIN, DONALD BAIN, GEORGE LUCAS, WILLIAM LUCAS.
WITNESSES: THO. MCLAIN, J. BRADLEY.

LUCAS, HENRY   APRIL 23, 1839.
    SONS: WM. B., JNO. J. D., ANNELIN B., HENRY L.
DAUGHTERS: MARY JANE, ELIZABETH R., MARGARET ANN KING.
OTHER LEGATEE: HELEN S. BRANTLEY OF SOUTH CAROLINA.
EXECUTORS: WILL B. LUCAS, JOHN J. D. LUCAS (SONS).

WITNESSES: JNO. O. DANIEL, WM. S. JOHNSON, WILL S. ANDRES.

LUCAS, HENRY L.   OCTOBER 18, 1855. AUGUST TERM 1859.
    (WIFE NOT NAMED) BROTHER & ADMINISTRATOR: WILLIAM 9
B. LUCAS. WITNESSES: WILLIAM WILSON, A. B. LUCAS. CLERK:
A. K. CROMARTIE.

LUCAS, J. J. D.   (PROBATE DATE) FEBRUARY 18, 1884.
    WIFE & EXECUTRIX: VIRGINIA T. SONS: WILLIAM H. G.,
JOHN D. A., THOMAS A. E. M., OWEN M. DAUGHTER: MARY A.
MELVIN (HEIRS OF MARY A. MELVIN: MARY E/, URA M., ADA
D. & RENA G MELVIN). EXECUTOR: WILLIAM H. G. LUCAS (SON).
WITNESSES AS TO HANDWRITING: EVAN ROTHWELL, C. C. LYON,
L. J. HALL. CLERK: G. F. MELVIN.

LUCAS, THOMAS   JUNE 27, 1792.
    WIFE & EXECUTRIX: PRISCILLA. WIFE'S DAUGHTERS: MARY
LUCAS & SARAH LUCAS. (MY 2 CHILDREN): SUSAN & WILLIAM.
NEPHEW: JOHN LUCAS. EXECUTOR: GEORGE _____
WITNESSES: DANIEL BERRY, RICHARD SALTER, RICHARD CLAYTON.

LUCAS, THOMAS   JUNE 6, 1772.
    WIFE & EXECUTRIX: PRISCILLA. DAUGHTERS: MARY LUCAS,
SARAH LUCAS. BROTHER'S SON: JOHN LUCAS. OTHER LEGATEES:
MILLY'S TWO CHILDREN, LENORA & WILLIAM. EXECUTOR:
GEORGE LUCAS.

LYON, ELEANOR   FEBRUARY 22, 1844. NOV. TERM 1846.
    BROTHERS: ITHAMORE SINGLETARY, JAMES B. SINGLETARY,
EVAN SINGLETARY, OWEN SINGLETARY, FITZRANDOLPH SINGLETARY.
SISTER: MARY HOWELL. NIECE: LOUISA HOWELL. EXECUTORS:
JAMES W. LESESNE, JAMES ROBESON, JR. WITNESSES: DURRUM
LEWIS, JOSHUA L. NANCE. CLERK: H. H. ROBINSON.

LYON, ROBERT H.   DECEMBER 22, 1892. SEPTEMBER 19,
    1895. (OF ELIZABETHTOWN) WIFE & EXECUTRIX: SALLIE.
SONS: KARL, HENRY, ROY. PROTEGE: "PEARL" OTHER
LEGATEES: PEGGY HALL, HENRIETTA NORMAN, E. D. BIZZELL,
TOM RUSSELL. TRUSTEES, EXECUTORS & GUARDIANS: C. C.
LYON, C. W. LYON, R. HENRY LYON, B. G. WORTH. WITNESSES:
B. M. ROBERTS, W. J. SUTTON, F. M. WILLIS, T. V. BUTLER,
G. W. STARLING, D. T. PERRY. CLERK: W. J. SUTTON.

MANLEY, LYDIA   SEPTEMBER 4, 1809.
    DAUGHTER: MOLSEY SHAW. GRANDDAUGHTERS: REBECCA
SHAW, JANE SHAW. SON-IN-LAW & EXECUTOR: MALCOM SHAW.

OTHER LEGATEES: BAZIL MANLEY, ROBERT DEWEY, ANN MCKAY.
WITNESSES: ARCHIE CAMPBELL, DANIEL CAMPBELL, DANIEL
GOODEN.

MARSHBURN, DANIEL H.   SEPTEMBER 1, 1873. MARCH 24, 1874.
     WIFE: MARIAN. SONS: JAMES M., ROBERT M., JACOB W.,
FRANKLIN M. DAUGHTERS: JULIA WILLIAMS WIFE OF OWEN W.
WILLIAMS, SARAH E. MARSHBURN, MARY P. PETERSON, MATILDA
MARSHBURN, MARION L. MARSHBURN, SUSAN, LAURA & EMMA MARSH--
BURN. EXECUTORS: JAMES W. MARSHBURN (SON), OWEN W. WILL-
IAMS AND ROBERT HIGHSMITH (BROTHER-IN-LAW). WITNESSES:
WM. H. RUSS, M. MERRITT. CLERK: EVANDER SINGLETARY.

MASSINGAE, JOSEPH (PLANTER) SEPTEMBER 2, 1804.
     WIFE: MARY. WITNESSES: JOHN WRIGHT, WILLIAM PENNY.

MAULTSBY, ANTHONY   DECEMBER 14, 1800.
     SONS: WILLIAM ALEXANDER MCFATTER, SAMUEL CARVER
MCFATTER, JOHN SAVAGE MCFATTER. OTHER LEGATEES: ISABELLA
MCFATTER, ANNA JANE MCFATTER, MARY ANN MCFATTER, WILLIAM
MAULTSBY HEIRS, JAMES MAULTSBY HEIRS, SAMUEL MAULTSBY
HEIRS, THOMAS MAULTSBY. WITNESSES: HENRY STEWART,
DUNCAN MCKEITHAN, J. MCKAY.

MAULTSBY, SAMUEL   JANUARY 1, 1867. SEPT. 5, 1892.
     WIFE: DEALA. OTHER LEGATEE: W. M. BROWN. WITNESS-
ES: GRADY DRY, W. J. JOHNSON. CLERK: GEO.F. MELVIN.

MAULTSBY, THOMAS   FEBRUARY 28, 1812. CODICIL:
     MARCH 10, 1812. WIFE & EXECUTRIX: SARAH. SON & EX-
ECUTOR: JOSIAH MAULTSBY. DAUGHTERS: (NOT NAMED)
EXECUTORS: DAVID LLOYD, BENJAMIN LOCK. WITNESSES: JOHN
SIMPSON, DAVID D. CARPENTER, JOHN RUSS, BENJAMIN EVANS.

MAXFIELD, MARY (GENTL WOMAN) MAY 14, 1778.
     DAUGHTER: LITTICE TOWNSEND. SON & EXECUTOR: ROBERT
CONKEY. WITNESSES: DAVID WHITE, THOMAS TOWNSEND, BEN'J.
HUMPHREY.

MEARS, ELIHUE   JUNE 5, 1860. CODICIL: NOV. 3,
     1870. APRIL TERM 1871. WIFE: CHARLOTTE. NEPHEW:
ELIHUE MEARS, NIECE: FRANCES MEARS, CHILDREN OF MY
BROTHER JOHN MEARS. NEPHEW & NIECE: JOHN W. ELLIS &
PENELOPE ANN MARIAH ELLIS. OTHER LEGATEE: JACK MEARS,
NOW A FREE MAN. EXECUTORS: JOHN W. ELLIS, MALCOM MCLEOD.

WITNESSES: THOS. M. KELLY, F. M. WOOTEN, JOHN D. CURRIE,
E. J. MCLEOD. CLERK: D. BLUE.

MEEK, GEORGE   NOVEMBER 15, 1789.
     WIFE & EXECUTRIX: MARY. EXECUTORS: HENRY MCK. STUART,
A. MCNORTEN. WITNESSES: JAMES COUNCIL, PETER ROBESON.

MELVIN, BARBARA A.   19 JULY 1881. 18 DECEMBER 1882.
     (CERTIFIED COPY OF WILL FROM CUMBERLAND COUNCY, N. C.)
WIDOW OF DANIEL M. MELVIN. SON & EXECUTOR: B. SPURGEON
MELVIN. FATHER: JOHN MCCALL (DECEASED). DAUGHTER:
HELLEN J. MCLAURIN. (OTHER CHILDREN NOT NAMED) WITNESSES:
CHARLES H. BLOCKER, L. J. MCKAY.

MELVIN, DANIEL, SR.   NOVEMBER 15, 1844. NOV. TERM 1846.
     SONS: ROBERT, DANIEL, ARTHUR, JOHN, GEORGE W.
DAUGHTERS: ANN HERRINGTON, CATHERINE SMITH, SARAH MONROE,
JANE MONROE, ELIZABETH YOUNG. GRANDSON: ROBERT YOUNG
(SON OF ELIZABETH YOUNG). EXECUTORS: ROBERT, DANIEL,
ARTHUR & GEORGE W. MELVIN (SONS). WITNESSES: KENNETH
MCLEOD, OWEN SMITH. CLERK: H. H. ROBINSON.

MELVIN, DEMARIS & ROSANA J. (SISTER) FEBRUARY 13, 1880.
     SEPTEMBER 22, 1882. BROTHERS: JONATHAN MELVIN, JAMES
MELVIN, ROBERT MELVIN. SISTER: CATHERAN BULLARD. OTHER
LEGATEES: ELIZABETH TATOM WIFE OF JOSHUA TATOM, HENRY
MELVIN. EXECUTOR: DANIEL MILES MELVIN. WITNESSES: W. B.
BAKER, W. F. MELVIN, W. S. MELVIN. JUDGE OF PROBATE:
G. F. MELVIN.

MELVIN, GEORGE W. (PLANTER AND SHERIFF AS OF THIS DATE,
     DECEMBER 20, 1845) MAY TERM 1847. WIFE: ANN JANE.
DAUGHTER: HANNAH JANE. WITNESSES: HEMAN H. ROBINSON,
G. I. MCMILLAN. CLERK: H. H. ROBINSON.

MELVIN, JAMES   SEPTEMBER 1, 1880. AUGUST 29,
     1881. WIFE: MARIAN. EXECUTOR: W. S. MELVIN.
WITNESSES: J. B. MELVIN, W. F. MELVIN. JUDGE OF PROBATE:
N. A. STEDMAN, JR.

MELVIN, JOHN   NOVEMBER 9, 1839.
     WIFE: SARAH ANN. DAUGHTERS: MARGARET ANN, ELIZA J.,
ELIZABETH POYNTER. SONS: WASHINGTON A., JAMES KELLY,
JOHN BEATTY. EXECUTOR: G. W. MELVIN. WITNESSES: A.
MONROE, SANDERS SIMMONS.

MELVIN, JOHN   FEBRUARY 24, 1851. MAY TERM 1853.
    SONS: EDWARD (DECEASED), SAMUEL (DECEASED), DUNCAN,
GEORGE, ANDREW, JOSHUA, JOSEPH, JAMES, ROBERT, JONATHAN,
DAVID T. (DECEASED). GRANDSONS: JOHN, GEORGE & EDWARD
MELVIN, CHILDREN OF MY SON EDWARD. DAUGHTERS: JANE
REEVES, NANCY REEVES, SARAH SMITH, CATHERINE BULLARD,
ELIZABETH TATOM, DAMARIS MELVIN, ROSANNA JANE MELVIN AND
SARAH MELVIN, WIDOW OF MY SON DAVID T. EXECUTORS: DUNCAN
& JAMES MELVIN (SONS). WITNESSES: JNO. S. RICHARDSON,
DANIEL MCDUFFIE. CLERK: J. I. MCREE.

MELVIN, JONATHAN   FEBRUARY 26, 1875. MAY 21, 1875.
    SISTERS: DEMARUS MELVIN, ROSANA MELVIN. EXECUTOR:
WILLIAM S. MELVIN. WITNESSES: R. A. MELVIN, D. R. MELVIN,
N. J. BIRK. JUDGE OF PROBATE: EVANDER SINGLETARY.

MELVIN, JOSHUA   NOVEMBER 8, 1854. NOVEMBER 23,1856.
    (DIED IN PARISH OF BIENVILLE, STATE OF LOUISIANA ON
NOV. 14, 1854) WIFE: ELIZABETH. SON: GEORGE W.
DAUGHTER: ELIZA JANE. EXECUTORS: JACOB EVANS, JAMES
BRYAN, JAMES J. VICKERS. WITNESSES: W. M. D. CAWTHON,
JOHN DENNARD, A. T. CAWTHON, J. D. CAWTHON, HOWELL AL-
BRITTAIN, JAMES J. VICKERS, LUKE ALBRITTAIN. PROBATED IN
LOUISIANA.

MELVIN, ROBERT,SR.   NOVEMBER 15, 1844. NOVEMBER TERM,
    1846. WIFE: ELIZABETH (MY CHURCH BIBLE AND DOSSEYS
CHOICE HYMN BOOK). SONS: JOHN S., JOSEPH M., GEORGE F.,
JAMES H., DAVID B., DANIEL MARSHALL, WILLIAM, ARTHUR W.,
ROBERT P. DAUGHTER: ELIZA ANN MELVIN. GRANDCHILDREN:
ROBERT M., ELIZABETH AND AMOS JESSUP. "MY BODY TO BE
INTERED IN THE BURYING GROUND AT MY FATHER'S." (LANDS
BOUGHT OF CADE WEATHERSBEE, EXEKIEL SUGGS, WILLIAM T.
JESSUP, OWEN SMITH, ATTORNEY FOR LEWIS SUGGS, ARTHUR FORT,
ELIAS MCLEMORE, PETER MCLEAN, ISHAM CAIN, WM. ATKINSON)
EXECUTORS: JAMES H. & DAVID B. MELVIN (SONS) AND GEORGE
W. MELVIN (BROTHER). WITNESSES: KENNETH MCLEOD, J. JONES.
CLERK: H. H. ROBINSON.

MEMORY, GEORGE   1806.
    WIFE & EXECUTRIX: SARAH. SON: THOMAS. DAUGHTERS:
CELIA MEMORY, ELLENDER WARD. EXECUTORS: JAMES KELLY.
WITNESSES: MATTHEW MCEWEN, JANE MCEWEN.

MEREDITH, JAMES   JUNE 22, 1850. NOV. TERM 1863.
   WIFE: SARAH. SON & EXECUTOR: JAMES H. DAUGHTERS:
SARAH ANN ANDERS, ELEANOR (ELLEN) JANE COLINS. WITNESSES:
GEORGE W. BANNERMAN, WILLIAM J. PARKER, ARCHIBALD MURPHY.
CLERK: D. BLUE.

MILLER, AUGUSTE S. (FARMER) SEPTEMBER 26, 1883. OCT.
   26, 1885. WIFE & EXECUTRIX: MAREY E. SON: LEOPOLD
MILLER. DAUGHTER: MARY MILLER. WITNESSES: W. H.
BROWN, J. B. BROWN, WM. MONROE, S. B. KING. CLERK: G. F.
MELVIN.

MILLER, FREDERICK   APRIL 4, 1834.
   WIFE: HANNAH. SON: WILLIAM L. DAUGHTERS: EMILY
R. GAUSE, WIFE OF J. I. GAUSE, JANE D. BYRNE. GRANDSON:
WILLIAM L. GILMORE (LANDS IN CUMBERLAND COUNTY ON WILLIS
C.. EEK LEFT TO DAUGHTER JANE D. BYRNE). EXECUTORS:
WI   .AM L. MILLER (SON) & JAMES A. BYRNE. WITNESSES:
JO   PATTERSON, ARCH'D CRAWFORD.

MOORE, BERENGER   JANUARY 4, 1775.
   WIFE & EXECUTRIX: MARY. NEPHEW: NATHAN MOORE.
 THER LEGATEES: JOHN HILL SON OF WILLIAM HILL OF BRUNSWICK
 OUNTY, JOHN DAVIS SON OF ROGER DAVIS OF BRUNSWICK COUNTY.
 XECUTORS: WILLIAM HILL, ROGER DAVIS. WITNESSES: ROBERT
TUCKER, WILL DRY, JR., THO. BROWN.

MOORE, JAMES   MAY 21, 1793.
   DAUGHTERS: EARDICE, LYDIA, HANNAH. OTHER LEGATEE:
ABIGAL CHAVIS. EXECUTORS: ABRAHAM FREEMAN, ABAGIL CHAVIS.
WITNESSES: A. SIMPSON, DAVID CLARK, RICHARD STUBBS.

MOORE, MAURICE (PLANTER) FEBRUARY 15, 1832.
   DAUGHTER: SARAH ROBESON WIFE OF JAMES ROBESON. (IF
NO ISSUE OF SARAH AND JAMES, MY EXECUTORS TO SELL PLAN-
TATION AND HIRE OUT NEGROES AND THE PROCEEDS TO BE APPLIED
TO BENEVOLENT PURPOSES, AS WORTHY PREACHERS OF THE GOS-
PEL, REPAIRING CHURCHES, ETC. AND TO THE RELIEF OF WIDOWS
AND ORPHANS THAT THEY MAY THINK IN NEED) OTHER LEGATEE:
ROBERT MOORE. EXECUTORS: JOHN OWEN & JOSEPH R. KEMP
(MY FRIENDS). WITNESSES: ALEX J. BYRNE, B. ROBESON,
WILLIS COUNCIL.

MOORE, WILLIAM   NOVEMBER 5, 1767. MAY COURT 1768.
   WIFE AND TWO DAUGHTERS MENTIONED, BUT NOT NAMED.

SONS: JAMES, SKENKINE. BROTHER & EXECUTOR: JOHN MOORE.
EXECUTOR: PETER BYRON. WITNESSES: LAWRENCE BYRNE,
JOHN LOCK, WILLIAM PLUMMER. CLERK: ARTHUR MOORE.

MOORE, WILLIAM   AUGUST 18, 1773. AUGUST TERM 1774.
    SONS: WILLIAM, JOHN, MATTHEW, HAMES. EXECUTOR:
JAMES MOORE (SON). WITNESSES: JESSE MOSS, RICHARD
RESGOW. CLERK: ALFRED MOORE.

MOOREHEAD, JAMES   JULY 28, 1807.
    DAUGHTERS: ELIZABETH WIFE OF ISAAC WRIGHT (LAND KNOWN
BY THE OLD COURT HOUSE), SARAH WIFE OF HINTON JAMES
(PLANTATION LANDS ADJOINING BROMPTON, BOUGHT OF WILLIAM
ROBESON). EXECUTORS: HINTON JAMES, ISAAC WRIGHT. HAND-
WRITING PROVED BY JAMES B. WHITE & J. S. PURDIE.

MOOREHEAD, MARY   AUGUST 5, 1787.
    HUSBAND & EXECUTOR: JAMES MOOREHEAD. SONS: BARTRAM
ROBESON, JONATHAN ROBESON, WILLIAM ROBESON. DAUGHTERS:
ELIZABETH ROBESON, SARAH, MARY. (FORMER LATE HUSBAND,
THOMAS ROBESON) EXECUTORS: BARTRAM ROBESON & JONATHAN
ROBESON. WITNESSES: JOSEPH CAIN, JAMES COUNCIL.

MONROE, ARCHIBALD   21 MARCH 1832.
    WIFE: NANCY. SONS: PETER, JAMES, ARCHIBALD, COLIN.
DAUGHTERS: MARGARET KELLY, CATHERINE MONROE, MARY MONROE.
EXECUTOR: COLIN MONROE (SON). WITNESSES: DANIEL MONROE,
WILLIAM WILLIS, ALEX PATTERSON.

MONROE, COLIN   MAY TERM 1868. FEB. TERM 1865.
    WIFE: SARAH I. MOTHER: NANCY MONROE. SISTERS:
MARGARET KELLY, CATHERINE MCKEE, MARY G. MONROE. NEPHEW:
COLIN KELLY. BROTHERS: DUGOLD, JOHN, PETER, DAVID,
JAMES. OTHER LEGATEES: JOHN W. MONROE SON OF DANIEL
MONROE, COLIN SINGLETARY, SON OF ROLAND SINGLETARY, COLIN
MONROE SON OF PETER MONROE, MALCOM MONROE, MARY JANE
BROWN, WILLIAM JOHNSON AND WIFE. (TOMBSTONES TO BE PUT
AT WILLIAM JOHNSON & WIFE'S GRAVES) EXECUTORS: THOS.
D. MCDOWELL, H. H. ROBINSON. CLERK: D. BLUE.

MONROE, DUNCAN (OF BROWN MARSH)   DECEMBER 1, 1777.
    WIFE: ELIZABETH SILLER. SON: ANGUS. WITNESSES:
IONALD MCCOLLUM, NEILL CURRIE, ARCHIBALD CAMPBELL.
EXECUTOR: ANGUS MONROE.

MONROE, JOHN   MARCH 19, 1877. DECEMBER 6, 1878.
    WIFE: JANE. SONS: GEORGE W., ARCH WILLIAM.
DAUGHTERS: HARRIET J., ANN E., SARAH E., NANCY C., MAR-
GARET E. MELVIN. GRANDCHILDREN: JANE HUNT, JOHN HUNT,
ROBERT HUNT, GASTON HUNT. EXECUTOR: NATHAN BRYAN.
(LANDS JOINING THE VILLAGE OF MAYESVILLE) WITNESSES:
A. MUNN, D. MUNN. JUDGE OF PROBATE: E. SINGLETARY.

MONROE, NANCY   JANUARY 12, 1857. CODICIL: APRIL
    30, 1859. SONS: JAMES, COLIN, MALCOM, DUGALD,
DANIEL, JOHN & PETER. DAUGHTER: MARY G. MONROE. EXECU-
TOR: COLIN MONROE (SON). WITNESSES: JOHN S. WILLIS,
WM. WILLIS.

MONROE, SARAH J.   JUNE 6, 1883. DECEMBER 15, 1883.
    BROTHER: WILLIAM S. JOHNSTON. SISTER: MARGARET
WILLIAMS. OTHER LEGATEES: MARY J. BROWN, GEORGE W. TAIT,
ROBERT TAIT, N. A. & COLIN MCLEAN, SONS OF DUNCAN MCLEAN,
JOHN N. KELLY (MY PENSION MONEY). METHODIST E. CHURCH
OF ABBOTTSBURG, N. C. EXECUTORS: JOHN M. JOHNSTON,
JOHN N. KELLY. WITNESSES: A. K. CROMARTIE, SNOWDEN
HESTER. CLERK: G. F. MELVIN.

MORGAN, WILLIAM   SEPTEMBER 3, 1823. OCTOBER 21, 1823.
    (NUNCUPATIVE WILL) LEGATEES: WADE HAMPTON CAIN,
SAMUEL CAIN, RICHARD CAIN. EXECUTORS: SAMUEL A. RICHARD-
SON, JOSEPH CAIN. (JOSEPH CAIN BEFORE JOHN BEARD, JUSTICE
OF THE PEACE, PURDIE RICHARDSON & ALLEN BROWN WITNESSES
BEFORE JOHN BEARD, JUSTICE OF PEACE)

MORRISON, JOHN   MARCH 28, 1801.
    WIFE: FLORA. DAUGHTER: MARION. SON: KENNETH.
SON-IN-LAW: BENJAMIN WILLIS. GRANDSONS: DANIEL CAMPBELL,
NEILL MORRISON. EXECUTORS: JOHN CAMPBELL, DUNCAN CAMP-
BELL. WITNESSES: A. H. BRIDE, JEREMIAH WILLIS, BENJAMIN
WILLIS.

MOSICK, JACOB   FEBRUARY 13, 1788.
    FRIENDS: ELIZABETH BERRY, LUCY STREATY. EXECUTORS:
WILLIAM JONES, WILLIAM STREATY. WITNESSES: WILLIAM JONES,
JAMES RUSS.

MULFORD, ELIZABETH   FEBRUARY 14, 1798.
    HUSBAND: EPHRIAM. SONS: DAVID, THOMAS, JOHN
EPHRIAM. DAUGHTER: ABIGAL. GRANDDAUGHTER: ELIZABETH

PEMBERTON. GRANDSON: THOMAS MULFORD (THE YOUNGER).
EXECUTORS: GENL. THOMAS BROWN, THOMAS SMITH. WITNESSES:
J. R. GUTRIER, ANNAH RUSS.

MULFORD, EPHRIAM   APRIL 8, 1805.
        EXECUTORS: JAMES PEMBERTON, JOHN MCPHERSON,
JONATHAN SMITH. WITNESSES: P. KELLY, MARGARET KELLY,
FLOOD FOLEY.

MULFORD, SARAH   10 NOVEMBER 1824.
        (WIDOW OF EPHRIAM MULFORD) DAUGHTERS: REBECCA ANN
MULFORD, MARY THOMAS, SARAH NEILL DUNCAN. OTHER LEGATEES:
PEYTON DUNCAN, ARCHIBALD MURPHY, JOHN THOMAS. BROTHER &
EXECUTOR: RICHARD GARVAN. WITNESSES: JAMES RUSS, P.
KELLY.

MULLINGTON, RICHARD MAY 13, 1776.
        GRANDSONS: JOSIAH (JOSIE) LEWIS, RICHARD MULLING-
TON LEWIS, AARON & MOSES LEWIS. GRANDDAUGHTERS: SILENCE
GREEN, ANN GREEN, LUCY LEWIS. EXECUTOR: JOSIAH LEWIS.
WITNESSES: JOHN POYNTER, RALPH MILLER, STEPHEN DOWNING.

MUNN, MARY   5 SEPTEMBER 1894. 20 APRIL 1895.
        NEPHEW: FRANK P. MUNN. UNCLE: DUNCAN CAMPBELL.
WITNESSES: D. MUNN, W. A. MUNN. CLERK: W. J. SUTTON.

MURCHISON, IDA F. (OF HOLLY HILL) MARCH 3, 1883.
        JANUARY 27, 1886. SISTER: LUCY G. MURCHISON
(MY LISBURNE PLANTATION) AFFIDAVIT OF A. B. WILLIAMS
BEFORE T. S. LUTTERLOH, CLERK OF THE COURT OF CUMBERLAND
COUNTY, N. C. ON NOVEMBER 2, 1885. CLERK: G. F. MELVIN.

MURPHY, HUGH   MARCH 16, 1835.
        WIFE: CATHERINE. SONS: ARCH'D. MURPHY (LANDS ON
CAPE FEAR RIVER BEING LOT NO. 2 IN DIVISION OF EPHRIAM
MULFORD, JR., AND THE SHARE OF THE DOWER, SARAH MULFORD,
NOW DECEASED WIDOW OF THE SAID EPHRIAM MULFORD, WHICH I
PURCHASED FROM PEYTON DUNCAN AND WIFE AND LANDS BOUGHT
OF JOHN MCPHERSON, FROM THE APPLE TREE TO THE RIVER),
ROBERT MURPHY, PATRICK MURPHY. DAUGHTERS: MARGARET,
WORTHLY, MARY JANE, JANNETT PRIDGEN. NEPHEW: PATRICK
MURPHY. SON-IN-LAW: JAMES MCDUGALD. GRANDCHILDREN:
HANSON F., CATHERINE, JANE & ELIZABETH MURPHY, HUGH MURPHY,
SON OF PATRICK, JOHN MURPHY (MY TENNESSEE LANDS).
EXECUTORS: ROBT. MURPHY, ESQ., PATRICK MURPHY,

58

WITNESSES: J. P. REEVES, WORTHELY MCDUFFIE.

MURPHY, JOHN A.   PROBATED 13 MARCH 1893.
     WIFE: MARY LOU. SISTER: ANN E. MURPHY. BROTHERS:
P. H., W. B., R. J. WITNESSES: MARGARET A. MCDOUGALD,
DR. W. K. ANDERS, L. J. HALL. CLERK: GEO. F. MELVIN.

MURRELL, ZACKARIAH, SR. NOVEMBER 29, 1807.
     WIFE: REBECCAH. SONS: SAMUEL, MATTHEW, ZACKARIAH,
JOHN. DAUGHTERS: MARGARET BROWNING, MOLSEY, REBECKAH.
EXECUTORS: JOHN & ZACKARIAH (SONS). WITNESSES: EDWARD
HARRISS, MATTHEW MURRELL.

MUSTLEWHITE, THOMAS SEPTEMBER 14, 1770.
     WIFE & EXECUTRIX: MARY. SONS: JESSE, THOMAS,
MILBAY, NATHAN, ALEXANDER. DAUGHTERS: AMEY, ELIZABETH,
WINNEY, ELLEN, BRIDGET, MARY, AMELIA, PATIENCE, SARAH.
EXECUTOR: MILBAY MUSTLEWHITE (SON). WITNESSES: ITHAMA
SINGLETARY, RICHARD THOMAS, CAROLINE SINGLETARY.

MCBRIDE, MATHEW   OCTOBER 21, 1875. AUGUST 2, 1880.
     WIFE: SARAH. DAUGHTER: CATHARINE ELIZABETH.
GRANDCHILDREN: WILLIAM RICHARDSON MCBRIDE, ELLA FRANCES
MCBRIDE. EXECUTOR: W. J. PARKER. WITNESSES: THOMAS
BRANCH, J. SANDFORD. JUDGE OF PROBATE: EVANDER SINGLE-
TARY.

MCCALL, DUNCAN   JUNE 11, 1841.
     SON & EXECUTOR: JOHN MCCALL. DAUGHTERS: CATHERINE
& ANN. GRANDCHILDREN: DANIEL, CHRISTIAN & ELIZA MC-
KEITHAN (CHILDREN OF MY DECEASED DAUGHTER MARY), DUNCAN,
NEILL & ISABELLA ANN (CHILDREN OF MY DECEASED SON NEILL
MCCALL). WITNESSES: A. TAYLOR, WM. C. BURNEY.

MCCALL, HARRIET   APRIL 5, 1882. JANUARY 15, 1884.
     HUSBAND: JOHN MCCALL, (DECEASED) GRANDSON OF MY
LATE HUSBAND: RANDALL MCCALL. GRANDDAUGHTER OF MY LATE
HUSBAND: MINERVA MCKAY WIFE OF CHAS. MCKEY. OTHER
LEGATEE: FLORA CLARK. (MCCAULSKEY GRAVEYARD) EXECUTOR:
A. K. CROMARTIE. WITNESSES: JOHN Q. ELKINS, JAMES KELLY.
CLERK: G. F. MELVIN.

MCCALL, JOHN   MAY 1875. AUGUST 6, 1877.
     WIFE & EXECUTRIX: HARRIET. SON: JOHN NEILL.
DAUGHTER: BARBARA ANN MELVIN, WIDOW OF THE LATE MARSHALL
MELVIN. (2 ACRES TO BE LAID OFF AS TO INCLUDE THE GRAVE
YARD & BE EVER RESPECTED & HELD AS A BURIAL PLACE)

(LANDS WHICH WERE GRANTED TO NEILL McCOALSKEY, DUNCAN McCOALSKEY, NEIL McCOALSKEY, ANN McCOALSKEY, DUNCAN McCALL) EXECUTOR: DOCTOR NEILL GRAHAM. WITNESSES: JAMES KELLY, A. K. CROMARTIE. JUDGE OF PROBATE: EVANDER SINGLETARY.

McCONKEY, ROBERT (PLANTER) SEPTEMBER 10, 1790.
WIFE & EXECUTRIX: RUTH. COUSINS: ANN COVINGTON, JOHN FOWLER, WILLIAM FOWLER. NIECE: LYDIA FREEMAN. EXECUTORS: THOMAS LOCK, JAMES MOREHEAD. WITNESSES: JAS. MOOREHEAD, JOSIAH HENDON, LYDIA HENDON.

McCOULSKY, DUNCAN (PLANTER) MAY 5, 1807.
SONS: NEILL, DUNCAN, DANIEL. DAUGHTERS: MARY, ANN, SARAH. EXECUTORS: DUNCAN McCALL, AARON LEWIS. WITNESSES: DUGALD McKEITHAN, JOHN MUN, D. McCALL.

McCULLOCH, ROBERT MAXFIELD JANUARY 15, 1801. JAN. 21, 1808. LEGATEES: ESTATE OF JOHN LOCK, JR., MARY BYRNE DAUGHTER OF PETER BYRNE (WHOM I INTENDED TO MARRY). HOLOGRAPH WILL PROVEN BY JOSEPH THOMAS, THOMAS LOCK, THOMAS BYRNE BEFORE JAS. S. PURDIE, J. P. (MARY LOCK DAUGHTER OF JOHN LOCK, JR., DEC'D.) McCULLOCH DEPARTED THIS LIFE ON THE 10TH INSTANT.

McDANIEL, JAMES I. (PLANTER) NOVEMBER 17, 1779.
WIFE & EXECUTRIX: AGNES. SONS: WILLIAM GRAY, JAMES, ABSALOM, DANIEL. DAUGHTERS: MARGARET, AGNES, MARY. EXECUTORS: WILLIAM GRAY McDANIEL (SON). WITNESSES: RICHARD WILKINSON, JAMES BEARD, ROBERT EDWARDS.

McDANIEL, JOHN
WIFE & CHILDREN MENTIONED, BUT NOT NAMED. EXECUTORS: THOMAS SMITH, ISHAM SMITH. WITNESSES: ENOCH HALL, DANIEL PERRY.

McDONALD, MRS. MARY A. 27 JUNE 1894. 4 JULY 1894.
NIECES: MRS. ANNA S. RUSS, EMILIA McKAY KEMP. NEPHEWS: WILLIAM J. KEMP, ANDREW S. KEMP (CHILDREN OF MY DECEASED BROTHER STRANGE). EXECUTOR: WILLIAM J. KEMP. WITNESSES: A. H. WILLIAMS, LIZZIE M. WHITTED, T. S. WHITTED. CLERK: GEO. F. MELVIN.

McDOUGAL, ALLEN (FARMER)   OCTOBER 9, 1771.
        WIFE & EXECUTRIX: MARY. SONS: RANDAL, HERR,
ALEXANDER. SISTER: ISABELLA LE SHAW. WITNESSES: DAVID
LOCK, THOMAS HOWARD.

McDOWELL, ALEXANDER   20 JUNE 1846. AUGUST TERM ____.
        WIFE: MARY JANE. SONS & EXECUTORS: THOMAS DAVID,
JOHN ALEXANDER. "...LARGE ADVANCEMENTS TO MY SON THOMAS
D. McDOWELL WHEN HE COMMENCED MERCHANDIZING." WITNESSES:
THOMAS C. SMITH, WILEY ATKINSON, JAMES ROBESON, JR. CLERK
OF COURT: H. H. ROBINSON.

McDOWELL, THOMAS D.   12 MARCH 1896. 21 MAY 1898.
        SONS: ALEXANDER, JOHN. WITNESSES: R. B. CROMARTIE,
G. S. SINGLETARY. CLERK: W. J. SUTTON.

McDUFFIE, DANIEL, SR. SEPTEMBER 14, 1828.
        WIFE: MARY. SONS: JAMES, JOHN, DANIEL,ROBERT.
4 DAUGHTERS NOT NAMED. EXECUTOR: JAMES McDUFFIE (SON).
WITNESSES: ROBERT MELVIN, GEORGE CAIN, JOHN MELVIN.

McDUFFIE, JOHN   (DIED NOV. 22, 1773) JANUARY 26,
        1774. SON: DUGAL. (ELDEST SON IN ISLAND OF JAMAICA)
NUNCUPATIVE WILL, PROVEN BY WILLIAM McNEILL, ARCHIBALD
SHAW AND ALEXANDER SHAW BEFORE JAMES BAILEY, ONE OF HIS
MAJESTY'S JUSTICES OF THE PEACE. (DIED AT THE HOUSE OF
WILLIAM McNEILL)

McDOUGALD, ANN   OCTOBER 4, 1825.
        SON & EXECUTOR: HUGH McDUGALD. DAUGHTER: CATHER-
INE CAMPBELL WIFE OF DUNCAN CAMPBELL. GRANDDAUGHTER:
MARY ANN CAMPBELL DAUGHTER OF CATHERINE. GRANDSON:
NEILL McDUGALD. OTHER LEGATEES: CALL McDUGALD, JAMES
McDUGALD, EMILY McDUGALD. WITNESSES: DAVID THOMAS,
WILLIE ATKINSON.

McDUGALD, MARGARET   SEPTEMBER 16, 1861. AUGUST TERM
        1862. SONS: CALL (DECEASED), JAMES I., NEILL.
DAUGHTERS: DELILA ANN McMILLAN, EMILY McALLISTER, ELIZA
ANN McDUFFIE, MARGARET KING. GRANDCHILDREN: WILLIAM J.,
JOHN G., EMILY J.,(CHILDREN OF MY SON CALL McDUGALD),
MARY ANN, JOHN IVER, MARGARET ANN & HUGH W. McMILLAN,
CHILDREN OF MY DAUGHTER DELILA ANN McMILLAN, MARTHA W.,
MARGARET R., MICHAEL & WILLIAM ARTHUR KING, CHILDREN OF
MY DAUGHTER MARGARET KING, DECEASED, MARGARET ANN

McDUGALD, MARGARET G. McDUGALD, MARGARET ELENOR McDUGALD
& DUGALD McDUGALD. FRIEND & TRUSTEE: WILLIAM A. SAVAGE.
EXECUTORS: "MY ONLY TWO SURVIVING SONS", JAMES I. &
NEILL McDUGALD. WITNESSES: W. A. SAVAGE, IVER McMILLAN,
D. J. CLARK. CLERK: D. BLUE.

McEWEN, JOHN   SEPTEMBER 1, 1786.
     SONS: ROBERT, WILLIAM, MATTHEW. DAUGHTERS:
MARGARET, JANE. EXECUTOR: MATTHEW McEWEN (SON).
WITNESSES: ARCHIBALD KELLY, WILLIAM McEWEN, ROBERT
McEWEN.

McEWEN, ROBERT   JUNE 17, 1804.
     WIFE: MARY. DAUGHTER: JANE. SONS: JOHN, JAMES,
MATTHEW, ARCHIBALD, ROBERT, DANIEL, GEORGE, PATRICK
NEILL (TO HAVE TWO PARTS BECAUSE HE IS CRIPPLED).
WITNESSES: M. McEWEN, DANIEL CAMPBELL, ANN McEWEN.

McFAYDEN (McFADYEN), ANGUS 14 OCTOBER 1895. 3
     AUGUST 1896. (OF FRENCHES CREEK TOWNSHIP) (FARMER)
WIFE: MARGARET. CHILDREN: MARY E. HINES, JOHN B.,
H. B., A. W., E. G., THOMAS B. EXECUTORS: JOHN B. Mc-
FADGEN, C. V. HINES. WITNESSES: S. M. KING, J. H.
PORTER, W. J. KEITH. CLERK: W. J. SUTTON.

McINNIS, DUNCAN   OCTOBER 11, 1822. NOV. TERM 1822.
     WIFE: ANN. DAUGHTER: CATHERINE ANN. SISTERS:
CATHERINE McINNIS, CHRISTIAN McINNIS. BROTHER: ALEX-
ANDER McINNIS. OTHER LEGATEE: MARGARET JANE NICHOLSON.
EXECUTORS: MAJ. THOMAS BROWN, ISAAC WRIGHT. WITNESSES:
WILLIAM H. BEATTY, JEREMIAH NORMAN, WILLIAM J. CROMARTIE,
DANIEL McKEITHAN. CLERK: ALEX McDOWELL.

McINNIS, MALCOM   MARCH 18, 1858. AUGUST 30, 1882.
     NIECE: CATHARINE TATOM WIFE OF OLLEN TATOM AND
DAUGHTER OF THOMAS & MARY McINNIS. EXECUTOR: RICHARD
W. TATOM. WITNESSES: THOMAS McINNIS, J. S. TATOM.
(M. McI. TATOM SON OF CATHERINE TATOM) JUDGE OF PROBATE:
G. F. MELVIN.

McKAY, ANN   AUGUST 18, 1856. FEB. TERM 1862.
     SON: JOBEY McKAY. NIECE: ANN CLARK WIFE OF JOHN
K. CLARK. EXECUTOR: DANIEL JAMES CLARK. WITNESSES:
K. K. COUNCIL, NEILL GRAHAM, DAVID N. PERRY. CLERK:
D. BLUE. BROTHER: JOHN McKAY.

62

McKAY, ANN ELIZA   AUGUST 18, 1868.   MARCH 3, 1879.
      DAUGHTER: MARY ANN CROMARTIE. GRANDSON: LLOYD
McKAY CROMARTIE. GRANDDAUGHTERS: ELIZA, IDA, DELLA,
MARIAN, ELIZABETH, EMMELINE, ISABELLA. WITNESSES: THOS.
D. McDOWELL, W. H. WHITE. (WILL PRESENTED FOR PROBATE
BY DUNCAN CROMARTIE) JUDGE OF PROBATE: EVANDER SINGLETARY.

McKAY, IVER   APRIL 8, 1785.
      WIFE & EXECUTRIX: ANN. SONS: RALPH, JOHN, ALEX-
ANDER, ARCHIBALD, DANIEL. DAUGHTERS: ISABEL, ELIZABETH.
EXECUTORS: RALPH & JOHN McKAY (SONS). WITNESSES: JOHN
BLOCKER, JOHN McKAY, RALPH McKAY.

McKAY, JAMES I.   (NO DATES)
      WIFE & EXECUTRIX: ELIZA ANN. "HENDON PLANTATION",
"BELFONT PLANTATION","FERRY PLANTATION WITH FERRY",
"PHOEBUS PLANTATION". BROTHERS: WILLIAM J. McKAY,
JOHN L. McKAY. SISTER: EMILY S. KEMP. MY HONEY FIELDS
IN COLUMBUS COUNTY TO EMELINE WHITTED. MY ASHFORD AND
WHITE PLANTATIONS TO MY FRIEND, WILLIAM J. COWAN. OTHER
LEGATEES: ROBERT HARVEY, JAMES McKAY MARKS, JOHN T.
GILMORE, SALTER LLOYD. "AFTER THE TERMINATION OF MY
WIFE'S WIDOWHOOD, MY ABOVE NAMED BELFONT PLANTATION TO
WILLIAM J. COWAN AND MY EXECUTORS IN TRUST FOR THE COUNTY
OF BLADEN ON THE EXPRESS CONDITION THAT THE SAID PLAN-
TATION SHALL BE USED AS AN EXPERIMENTAL FARM AND THAT THE
POOR OF THE COUNTY AND POOR AND INDIGENT ORPHANS WHO ARE
DIRECTED BY LAW TO BE BOUND OUT SHALL BE KEPT, MAINTAINED
AND EMPLOYED ON SAID PLANTATION UNDER SUCH RULES AND
REGULATIONS AS THE COUNTY COURT OF SAID COUNTY SHALL PRE-
SCRIBE." EXECUTOR: WILLIAM J. McKAY. WITNESSES:
PEYTON DUNCAN, NEILL PATTERSON.

McKAY, JOHN   SEPTEMBER 17, 1820.
      SONS: DUGAL, NEILL, JOHN. DAUGHTERS: NANCY,
EFFIE, MARY, FLORA, MARGARET. GRANDSONS: ZEBAN McKAY,
JOHN SON OF NEILL, JOHN SON OF EFFIE. EXECUTOR: NEILL
McKAY (SON). WITNESSES: JOHN DARRAH, ARCHIBALD DARRAH.

McKAY, RALPH   AUGUST 7, 1790.
      MOTHER: ANN McKAY. BROTHERS & EXECUTORS: ARCHI-
BALD & DANIEL McKAY. WITNESS: JOHN McKAY.

McKEITHAN, DANIEL T. NOVEMBER 29, 1862. AUGUST TERM
      1863. WIFE: M. A. McKEITHAN. (CHILDREN MENTIONED

BUT NOT NAMED) EXECUTOR: HAYES C. McCALLUM. WITNESSES: GEORGE W. BALLENTINE, D. F. McKEITHAN. SURETIES: NEILL GRAHAM, BOND $30,000.00. CLERK: D. BLUE.

McKEITHAN, DUNCAN   SEPTEMBER 23, 1774.
      WIFE & EXECUTRIX: ELIZABETH. SON: DUNCAN. DAUGHTERS: MARGARET McFATTER, ELIZABETH McDANIEL. EXECUTOR: IVER McKOY. WITNESSES: MARY SMITH, JOHN SMITH, SAMUEL SMITH.

McKEITHAN, WILLIAM JAMES OCTOBER 30, 1883. NOVEMBER 19, 1883. SISTERS: MATILDA McKAY (MY WADDELL FERRY PLANTATION), MARY J. BLUE. NEPHEWS: J. L. McKAY, W. J. McKAY, A. S. McKAY, A. A. McKAY. NIECES: LIZZIE LUCAS, SALLIE MELVIN. OTHER LEGATEES: SANDY, GRADY & VANCE McKAY. EXECUTORS: W. J. PARKER, A. S. KEMP. WITNESSES: S. G. VAUGHN, D. L. SMITH. CLERK: G. F. MELVIN.

McLEARN, JOHN (PLANTER) MARCH 8, 1801.
      SON: MALCOM. SISTER: CATHERINE SHAW. EXECUTORS: DUNCAN McCOULSKEY, DUGALD BLUE, SR. WITNESSES: JOHN BLUE, SR., DUNCAN McCALL, JOHN BLUE, JR.

McLELLAND, ANDREW   JUNE 26, 1845. NOVEMBER TERM 1846.
      SON: THOMAS. GRANDSON: ANGUS McLELLAND. EXECUTOR: COLIN MONROE. WITNESSES: ROWLAND SINGLETARY, SNOWDEN SINGLETARY. CLERK: H. H. ROBINSON.

McLELLAND, SAMUEL   JULY 25, 1857. FEBRUARY 6, 1886.
      DAUGHTER: MARY ANN PORTER WIFE OF WILLIAM H. PORTER. EXECUTORS: T. D. McDOWELL, J. A. McDOWELL, THOMAS J. NORMAN. WITNESSES: R. S. GILLESPIE, W. H. WHITE, JAMES F. GILLESPIE. CLERK: G. F. MELVIN.

McLEOD, LAUCHLIN   SEPTEMBER 7, 1849.
      WIFE: SARAH. (LANDS LYING ON THE HEAD WATERS OF PLUMMERS RUN ON THE SOUTH SIDE OF CARVERS CREEK AND WEST OF THE CAPE FEAR RIVER) EXECUTORS: JOHN B. BROWN, THOS. O. BROWN. WITNESSES: CHAS. McNORTON, W. WESTBROOK.

McLEOD, MALCOM   APRIL 12, 1875. AUG. 7, 1876.
      DAUGHTER: SALLIE ANN. SONS & EXECUTORS: JOHN WILLIAM, EVANDER JAMES, MALCOM GIFFORD. WITNESSES: MALCOM G. McLEOD, EVANDER J. McLEOD, JOHN N. KELLY. JUDGE OF PROBATE: EVANDER SINGLETARY.

McMASTER, FELIX   JULY 9, 1793.
     WIFE: NOT NAMED. MOTHER: CAROLINE MCMASTER.
DAUGHTER: CATHRON. EXECUTORS: JOHN DEVANE, JR., FRANCIS
DAVIS, JAMES HENRY. WITNESSES: HECTOR MCALLISTER, JAMES
HENRY, ELIZABETH HENRY.

McMILLAN, DUGALD   MAY 19, 1835.
     WIFE: ELIZABETH. SONS: DUNCAN, DUGALD, JOHN IVER.
DAUGHTERS: ELIZABETH LEWIS, JANE SHAW, MARGARET SHAW.
GRANDSON: DUGALD MCMILLAN LEWIS. OTHER LEGATEE:
JANNETT DUNCAN. EXECUTORS: JOHN IVER MCMILLAN, DUNCAN
MCMILLAN (SONS) WITNESSES: W. D. MCNEILL, MOSES LEWIS.

McMILLAN, DUNCAN   AUGUST 9, 1806.
     WIFE & EXECUTRIX: EFFE. SON: JOHN. DAUGHTERS:
NANCY, ESEBET. WITNESSES: I. MCMILLAN, SR., SAM'L. BOOZ-
MAN.

McMILLAN, EDWARD (PLANTER) NOVEMBER 20, 1778.
     WIFE: MARGARET. SONS: NEILL, DUGAL. DAUGHTERS:
JACK, MARGARET, NANCY, MILLY. EXECUTORS: JOHN TYLER,
JOHN MCMILLAN, ARCHIBALD CAMPBELL. WITNESS: JOHN TAYLOR.

McMILLAN, IVER   JULY 21, 1839.
     WIFE: MARY. SONS: RANALD, IVER, DUGALD, ARCHEY.
EXECUTORS: DUGALD & RANDAL MCMILLAN (SONS). WITNESSES:
NEILL MCDUGALD, JAMES I. MCKAY.

McMILLAN, JANNETT   DECEMBER 4, 1883.
     NIECE: MARGARET ELIZABETH MCMILLAN. NEPHEW: DANIEL
N. MCMILLAN. SISTERS: MARGARET CARR, ELIZABETH MCMILLAN.
EXECUTORS: REV. WILLIAM BROBSTON AND MY SISTER BETSEY.
WITNESSES: WM. BROBSTON, ELIZABETH MCMILLAN.

McMILLAN, JOHN   APRIL 22, 1801.
     (SEAMAN FORMERLY OF ARGISHSHIRE IN GREAT BRITAIN,
ON BOARD THE REVENUE CUTTER OF THE UNITED STATES COMMANDED
BY CAPT. JOHN BROWN) LEGATEE: JOHN MCMILLAN, MY GOOD
FRIEND OF ELIZABETHTOWN, ALL MY PROPERTY IN STATE OF NORTH
CAROLINA. WITNESSES: F. BLAKE, B. GOODEN.

McMILLAN, JOHN   NOVEMBER 22, 1820.
     DAUGHTERS: ANN MCINNIS WIFE OF DUNCAN MCINNIS,
MARGARET MCREE. SON & EXECUTOR: IVER MCMILLAN. GRAND-
DAUGHTER: MARGARET JANE NICHOLSON. (SLAVES IN POSSESSION

OF JAMES P. McREE) (LANDS IN TURNBULL TOWNSHIP ON WHICH
JESSE TATOM NOW LIVES) (LANDS NEAR CYPRESS CREEK ON WHICH
JOHN McMILLAN, SCHOOL MASTER NOW LIVES) (LANDS KNOWN AS
HALE PARK) WITNESSES: JAMES CAMPBELL, DANIEL McKEITHAN.

McNAUGHTON, JOHN   JANUARY 21, 1851. MAY TERM 1853.
        NIECE: MARY STUBBS: SONS: JOHN, LEWIS, NEILL.
OTHER LEGATEE: DAVID JAMES HARGROVE. EXECUTORS: JOHN
& LEWIS McNAUGHTON (SONS). WITNESSES: J. G. McDUGALD,
W. J. SIKES. CLERK: J. I. McREE.

McNEILL, HECTOR   JANUARY 6, 1778.
        WIFE & EXECUTRIX: MARGARET. OTHER LEGATEES:
DUNCAN McNEILL, BLUFF JOHN NEILL, JOHN JOHNSTON, LOCHLINE
CAMERON AND HIS MOTHER ISABELA BOWIE. EXECUTORS: DUNCAN
McNEILL, SOULE McDANIEL (OF SOUTHILL). WITNESSES: JOHN
STEWART, SR., JOHN STEWART, JR., SOULE McDANIEL.

McNEILL, JOHN   MAY 25, 1833.
        WIFE: MARY. SON & EXECUTOR: WILLIAM D. McNEILL.
DAUGHTER: SARAH JANE SHIPMAN. GRANDCHILDREN: MARY REED,
DAVID REED, ELIZA ANN REED. WITNESSES: GUION LEWIS,
MOSES LEWIS.

McNEILL, MARY   APRIL 19, 1841.
        SON & EXECUTOR: WILLIAM D. McNEILL. GRANDSON:
JOHN KENNETH McNEILL. WITNESS: NEILL KELLY.

McNORTON, JOHN   MARCH 19, 1873. JUNE 2, 1873.
        LEGATEES: MARY STUBBS, SARAH A. BENSON, JOHN K.
CLARK FOR WHITE PLAINS CHURCH, DAVID J. HARGROVE, MARY E.
McNORTON, HARRIET C. McNORTON, ANN McKEITHAN. EXECUTOR:
JOHN A. EDWARDS. WITNESSES: D. J. CLARK, WM. J. MEARS.
CLERK: EVANDER SINGLETARY.

McREE, ANN   MARCH 22, 1828.
        NEPHEWS: HAYNES RICHARDSON, SAM'L RICHARDSON.
OTHER LEGATEES: CHILDREN OF JAMES B. PURDIE. EXECUTORS:
DR. JOHN SMITH, SAM'L RICHARDSON. WITNESSES: ALEXR
McDOWELL, ROBERT PLUMMER.

McREE, JAMES IVER   JANUARY 18, 1854. NOVEMBER TERM
        1854. WIFE: JULIA WRIGHT FLOWERS McREE (MY TOWN
LOTS IN THE TOWN OF ELIZABETHTOWN AND THE MANSION HOUSE).
UNCLE: JOHN IVER McMILLAN. EXECUTOR: DOCTOR HEMAN H.

ROBINSON. WITNESSES TO HOLOGRAPH WILL: KENNETH McLEOD, ESQ., JOHN A. RICHARDSON, JAMES MELVIN. CLERK: F. F. CUMMING.

McREE, ROBERT   FEBRUARY 9, 1793.
          WIFE: JANE. DAUGHTERS: ELIZABETH, SARAH CHRISTIAN, SUSANNAH, JEAN GUTHRIE, ALICE. SON: WILLIAM. GRANDSON: ROBERT McREE SON OF WILLIAM, ROBERT CHESHIRE, JOHN. GRANDDAUGHTER: HELEN McREE. EXECUTORS & SONS: WILLIAM McREE, WILLIAM CHESHIRE & WILLIAM GUTHRIE. WITNESSES: RICHARD SALTER, JNO. ELLIS.

McREE, SAMUEL   MAY 5, 1798.
          WIFE & EXECUTRIX: MARY. DAUGHTERS: SARAH GIBBS WIFE OF JOHN GIBBS, MARGARET McREE. SONS: JAMES, WILLIAM, ALEX, JOHN. EXECUTORS: WILLIAM BRYAN, JAMES MORHEAD. WITNESSES: A. WHITE, A. S. WHITE.

McREE, WILLIAM (PLANTER) JANUARY 18, 1789.
          WIFE & EXECUTRIX: MARGARET. SONS: GRIFFITH JOHN, JAMES, JOHN. DAUGHTER: SARAH. GRANDSON: WILLIAM SINGLE-TARY. EXECUTOR: GRIFFITH JOHN McREE (SON), & JOSEPH SINGLETARY.

NANCE, DANIEL   MAY 14, 1802.
          WIFE & EXECUTRIX: PATIENCE. SONS: JOSEPH, WYNNE. DAUGHTER: ELIZABETH COOK. GRANDDAUGHTER: SALLY MERCER. GRANDSON: DANIEL COOK. EXECUTOR: JOSEPH NANCE (SON). WITNESSES: WILLIAM HAWTHORNE, JOSEPH CARROLL, WINNEY POWERS.

NANCE, JOSEPH   JUNE 8, 1820.   JOSEPH I.
          WIFE: MARY. SONS: DANIEL M., JOSHUA L.,/DAVID T. DAUGHTERS: AMMY HESTER, FANNY BUTLER, PATIENCE NANCE, DOROTHY NANCE, ELIZABETH NANCE, MARY W. NANCE. (JOHN BUTLER HUSBAND OF FANNY) EXECUTORS: JONATHAN SINGLETARY, JOSEPH SINGLETARY. WITNESSES: JOSEPH SINGLETARY, JONATHAN SINGLETARY, DANIEL M. NANCE.

NELSON, JOHN   JANUARY 1, 1779.
          (NUNCUPATIVE WILL) LEGATEE: THOMAS SINGLETARY. AFFIANT: JAMES CAIN, SWORN BEFORE JOSEPH CAIN.

NORMAN, JEREMIAH   APRIL 11, 1840.
          WIFE: MARY. CHILDREN BY MARY NORMAN, SARAH BAILEY,

THOMAS, JAMES & CAROLINE EMILY NORMAN. (MY THREE CHILDREN IN SOUTH CAROLINA TO HAVE ALL THAT IS CONTAINED IN THEIR GRANDFATHER R. WOODBURY'S WILL, WITH THAT PORTION PASSED OVER BY MR. JOHN WOODBURY AS THEIR AGENT IN 1831) EXECUTOR: THOMAS JAMES NORMAN (SON).

OLDHAM, ELIZABETH   JULY 2, 1852. FEB. TERM 1853.
     BROTHERS: THOMAS J. ROBESON, BARTRAM ROBESON. SISTER: SARAH R. SMITH. NIECES: MARY ELIZABETH ROBESON, MARY B. SMITH, DAUGHTER OF SARAH R. SMITH. WITNESSES: JAMES ROBESON, JR., DR. JOHN S. RICHARDSON, MRS. ELIZABETH E. ROBESON. BARTRAM ROBESON APPOINTED ADM. C.T.A. UPON HIS ENTERING INTO A BOND IN THE SUM OF FIFTEEN THOUSAND DOLLARS WITH JAMES ROBESON AND THOMAS J. ROBESON AS SURE-TIES. CLERK: J. I. MCREE.

OWEN, JOHN   JUNE 27, 1841.
     WIFE & EXECUTRIX: LUCY ANN. DAUGHTER: ELLEN PORTERFIELD OWEN. EXECUTOR: THOMAS C. MILLER. WITNESSES: I. W. WRIGHT, JAMES CARMON.

OWEN, THOMAS   FEBRUARY 10, 1799.
     WIFE: ELEANOR. SONS: JAMES, JOHN. DAUGHTERS: MARY STEDMAN. EXECUTORS: JAMES MOOREHEAD, ELISHA STEDMAN.

PAGE, ABRAM   NOVEMBER 15, 1886. 1891.
     WIFE: SARAH. SON: W. C. DAUGHTERS: ELLEN SMITH, LAURA PETERSON, AMANDA NORRIS, EMMA PAGE, ANNA MCDANIEL. EXECUTOR: CHAR;ES P. PARKER. WITNESSES: W. J. PARKER, A. A. CROMARTIE. CLERK: GEO. F. MELVIN.

PARKER, WILLIAM   JULY 17, 1802.
     WIFE: MARY. SON: JOHN. (OTHER CHILDREN MENTION-ED BUT NOT NAMED) EXECUTORS: AARON PARKER, HENRY PARKER, SAMUEL SMITH. WITNESSES: JONATHAN PIERCE, JAMES SMITH, AARON PARKER.

PATTERSON, DANIEL   FEBRUARY 7, 1832. AUGUST 3, 1832.
     WIFE: NANCY. FOUR SONS: JOHN, ALEXANDER, NEILL, DANIEL. EXECUTOR: JOHN (ELDEST SON). WITNESSES: DANIEL MUNN, MARY LAMMON.

PEMBERTON, ELIZABETH JUNE 11, 1821. CODICIL: OCTOBER 22, 1821. SON: THOMAS PEMBERTON. DAUGHTERS:

ELIZABETH KEA, SOPHIA, ABIGAL, NANCY, ANN. TRUSTEES FOR DAUGHTERS: THOMAS BROWN, ESQ., JOHN BROWN. WITNESSES: THOMAS SMITH, MARGARET SMITH, MARY GAUSE.

PERRY, JOHN   SEPTEMBER 21, 1870. MAY 1, 1871.
       WIFE: NOT NAMED. SONS: ELIJAH M. (EXECUTOR), JAMES W. DAUGHTER: REBECCA. GRANDCHILDREN: HARRIET REBECCA, MARGARET, JAMES HARRISON, CHILDREN OF JAMES W. PERRY, MARGARET, DAUGHTER OF REBECCA. WITNESSES: J. A. EDWARDS, D. J. CLARK. CLERK: D. BLUE.

PHARES, SAMUEL   APRIL 1, 1837.
       WIFE: ELIZABETH. EXECUTOR: JOHN HAIR. WITNESSES: WILLIAM HAILS, DUNCAN BEDSOLE.

PITMAN, JACOB   FEBRUARY 9, 1779.
       WIFE & EXECUTRIX: HANNAH. SON: SAMPSON. DAUGHTER: BOTHANY. EXECUTORS & FRIENDS: JOSEPH SALTER, THOMAS LITTLE. WITNESSES: BRYANT BEST, FARLOW O'QUINN, JOHN BEST.

PLUMMER, ANN   MAY 16, 1798.
       (NOTE OF MUSGROVE JONES TO BE DIVIDED EQUALLY AMONG MY 5 CHILDREN) EXECUTOR: WILLIAM SINGLETARY. WITNESSES: JAMES BRYAN, MUSGROVE JONES

PLUMMER, JAMES   MAY 11, 1838. CODICIL.
       APRIL 30, 1841. WIFE: LUCY. BROTHER: SKINKIN M. PLUMMER. BROTHER-IN-LAW: JOSEPH THAMES. SISTER'S HUSBAND AND DAUGHTER: NEILL BEARD AND SOPHIA DOWNING. EXECUTORS: JONATHAN EVANS, JOHN SMITH. WITNESSES: JAS. A. ROBESON, A. J. BYRNE.

POINTER, JOHN
       DAUGHTERS: MARGARET & FRANCIS POINTER. SON: JOHN POINTER. EXECUTORS: WILLIAM SALTER, RICHARD SALTER. WITNESSES: BRAYTON SINGLETARY, BENJAMIN SINGLETARY.

POPE, AMEY   JULY 13, 1805.
       DAUGHTERS: MARY & ELIZABETH POPE. EXECUTORS: ARTHUR SIMPSON, JACOB HIGH. WITNESSES: WILLIAM LEWIS, K. LEWIS, NANCY LEWIS.

PORTER, JOHN   NOVEMBER 15, 1773.
       BROTHERS: HUGH, SAMUEL, (SANDY) PORTER. EXECUTORS:

EVAN ELLISS, WILLIAM MCREE. WITNESSES: ALEX'R HARVEY, JOHN HARRISON.

PORTER, JOHN C.   OCTOBER 1, 1845. NOVEMBER TERM 1845. WIFE: MARGARET ANN (PROPERTY LEFT TO WIFE DURING HER NATURAL LIFE AND THEN TO THE CHILD SHE IS NOW CARRYING). EXECUTOR: ROBERT MELVIN, SR. WITNESSES: GEORGE CAIN, D. B. MELVIN.

POWELL, JOHN   JUNE 13, 1789. WIFE & EXECUTRIX: ELIZABETH. DAUGHTERS: CHLORE THE WIFE OF ALEXANDER AVERY, CHARITY WILKINSON, MARY, ELIZABETH, EASTER, EDE, ZILPHIA. SONS: ISAAC, BARNABAS. EXECUTORS: ISAAC POWELL, (SON), BRITTON HARGRAVES (FRIEND). WITNESSES: JEREMIAH BIGFORD, JOHN CHANCY, DEMPSEY CHANCY.

POWELL, ZILPHIA   MARCH 11, 1794. MOTHER: ELIZABETH POWELL. SISTERS: MARY, EASTER, EDITH WHITE. BROTHER & EXECUTOR: ISAAC POWELL. EXECUTOR: WILLIAM WILKINSON. WITNESSES: JOHN CHANCY, JAMES WHITE.

PRIDGEN, HENRY   1862. AUGUST TERM 1866. SON & EXECUTOR: WILLIAM G. PRIDGEN. WITNESSES: D. A. MACMILLAN, P. H. PRIDGEN. CLERK: D. BLUE.

PRIDGEN, MATTHEW   SEPTEMBER 13, 1818. SONS: STEPHEN, TIMOTHY, EVAN. WIFE: HANNAH. DAUGHTERS: CATHERINE, ELIZABETH, JANNET. EXECUTORS: G. W. BANNERMAN, ENOCH HERRING. WITNESSES: G. W. BANNERMAN, THOMAS SIKES.

PRIDGEN, WILLIAM H.   NOVEMBER 10, 1884. SEPTEMBER 25, 1885. SISTER: ANNA PRIDGEN. NIECE: SUSAN C. WIFE OF JOHN H. SQUIRES. WITNESSES: M. P. PETERSON, JOHN H. SQUIRES. CLERK: G. F. MELVIN.

PURDIE, ANN M.   MAY 13, 1878. NOV. 14, 1878. SON: JOHN W. PURDIE. DAUGHTER: ELIZA JANE. GRANDSON: JAMES PURDIE NEPHEW OF COL. THOMAS J. PURDIE. BROTHER: THOMAS C. SMITH. OTHER LEGATEES: H. H. ROBINSON & WIFE HWLEN JANE. EXECUTOR: THOS. D. MCDOWELL. WITNESSES: DR. W. A. BIZZELL, N. MCI. TATOM, DR. JAS. S. ROBINSON. MRS. ELIZA J. DUNHAM, ADMRX. JUDGE OF PROBATE: EVANDER SINGLETARY.

PURDIE, JAMES B.   APRIL 19, 1834.
        WIFE & EXECUTRIX: ANNA MARIAH. SONS: JOHN
WESLEY & THOMAS. DAUGHTERS: ELIZA JANE & SARAH ANN.
EXECUTORS: THOMAS C. SMITH. WITNESSES: ALEXANDER MC-
DOWELL, ANN WILKINSON.

PURDIE, JAMES S.   DECEMBER 13, 1817.
        WIFE: MARY JANE (SECOND WIFE). SON: JAMES BAILEY
PURDIE. DAUGHTER: ELIZABETH BROWN. (A COMMODIOUS
DWELLING HOUSE 18 BY 30 FT., SINGLE STORY TO BE ERECTED
FOR USE & CONVENIENCE OF WIFE) CHILD OF WHICH MY WIFE IS
NOW PREGNANT. EXECUTORS: THOMAS BROWN, JAMES B. PURDIE.
WITNESSES: JOHN SMITH, JAMES P. MCREE.

PURDIE, JOHN W.   FEBRUARY 8, 1884. MARCH 26, 1884.
        WIFE & EXECUTRIX: SALLIE. SON: JAMES A. PURDIE.
(OTHER CHILDREN NOT NAMED) EXECUTORS: W. DOUGLAS SMITH,
EDWARD SMITH, HENRY E. SMITH. WITNESSES: THOS. D. MC-
DOWELL, C. C. LYON. CLERK: G. F. MELVIN.

RAY, DUGALD   MAY 11, 1840. FEB. TERM 1848.
        WIFE & EXECUTRIX: MARGARET. WITNESSES: ALEXANDER
MCDOWELL, ARCHIBALD MCCALL. CLERK: H. H. ROBINSON.

RAY, ISAAC   SEPTEMBER 20, 1870.
        WIFE & EXECUTRIX: MELIA. BROTHER-IN-LAW: PETER
LORD. OTHER LEGATEE: MARGARET WRIGHT. EXECUTORS: THOMAS
& PETER ROBESON. WITNESSES: JAMES COUNCIL, LAWRENCE
BYRNE, DAVID L. WHITE.

REEVES, EVAN   JUNE 10, 1823.
        WIFE: ELIZA. OTHER LEGATEE: JAMES REEVES, SR.
EXECUTOR: JAMES REEVES. WITNESSES: JOHN LONG, GEORGE
DOWNING.

REEVES, JOHN M.   7 FEBRUARY 1892. 2 JULY 1894.
        NIECE & EXECUTRIX: SUSAN J. LAND. OTHER LEGATEE:
GEORGE W. HOWARD. WITNESSES: C. P. PARKER, J. A. ROBESON.
CLERK: G. F. MELVIN.

REGAN, ALFORD   5 SEPTEMBER 1892. 20 NOVEMBER 1894.
        WIFE: MARIA. DAUGHTER: HARRIET REGAN. OTHER
LEGATEES: EMELITT WHITTED. WITNESSES: RUFUS WHITTED,
D. MUNN. CLERK: GEO. F. MELVIN.

REGAN, JOSEPH   JANUARY 4, 1773.
        WIFE: ANNA. SONS & EXECUTORS: RALPH, JOHN,
RICHARD. (MR. ABSALOM BARNES & MRS. SAMUEL CAIN TO DIVIDE
LANDS) WITNESSES: SAMUEL RICHARDSON, WILLIAM MOORE,
WILLIAM BIRD.

REGISTER, DANIEL   OCTOBER 16, 1882. JULY 2, 1885.
        WIFE & EXECUTRIX: JANE. SONS: W. O., D. J.
DAUGHTERS: Y. J. BROWN, C. L. SMITH, H. S. V. HOWARD,
M. E. NUNERY. (LEAVES HIS DAUGHTER Y. J. BROWN ONE PENNY)
WITNESSES: ISAAC A. DAVIS, A. J. FREEMAN.

REGISTER, MARY   NOVEMBER 5, 1857.
        LEGATEE: LUCY ANN SAVAGE, "ALL PROPERTY FOR THE
NATURAL LOVE AND AFFECTION THAT I HAVE FOR HER." WITNESS-
ES: A. S. KEMP, A. E. McKAY.

REGISTER, WILLIAM   MAY 5, 1802.
        WIFE & EXECUTRIX: ELIZABETH. SONS: JOHN, JOSIAH,
THOMAS, WILLIAM. GRANDDAUGHTERS: ELIZABETH & ANN REGISTER.
EXECUTOR: AARON PARKER. WITNESSES: HENRY PARKER,
JOSIAH T. RUSS.

REYNOLDS, RICHARD, JR. JANUARY 5, 1804.
        WIFE & EXECUTRIX: MARY. EXECUTOR: SAMUEL SMITH.
(HOLOGRAPH WILL PROVED BY SAMUEL SMITH, BENJAMIN SMITH.
RICHARD HOLMES, J. P.) RICHARD REYNOLDS, JR. DIED ON
DECEMBER 24, 1803.

RIALS, ELIZABETH   FEBRUARY 12, 1847. MAY TERM ____.
        BROTHERS: DUNCAN BEDSOLE, WILLIAM BEDSOLE. FRIEND:
MALCOM MONROE. OTHER LEGATEES: NOAH RIAL, HARDY RIAL,
DANIEL RIAL, OWEN RIAL, URITY POPE, THOMAS BEDSOLE, SON
OF DUNCAN, NANCY HALL, SARAH BLACKWELL, TRAVIS BEDSOLE,
F. FAIRCLOTH, RHODA PARKER. EXECUTORS: DUNCAN BEDSOLE,
(BROTHER), MALCOM MONROE. WITNESSES: BLUFORD SIMMONS,
DANIEL McDUFFIE. CLERK OF COURT: H. H. ROBINSON.

RIALLS, STEPHEN   29 NOVEMBER 1825.
        (FAYETTEVILLE) WIFE: BETSY. EXECUTOR: CHARLES
P. MALLETT. WITNESSES: A. DOUGLASS, THOMAS SMITH.

RICHARDSON, NATHANIEL(NO DATE)
        WIFE: (NOT NAMED). BROTHER & EXECUTOR: SAMUEL
RICHARDSON. WITNESSES: WILLIAM MOORE, JOSEPH REGAN, JOHN
BLOUNT.

RICHARDSON, RANSOM   MARCH 29, 1892.   JULY 11, 1892.
        LEGATEES: STEPHEN ARCHIE RICHARDSON (21 YEARS
OLD ON OCT. 11, 1906), MOSES RICHARDSON, GREEN RICHARDSON.
EXECUTOR: ALLIE BROWN. WITNESSES: A. MCA. COUNCIL,
D. J. MCALISTER. CLERK: GEO. F. MELVIN.

RICHARDSON, SAMUEL N. JULY 14, 1836.
        MOTHER: MARY NORMAN. BROTHERS: HAYNES RICHARDSON
AND THOMAS NORMAN. SISTERS: SARAH NORMAN & CAROLINE
NORMAN. OTHER LEGATEE: ANN MCREE (MY VERY DEARLY BELOVED)
EXECUTOR: HAYNES RICHARDSON (BROTHER). WITNESSES: S. N.
RICHARDSON, SR. & SAMUEL MCLELLAND.

RICHARDSON, SAMUEL NEAL   APRIL 25, 1848. CODICILS: MAY
        29, 1894, FEB. 20, 1850. MAY TERM 1851.
SONS: EDMUND B., JOHN L., JAMES, PURDIE. DAUGHTERS:
ELIZA N. MARSHALL, HELEN MAHONEY, MARY ANN SMITH, SOPHIA
BLAKE. GRANDDAUGHTER : SARAH ANN BRIDGERS (DAUGHTER OF
JAMES). GRANDSON: JOHN A. RICHARDSON (SON OF JAMES).
GRANDDAUGHTER: MARY MCNEILL. (MY LATE LAMENTED WIFE,
LUCY G.) JAMES MAHONEY HUSBAND OF HELEN. EXECUTORS:
PURDIE, JOHN S. & EDMUND B. RICHARDSON (SONS). WITNESSES:
A. J. BYRNE, JOHN SMITH, WILLIAM J. DUNHAM, THOS. C. SMITH.
CLERK OF COURT: J. I. MCREE.

ROBESON, ALEXANDER   JUNE 7, 1875. NOVEMBER 15, 1881.
        BROTHERS: HESSICK L. ROBESON, FRED ROBESON.
SISTERS: LYDIA & RACHELL ROBESON. EXECUTOR: JAMES TOLAR.
WITNESSES: HARY KING, HESSIC L. ROBESON, JAMES TOLAR.
JUDGE OF PROBATE: N. A. STEDMAN, JR. (PETER W. KING
APPOINTED ADMINISTRATOR, JULIA TOLAR & CALVIN HOWARD,
WITNESSES)

ROBESON, BARTRAM   JANUARY 22, 1818.
        WIFE & EXECUTRIX: MARGARET. SONS: THOMAS, RAI-
FORD, BARTRAM. DAUGHTERS: ELIZA, MARGARET, SARAH.
EXECUTOR: JAMES I. MCKAY. WITNESSES: JAMES A. BYRNE,
ISAM ALLEN.

ROBESON, ELIZA A.   JUNE 30, 1891. OCTOBER 29, 1891.
        SONS: JAMES, J. MCK., CAD, W. I., J. D. DAUGH-
TER: EMMA S. LOVE. EXECUTOR: JAMES ROBESON (SON).
WITNESSES: E. N. ROBESON, W. B. SINGLETARY. CLERK OF
COURT: GEO. F. MELVIN.

ROBESON, JAMES   APRIL 25, 1854. MAY TERM 1864.
        WIFE & EXECUTRIX: ELIZA. EXECUTORS: THOMAS D.
MCDOWELL, JOHN A. MCDOWELL. WITNESSES TO HOLOGRAPHIC
WILL: DURRUM LEWIS, BENJAMIN FITZRANDOLPH, COLIN MONROE.
CLERK: D. BLUE.

ROBESON, MARGARET   28 MAY 1839.
        MOTHER (NOT NAMED). BROTHERS & EXECUTORS: ROBERT
RAIFORD ROBESON, THOMAS, BARTRAM. SISTERS: ELIZABETH
ROBESON, SARAH R. SMITH. WITNESSES: JAMES ROBESON,
WILLIS COUNCIL.

ROBESON, PETER   JULY 22, 1792. CODICIL: OCTOBER
        2, 1793. WIFE: ELIZABETH. CHILDREN: MARY,
THOMAS, PETER, WILLIAM, JOHN LORD ROBESON. EXECUTORS:
WILLIAM LORD, FREDERICK MILLER, JAS. S. PURDIE, SAMUEL A.
RICHARDSON. WITNESSES: RICHARD SINGLETARY, SR., JAMES
SINGLETARY, SR., ALICE SINGLETARY.

ROBESON, SAMUEL   JUNE 12, 1839. JAN. 10, 1844.
        MAY TERM 1846. WIFE & EXECUTRIX: ELIZABETH.
CHILDREN MENTIONED BUT NOT NAMED. WITNESSES: JAMES
ROBESON, WILLIAM ROBESON, THOMAS J. ROBESON.

ROBESON, THOMAS, SR. OCTOBER 29, 1775. NOVEMBER 9, 1775.
        (NUNCUPATIVE WILL) SONS: PETER, THOMAS. OTHER
LEGATEE: JAMES COUNCIL. WITNESSES: WILLIAM CAIN AND
WIFE, OLIVE CAIN, JOSEPH CAIN AND WIFE ANN CAIN. SWORN
BEFORE THOMAS OWEN, ESQ., ONE OF HIS MAJESTIES JUSTICES OF
THE PEACE.

ROBESON, THOMAS   JUNE 1, 1780.
        WIFE & EXECUTRIX: MARY. CHILDREN: BARTRAM,
JONATHAN, WILLIAM, ELIZABETH, SARAH. EXECUTORS: BARTRAM
ROBESON (SON), PETER ROBESON (BROTHER), JAMES COUNCIL,
WM. SALTER, JAMES SMITH. WITNESSES: SAMUEL CAIN, RICHARD
SINGLETARY, JAMES SINGLETARY, SR.

ROBESON, COL. THOMAS AUGUST TERM 1785.
        (NUNCUPATIVE ALTERATION 2 OR 3 DAYS BEFORE HE
DIED) PROPERTY IN WILMINGTON FORMERLY BELONGING TO WOL.
WILLIAM BARTRAM, DEC'D. TO BE EQUALLY DIVIDED BETWEEN
THREE SONS, BARTRAM, JONATHAN & WILLIAM ROBESON. WIFE:
MRS. MARY ROBESON. DAUGHTERS: ELIZABETH, SARAH.
BROTHER: PETER ROBESON. EXECUTOR: JONATHAN ROBESON(SON).

WILL PROVED BY OATH OF JAMES COUNCIL.

ROBESON, WILLIAM   1825.
        WIFE & EXECUTRIX: ANN. SONS: JOHN A., WILLIAM
P., JAMES, THOMAS. DAUGHTERS: MARY, SARAH (WIFE OF
WILLIAM M. SINGLETARY), ANN, CATHERINE, ELIZABETH, MAR-
GARET. EXECUTORS: JOHN A. ROBESON, WILLIAM P. ROBESON
(SONS). WITNESSES: JOHN OWEN, WILLIAM LOCK, JAMES SMITH,
ESQ. CLERK OF COURT: ALEXANDER MCDOWELL.

ROBINSON, JOHN A.   MAY 27, 1863. AUGUST TERM 1866.
        WIFE & EXECUTRIX: ELIZA S. (ASHFORD PLANTATION).
SON & EXECUTOR: DAVID G. ROBESON. GRANDSON: JAMES A.
PURDIE, SON OF MY DECEASED DAUGHTER, FRANCIS PURDIE, WIFE
OF J. W. PURDIE. DAUGHTERS: SARAH ANN ROBINSON, MARY
M. C. HARRIS, ELIZABETH B. ROBINSON, JANE W. ROBINSON.
WITNESSES: THOS. F. ROBINSON, H. L. HOLMES. CLERK:
D. BLUE.

ROWLAND, JAMES   APRIL 10, 1782. AUGUST TERM 1782.
        WIFE & EXECUTRIX: ELIZABETH. SONS: JOHN, THOMAS,
JAMES, SAMUEL, DAVID. DAUGHTERS: SARAH, ELIZABETH, MARY.
EXECUTOR: JOHN ROWLAND. WITNESSES: JAMES JACKSON, THOMAS
ROWLAND. CLERK: SAMUEL CAIN.

RUSS, JOHN   MAY 12, 1791. BROTHERS: THOMAS
        RUSS, ELEAZER RUSS. SISTER: NANCY LLOYD, MAR-
GARET THOMAS. NEPHEW: JAMES RUSS, SR. COUSIN: SHEPHARD
RUSS. OTHER LEGATEES, EXECUTORS AND FRIENDS: DANIEL
LLOYD, GEORGE THOMAS. WITNESSES: JOHN SINGLETARY, JOHN
WINSOR, DEBORAH SINGLETARY.

RUSS, JOHN   MARCH 25, 1817. MAY TERM 1838.
        WIFE & EXECUTRIX: LYDIA. SON & EXECUTOR: JOHN
A. (OTHER CHILDREN MENTIONED BUT NOT NAMED). OTHER
LEGATEES: JAMES P. RUSS, ARGLUS P. RUSS. (MY SION RUSS
LANDS AND LANDS PURCHASED FROM DR. GEORGE LUCAS) WIT-
NESSES: ANN MARIA JONES, BENJAMIN LOCK, JAMES ALLEN.

RUSS, JOHN D.   JULY 18, 1865. DEC. 1, 1879.
        LEGATEE & EXECUTOR: ANDREW J. MESHAW. WITNESSES:
N. T. HARRIS, D. J. CLARK, JNO. M. BENSON. JUDGE OF
PROBATE: EVANDER SINGLETARY.

RUSS, JOSEPH   FEBRUARY 28, 1797.
        WIFE & EXECUTRIX: SARAH. CHILDREN: THOMAS,
JOSIAH, ANN ELIZA. OTHER LEGATEES: JOHN WILSON, SARAH
TAYLOR, MARY TAYLOR. EXECUTORS: JOHN SINGLETARY, THOMAS
LLOYD. WITNESSES: JOHN SINGLETARY, ANN RUSS, SUSAN
RUSS.

RUSS, MARY (WIDOW) AUGUST 25, 1772.
        SONS: THOMAS, JONADAB, ALEAZER, JOHN. DAUGHTERS:
MARY POYNTER, SARAH OLIPHANT, NANCY LLOYD, MARGARET
SMITH. EXECUTOR: JOHN RUSS (SON). WITNESSES: BRATON
SINGLETARY, WILLIAM SINGLETARY, MARY WILLIAMSON.

RUSS, THOMAS   AUGUST 31, 1795.
        WIFE (NOT NAMED). DAUGHTERS: MARGARET THOMAS,
HANNAH RUSS, RACHEL RUSS, MARY ANNAH, ANN, SUSAN, SARAH.
SONS: THOMAS, JOSEPH, JOHN SINGLETARY, JAMES. EXECUTORS:
JOSEPH RUSS & JOHN SINGLETARY RUSS (SONS). WITNESSES:
JOHN SINGLETARY, JOSEPH RUSS, WILLIAM RUSS, ANN RUSS.

SALKELD, ISAAC (OF SAMPSON COUNTY) FEBRUARY 25, 1795.
        WIFE & EXECUTRIX: RUTH. WITNESSES: JOAN BLACKMAN,
ABRAHAM NAYLOR, MARY BLACKMAN.

SALTER, JOHN D.   MAY 3, 1846. AUG. TERM 1852.
        SISTERS: SARAH BRYAN, ELIZABETH SALTER. OTHER
LEGATEES: JAMES SALTER, J. BRYAN'S CHILDREN. EXECUTOR:
JOSEPH R. KEMP. WITNESSES: JAMES W. CROMARTIE, JAMES
S. MELVIN, GEORGE T. BARKSDALE, DURHAM LEWIS. CLERK:
J. I. McREE.

SALTER, RICHARD   MAY 14, 1796.
        WIFE: ANN. CHILDREN: WILLIAM JAMES, MARY, JANE,
SARAH. FATHER & EXECUTOR: WILLIAM SALTER. EXECUTORS:
JOHN McKAY, JOHN COWAN. WITNESSES: J. A. McREE, SARAH
SALTER.

SALTER, RICHARD, SR. JULY 12, 1795.
        WIFE: ANN. SONS & EXECUTORS: RICHARD, JOHN,
JAMES, WILLIAM. DAUGHTERS: MARY, ANN. NEPHEW: RICHARD
HARRISON. WITNESSES: J. ELLIS, J. ROBESON, T. W. HARVEY.

SALTER, SARAH   AUGUST 18, 1797.
        BROTHERS: GEORGE THOMAS, JOHN THOMAS, WILLIAM
THOMAS, JONATHAN THOMAS. SISTERS: ELIZABETH PURNELL,

MARY CROWSON, SUSANNAH RUSS, NANCY McCULLOCK. NIECES: MARY J. PURNELL, SARAH I. THOMAS, JANE RUSS. EXECUTORS: JOHN THOMAS, JONATHAN THOMAS. WITNESSES: ISAACK SIKES, MARY HARVEY, JOHN McKAY.

SALTER, WILLIAM   MAY 17, 1797.
        WIFE & EXECUTRIX: SARAH. SON: RICHARD. DAUGHTERS: SARAH, ANN, MARGARET. GRANDSONS: WILLIAM JAMES SALTER, WILLIAM JAMES SALTER COWAN, WILLIAM JAMES McKAY. (PLANTATION "GEORGIA") OTHER LEGATEES: JOHN COWAN'S CHILDREN, WILLIAM JAMES COWAN, JOHN CARVER & ELIZABETH COWAN, JOHN McKAY. EXECUTORS: JOHN COWAN, JOHN McKAY.

SALTER, WILLIAM   JULY 6, 1836
        WIFE & EXECUTRIX: ELIZABETH. SONS: JOHN D., JAMES, JOSEPH R. DAUGHTERS: ELIZABETH SALTER, SARAH BRYAN. EXECUTOR: JOHN D. SALTER (SON). WITNESS: DAVID LEWIS.

SANDERS, CHRISTOPHER APRIL 27, 1778.
        WIFE & EXECUTRIX: SARAH. SONS: THOMAS, CHRISTOP-HER: DAUGHTERS: SARAH, AMELIA, ELVIRA, ELIZABETH. EXECUTOR: JOHN BALDWIN, JR. WITNESSES: JOHN FOKES, WILLIAM FOKES, JAS. SHIPMAN.

SANDERS, THOMAS   NOVEMBER 16, 1776.
        WIFE: EMILIA. SON: CHRISTOPHER SANDERS. CHILDREN: ELIZABETH BOSWELL, ELIZABETH ELLIS, AMILI MOSLY, THOMAS BROWDER. DAUGHTER-IN-LAW: ELCY SANDERS. WITNESSES: DUNCAN MORRISON, LOUVILL HARDWICK. CLERK: JOHN WHITE.

SAWREY, HENRY, SR.   (OF NORTH HAMPTON COUNTY)
        NOVEMBER 20, 1775. SONS: JOHN, EDWARD, HENRY. DAUGHTERS: MILDRED SAWREY, ANN SAWREY, ELIZABETH JUSTICE, MARY BRITT, LUCY PHILLIPS. EXECUTORS: HENRY & EDWARD SAWREY (SONS). WITNESSES: SIMON SIMPSON, JACOB SIMPSON, SEGMORE SIMPSON.

SCRIVEN, JOHN   NOVEMBER 25, 1822.
        BROTHERS: THOMAS SCRIVEN, JAMES SCRIVEN, JAMES SCRIBEN, JONATHAN & HIS WIFE MARGARET ALLEN. OTHER LEG-ATEES: E. W. ALLEN, JAMES JACKSON, MATTHEW MUNCE, J. NORMAN. EXECUTORS: SAMUEL ROBESON, COLIN MONROE.

WITNESSES: JOHN ALLEN, WILLIAM CAIN, SR.

SEYMORE, SARAH   SEPTEMBER 23, 1793.
        SON: EDWARD FOGARTIE. FRIENDS: JOHN HALL,
DUNCAN MCCULLOCH. EXECUTORS: BENJAMIN LOCK, DONALD BAIN.
WITNESSES: THOMAS FLOWERS, THOMAS F. JONES, JOHN P.
GRANGE.

SHAW, ARCHIBALD   20 DAY OF   1799.
        WIFE & EXECUTRIX: CATHERINE. OTHER LEGATEES:
JOHN SHAW SON OF MY BROTHER DANIEL SHAW, MALCOM AND
DANIEL SHAW SONS OF DANIEL SHAW, JOHN MCKAY HUSBAND OF
ANN MCKAY, DAUGHTER OF MY BROTHER DANIEL SHAW, MARTHA
MCEWEN HUSBAND OF JEAN MCEWEN DAUGHTER OF MY BROTHER
DANIEL SHAW, ANGUS AND JOHN, SONS OF MY BROTHER JOHN SHAW,
CHARLES MCNORTON, HUSBAND OF THE LATE MARY MCNORTON,
DAUGHTER OF MY BROTHER JOHN SHAW, WILLIAM MCEWEN, HUSBAND
OF CATHERIN MCEWEN, DAUGHTER OF JOHN SHAW, JOHN MCMILLAN,
HUSBAND OF MARRION MCMILLAN, DAUGHTER OF JOHN SHAW, DANIEL
SHAW, SON OF NEILL SHAW, ARCHIBALD BUIE AND CATHERIN,
HIS WIFE, MARION SHAW, RELIC OF MY BROTHER COLIN SHAW,
JAMES MCCONLSKEY, HUSBAND OF MARGARET MCCONLSKEY, DEC-
EASED DAUGHTER OF NEILL SHAW, CHRISTOPHER AND DANIEL GOODEN,
GRANDSONS OF MY BROTHER NEILL SHAW. WITNESSES: JOHN
MCKAY, DUNCAN MCCALL, ANGUS LAMON, JR.

SHAW, CATHERINE   DECEMBER 28, 1804.
        LEGATEES: JOHN SHAW, JR., DANIEL SHAW, JOHN MC-
KAY MARSH, MATTHEW MCEWEN, MALCOM MCLEANEN, MALCOM SHAW.
WITNESSES: DANIEL CAMPBELL, JR., JAMES CAMPBELL, DUNCAN
RAY.

SHAW, DANIEL   FEBRUARY 16, 1780.
        WIFE: JANE. SONS: DUNCAN, ANGUS, MALCOM, DANIEL,
JOHN. DAUGHTERS: ANN, JANE. WITNESSES: JOHN CAMPBELL,
DUGALD BLUE, ALEXANDER SHAW.

SHAW, DANIEL   NOVEMBER 23, 1869. CODICIL:
        DECEMBER 1, 1869. PROBATED JANUARY 3, 1870.
SIX HEIRS (NOT NAMED) EXECUTORS: JAMES A. ELKINS, A. J.
FORMEE (FORMEDUVAL). WITNESSES: H. C. MCCOLLUM, D. F.
SHAW. JUDGE OF PROBATE: D. BLUE

SHAW, DANIEL, SR.   NOVEMBER 6, 1846. AUG. TERM 1848.
        SONS: WILLIAM, RANDALL, DANIEL, DUNCAN, ARCHI-
BALD. EXECUTORS: DANIEL & ARCHIBALD (SONS). WITNESSES:
DURRUM LEWIS, CHARLES H. BURNEY. CLERK OF COURT: H. H.
ROBINSON.

SHAW, JOHN, SR.   JANUARY 18, 1842. MAY TERM 1847.
        WIFE: MARY ANN. SONS: ALEXANDER, JOHN, ARCHIBALD,
WILLIAM. DAUGHTERS: CHRISTIAN, MARGARET, ANN. GRAND-
SONS: ARCHIBALD CAMPBELL, JOHN DOVE. GRANDDAUGHTER:
CATHERINE CAMPBELL. EXECUTOR: ALEXANDER SHAW (SON).
WITNESSES: COLIN MONROE, DAVID PATE. CLERK OF COURT:
H. H. ROBINSON.

SHAW, PENELOPE   FEBRUARY 4, 1849.
        (WIFE OF DANIEL SHAW, SR.) CHILDREN: CHARLES
FORMYDUVAL, DEMOSTHAIN FORMYDUVAL, SARAH ANN PIERCE WIFE
OF JAMES C. PIERCE, JOHN PAUL FORMYDUVAL, JANE ROSELINE
LENNON WIFE OF WILLIAM LENNON, MARY JANE CAROLINE SHAW
WIFE OF DUNCAN SHAW. EXECUTOR: JAMES C. PIERCE. WIT-
NESSES: JOHN J. PIERCE, BENJAMIN F. PIERCE.

SHERIDAN, THOMAS   APRIL 29, 1863. FEB. TERM 1864.
        (WIFE NOT NAMED) DAUGHTER: MARTHA. OTHER LEGATEE:
ALMIRA CARTER. "I LEAVE MY CARPENTER TOOLS AND MY GUN TO
BE SOLD TO PAY MY FUNERAL EXPENSES....THE LUMBER IN MY
SHOP LOFT I LEAVE IT TO MAKE MY COFFIN." EXECUTOR: COLIN
MONROE. WITNESSES: JOHN B. WARD, COLIN MONROE. CLERK:
D. BLUE.

SHIPMAN, DANIEL (PLANTER)   MARCH 28, 1772.
        SONS & EXECUTORS: JAMES SHIPMAN, DANIEL SHIPMAN.
WIFE: ELENORE. OTHER LEGATEES: ELIZABETH BURNEY, EL-
ELENORE BURNEY, SARAH SANDERS, ELENORE SANDERS. WITNESSES:
HARTRAN LEWIS, MATTHEW MOORE, JAMES CUNNINGHAM.

SHIPMAN, DANIEL   SEPTEMBER 18, 1799.
        WIFE & EXECUTRIX: ANN. DAUGHTERS: ANN AMES,
FRANCES ELENOR, REBECCA. BROTHER & EXECUTOR: JAMES
SHIPMAN. EXECUTORS: JOHN WADDELL, JAMES MOOREHEAD.
WITNESSES: ELISHA MOORE, ESAW HIGH, ELIZABETH LUNIES.

SHIPMAN, DANIEL   OCTOBER 19, 1844.
        WIFE & EXECUTRIX: DOREAS. SONS: JOHN D., ANDREW
J., JAMES W., HAYES F. DAUGHTERS: MARIAH LENNON, CARO-
LINE HOLLINGSWORTH, LUCY MCDANIEL, EMILY MCRACKEN, FLORINA
D. SHIPMAN. EXECUTOR: RICHARD WOOTEN. WITNESSES: ABNER
SHIPMAN, JAMES BROWN, JR.

SHIPMAN, HAYES F.   NOVEMBER 2, 1844. NOV. TERM 1845.
        WIFE & EXECUTRIX: SARAH JANE. CHILDREN: MARY

ELIZA, HAYES MCNEILL, SARAH DORCAS, ELIZA ANN. "MY AGED
GRANDFATHER", JOHN WINGATE. WIFE APPOINTED GUARDIAN OF
ALL CHILDREN WHO ARE MINORS UNLESS SHE DIES OR MARRIES
AGAIN AND THEN ROBERT MCRACKEN OF BRUNSWICK COUNTY AND IF
HE DIES DR. WILLIAM ANDERS. EXECUTORS: JAMES C. KELLY,
NEILL KELLY. WITNESSES: WILLIAM D. MCNEILL, THOMAS M.
KELLY, HAYNES LENNON, COLIN MONROE.

SIKES, ALEXANDER J. OCTOBER 18, 1883. 1887.
        SISTERS: ANN BENSON, MARIAH SIKES. NEPHEWS: TOM
WARD, JOHN WARD, DAVID R. SIKES. NIECE: PHOEBE HAMMONDS.
OTHER LEGATEES: SARAH ELIZABETH ANDERS WIFE OF D. J.
ANDERS. EXECUTOR: W. W. ANDERS. WITNESSES: W. IRVING
SHAW, THEO SESSOMS, WM. B. MURPHY. CLERK: GEO. F. MELVIN.

SIKES, DAVID   FEBRUARY 4, 1860. FEB. TERM 1864.
        WIFE: ISABELLA. DAUGHTER: MARY ANN EVANS WIFE OF
JACOB A. EVANS. SON & EXECUTOR: THEODORE M. SIKES.
WITNESSES: T. D. LOVE, SR., J. B. ALLEN. (SON ENTERED
INTO A BOND OF TWENTY THOUSAND DOLLARS WITH J. W. RUSS
AND THOMAS O. BROWN AS SURETIES) CLERK: D. BLUE.

SIKES, JOHN   JANUARY 23, 1866. MAY TERM 1868.
        WIFE: EMELIA. SON & EXECUTOR: GILES SIKES.
GRANDCHILDREN: JOHN RICHARD, JOEL, EMELIA ALLIS, CHILDREN
OF EDMON SIKES. WITNESSES: OWEN SMITH, DANIEL MCGHEE,
EMILY MCGHEE. CLERK: J. W. PURDIE.

SIKES, JONATHAN   JULY 4, 1818.
        WIFE: SARAH. SONS: SAMUEL, JOHN, RICHARD, JOSHUA,
ISIAH, CALEB, AMOS. DAUGHTERS: LUCY WIFE OF WILLIAM
KEMP, & CATHERINE. "WATERY LAKE SOMETIMES CALLED HARRI-
SONS LAKE". NIECE: ELIZABETH TURNER WIFE OF BENJAMIN
TURNER & DAUGHTER OF MY BROTHER, JONAH SIKES. BROTHER:
JOSEPH SIKES' CHILDREN: COLIN, MARY & JAMES SIKES.
EXECUTOR: JOHN SIKES (SON). WITNESSES: JOHN DICKSON,
J. CAIN.

SIKES, JOSIAH   MAY 23, 1812.
        WIFE & EXECUTRIX: ELIZABETH. OTHER LEGATEES:
LUKE SIKES & DAVID SIKES, SONS OF JOSIAH SIKES, JR.
EXECUTOR: DAVID LLOYD. WITNESSES: JOHN LUCAS, JOHN
RUSS.

SIMMONS, SANDERS   OCTOBER 25, 1836.

WIFE: ANN MARIAH (THE REMNANT OF MY PENSION MONEY COMING AFTER MY DEATH). EXECUTOR: JOHN HAIR, SR. WITNESSES: JOHN R. MCLEMORE, STEPHEN HAIR.

SIMPSON, JOHN   JULY 14, 1838.
WIFE & EXECUTRIX: MARY. SONS: FREDERICK, RICHARD M., WILLIAM, JOSEPH, JAMES B. DAUGHTERS: MARGARET ANN RUSS, EMELINE SIMPSON. EXECUTOR: SALTER JOHNSON. WITNESSES: DUGALD MCMILLAN, COLL MCDUGALD.

SINGLETARY, BENJAMIN (PLANTER)   AUGUST 22, 1765.
WIFE & EXECUTRIX: ELIZABETH. SONS: JOSEPH, JOHN, RICHARD, BENJAMIN, JAMES. EXECUTOR: RICHARD SINGLETARY (SON). WITNESSES: MITCHELL EUSTACE, THOMAS ROBESON, JR., MARY ROBESON.

SINGLETARY, BREYTON SEPTEMBER 7, 1790.
WIFE & EXECUTRIX: MARY. SONS: JOSEPH, BENJAMIN. DAUGHTER: DEBORAH. BROTHER & EXECUTOR: BENJAMIN SINGLETARY. LUCY STREATY, WILLIAM STREATY, BENJAMIN SINGLETARY, WITNESSES.

SINGLETARY, BRISTER   JUNE 17, 1884.
CODICIL: 12 DEC. 1884. PROBATED: JANUARY 10, 1885. GRANDSONS: BRISTER SINGLETARY, GENERAL SINGLETARY. SISTER: WINNIE SINGLETARY. DAUGHTERS: MARTHA, WIFE OF ED SINGLETARY, CAROLINE WIFE OF ELIAS MCKENZIE, BETSY, WIFE OF LARKIN POWELL. SON: GOODMAN SINGLETARY. OTHER HEIRS: NATHAN SINGLETARY, NEPAY SINGLETARY, HANNAH, WIDOW OF JACOB STEPHEN. EXECUTOR: C. W. WILLIAMS. WITNESSES: GEORGE W. JONES, MARY J. JONES. CLERK: G. F. MELVIN.

SINGLETARY, DAVID AUGUST 30, 1861. NOVEMBER TERM 1862.
WIFE & EXECUTRIX: ABAGIL. SONS: JAMES F., JONA-THAN, DAVID M., JOSIAH W., LENON P., GEORGE S. FATHER: JONATHAN SINGLETARY, SR. DAUGHTERS: SARAH E., HARRIET B., MARY F. WITNESSES: ROBERT M. SESSOMS, JAS. E. SINGLE-TARY. CLERK: D. BLUE.

SINGLETARY, EDWARD OCTOBER 1, 1863. NOVEMBER TERM 1863.
WIFE: MARY ANN. "ALL MY LAND, DURING THIS WAR, WHICH IS NOW GOING ON BETWEEN THE UNITED STATES AND THE CONFEDERATE STATES, EXCEPT THE OLD WILLIAM JONES PLANTAT-ION AND AT THE EXPIRATION OF SAID WAR, IF MY SONS SHALL RETURN AND STAY WITH MY WIFE, THEY CAN ALL WORK TOGETHER

FOR THE BENEFIT OF THE FAMILY . . .". SONS: CALVIN, WRIGHT, JOSHUA. DAUGHTERS: (NOT NAMED). EXECUTOR: CALVIN SINGLETARY, SON. WITNESSES: COLIN MONROE, SNOWDEN SINGLETARY, ROWLAND SINGLETARY. CLERK: D. BLUE.

SINGLETARY, ITHAMAR NOVEMBER 12, 1773.
WIFE: CAROLINA. SONS: ITHAMAR, JOH. DAUGHTERS: ELIZABETH, DEBORAH, MARY. BROTHERS & EXECUTORS: BENJAMIN FITZRANDOLPH, THOMAS OWEN. WITNESSES: JOHN ROBERTS, PHILLIP PAUL MATTOCKS, PRUDENCE ROBERTS.

SINGLETARY, JAMES, SR. FEBRUARY 20, 1810.
WIFE: NANCY. SONS: THOMAS, JAMES, SAMUEL. OTHER LEGATEES: HEIRS OF NANCY MCCALEB. EXECUTORS: BARTRAM ROBESON, THOMAS & JAMES SINGLETARY (SONS). WITNESSES: W. R. DUNHAM, RICHARD RICHARDSON.

SINGLETARY, JOHN · AUGUST 27, 1826.
WIFE & EXECUTRIX: DEBORAH. NIECE: KESIAH HESTER. NEPHEWS: JOSEPH SINGLETARY, JOHN S. WILSON, SON OF GEORGE. JOHN DUNHAM SINGLETARY SON OF JOHN SINGLETARY. THOMAS BENSON, NEPHEW OF MY WIFE. WITNESSES: WM. JOHNSON, ROBT. DEWEY, THOS. SMITH.

SINGLETARY, JOSEPH JULY 4, 1772. NOVEMBER COURT 1772.
WIFE: MARY. (CHILDREN NOT NAMED) BROTHERS & EXECUTORS: BENJAMIN FITZRANDOLPH, ITHAMAR SINGLETARY. WITNESSES: JOHN POYNTER, MARY POYNTER, BRAYTON SINGLETARY. CLERK: MATURIN COLVILL, C. C.

SINGLETARY, JOSIAH DECEMBER 14, 1841.
WIFE: SARAH (FORMERLY MARRIED). SONS: WILLIS, DAVID. DAUGHTERS: SUSAN WOOD WIFE OF WILLIAM WOOD AND AMELIA WOOD WIFE OF JOSEPH WOOD. EXECUTOR: COLIN MONROE. WITNESSES: ARCHIBALD KELLY, EDWARD LEWIS.

SINGLETARY, JOSHUA JANUARY 21, 1840.
WIFE: ANNA JANE. SONS: DENNIS (AND OTHERS NOT NAMED). ("I HAVE 40 BARRELS OF TAR AT ELIZABETHTOWN"). EXECUTORS: COLIN MONROE, JOHN M. LENNON. WITNESSES: JONATHAN SINGLETARY, JR., C. MONROE, EDWARD SINGLETARY.

SINGLETARY, MARY NOVEMBER 9, 1827.
NEPHEW & EXECUTOR: JAMES SNOWDEN DUNHAM. WITNESSES: SAMUEL ROBESON, WILLIAM DAVIS, MATTHEW MUNCE.

SINGLETARY, RICHARD (NUNCUPATIVE WILL) 31 MAY 1791.
1 JUNE 1791. LEGATEE: WILLIAM SINGLETARY CUNNING-
HAM SON OF RACHEL CUNNINGHAM. WITNESSES: WILLIAM SMITH,
SR., JOHN PEMBERTON, SAMUEL SMITH. EPHRIAM MULFORD,
JUSTICE OF THE PEACE.

SINGLETARY, RICHARD (NO DATES)
WIFE: SARAH. SONS: PETER, JOHN. DAUGHTERS:
SIDNEY, SOPHIA, NEPSY, AMELIA. GRANDSONS: WADE HAMPTON
CAIN, SAMUEL CAIN, RICHARD CAIN. EXECUTOR: PETER SINGLE-
TARY (SON). (LANDS WHERE JOSEPH CAIN NOW LIVES).
WITNESSES: JOSHUA SIKES, RICHARD SIKES.

SINGLETARY, RICHARD, SR. MARCH 8, 1773.
WIFE: JOYCE. SONS: BENJAMIN, WILLIAM, RICHARD.
DAUGHTER: ELIZABETH SINGLETARY, WIDOW OF JOHN SINGLETARY.
SON-IN-LAW: ELKANAH ALLEN. EXECUTORS: WILLIAM SINGLETARY
(SON), WILLIAM SALTER (NEPHEW). WITNESSES: GAINOR
HUMPHREYS, JOSEPH HUMPHREYS, BENJAMIN HUMPHREYS.

SINGLETARY, THOMAS APRIL 19, 1823. CODICIL: DECEMBER
9, 1825. WIFE: JANE (CALLED JANE WILSON, NAMED IN
CODICIL, HAVING MARRIED SINCE WILL WAS MADE). SONS:
JOHN H. SINGLETARY, GRANDSON OF JOHN HESTER, EPHRIAM
SINGLETARY, NEPHEW OF EPHRIAM HESTER, THOMAS SINGLETARY,
DANIEL M. SINGLETARY. DAUGHTERS: MARY, HANNAH. EXECU-
TORS: WILLIAM ROBESON, JOHN HENDRY, JOHN H. SINGLETARY.
WITNESSES: J. CAIN, MORRIS PLUMMER, WM. DAVIS.

SINGLETARY, WILLIAM JUNE 1, 1785.
WIFE: MARY. SONS: WILLIAM, COUNCIL. (LANDS KNOWN
AS SINGLETARY'S BLUFF, AND OLD PASTURE OR SUGAR LOAF POINT).
BROTHER: RICHARD SINGLETARY. EXECUTORS: JAMES COUNCIL,
RICHARD LLOYD. WITNESSES: JAMES BRADLEY, JOHN COWAN,
BENJAMIN HUMPHREY.

SMITH, DANIEL   JANUARY 20, 1876. JULY 1, 1878.
WIFE (NOT NAMED) SONS & EXECUTORS: JOHN, KINION
A. AND JAMES. DAUGHTERS: ELIZABETH ANN, ALICE HENRYETTA.
WITNESSES: LEVI BRYAN, JOHN CAIN. JUDGE OF PROBATE:
EVANDER SINGLETARY.

SMITH, DAVID J.   NOVEMBER 26, 1854. FEB. TERM 1855.
SISTERS: MARTHA, WIFE OF WILLIAM SMITH, MARGARET,
WIFE OF ROBERT SMITH, MOLSEY, WIFE OF GUILFORD NORRIS,

SUSANNA, WIFE OF JAMES LONG, TERCEY SMITH, SINGLE WOMAN.
BROTHERS: DANIEL, AMOS. FATHER & EXECUTOR: JOHN B.
SMITH. WITNESSES: JOHN CAIN, AMOS SMITH. CLERK: F. F.
CUMMING.

SMITH, JAMES   AUGUST 12, 1827. CODICILS: MARCH
        1, 1828, MAY 20, 1829, SEPT. 27, 1838. WIFE:
(NOT NAMED). SONS AND EXECUTORS: THOMAS AND JOHN.
DAUGHTER: SOPHIA LEONARD. OTHER LEGATEES: MAJOR BROWN,
JOHN LEONARD, WILLIAM B. MEARES, ESQ.

SMITH, JOHN   MAY 12, 1781. FEB. TERM 1782.
        SONS & EXECUTORS: SAMUEL, JAMES, THOMAS, JONATHAN.
DAUGHTER: ELIZABETH HAYNES. GRANDSON: JOHN SMITH, SON OF
MY DECEASED SON, JOHN SMITH. WITNESSES: MARGARET McREE,
GEORGE THOMAS, JOHN McFATTER. CLERK: SAMUEL CAIN.

SMITH, JOHN   JANUARY 25, 1792.
        MOTHER: MARGARET THOMAS. HALF-BROTHER: FRANCES
THOMAS. EXECUTORS: DAVID LLOYD, GEORGE THOMAS.
WITNESSES: JOHN GARSON, JONATHAN THOMAS, THOMAS LLOYD.

SMITH, JOHN SR.   JUNE 9, 1845.
        SONS: SHADRACH, DANIEL. DAUGHTERS: POLLY JANE
MOTE, WIFE OF JAMES MOTE, MARIAN SMITH, WIFE OF WILLIAM
SMITH, JANE SMITH, WIFE OF ALLEN SMITH. EXECUTORS:
DANIEL SMITH (SON), ALLEN SMITH (SON-IN-LAW). WITNESSES:
DANIEL McDUFFIE, JOHN CAIN.

SMITH, JONATHAN   AUGUST 31, 1822. NOVEMBER TERM 1823.
        SON & EXECUTOR: THOMAS F. SMITH. GRANDDAUGHTER:
EMELINE McKAY (HER UNCLE THOMAS F. SMITH TO BE HER
GUARDIAN). CLERK: A. McDOWELL.

SMITH, LUCY   JUNE 23, 1795.
        SONS: MALCOM SMITH, NOBLE SMITH (EXECUTOR).
WITNESSES: JOSEPH CAIN, LUCY WOOD. ACKNOWLEDGED JULY
20, 1795, BEFORE JOHN WHITE.

SMITH, MARGARET C.   OCTOBER 17, 1839.
        DAUGHTER: HARRIET V. BIDWELL. "MINERAL SPRINGS
PLANTATION". SON: SAMUEL G. GAUSE. GRANDSON: WILLIAM
TOON. GRANDDAUGHTERS: PRINCESS ANN TOON, MARY JANE
GAUSE. EXECUTOR: THOS. C. SMITH. WITNESSES: JOHN L.
McKAY, A. E. McKAY.

SMITH, MARY   MAY 24, 1862. MAY 19, 1871.
          SONS: J. J. SMITH, JOHN B. SMITH. DAUGHTERS:
DELILAH LONG, ELIZABETH J. SMITH, SUSAN SMITH, ELIZA
SMITH. SON-IN-LAW: ALEXANDER AUTRY. GRANDCHILDREN:
HENRY E. SMITH, MARY MATILDA AUTRY, MARGARET ANN SMITH.
EXECUTORS: ELIZABETH J. SMITH, SUSAN SMITH. WITNESSES:
MALCOM MONROE, JOHN G. SUTTON. CLERK: D. BLUE.

SMITH, RICHARD   8TH YEAR OF AMERICAN INDEPENDENCE.
          WIFE: LUCY. CHILDREN: MACOM, TRYON, NOBLE, ELIZA-
BETH, MARY, SARAH, TOBITHA, MASSEY. EXECUTORS: JOHN
WILLIS, ELIAS BURRUS, SAMUEL PORTER, ESQ. WITNESSES:
JAMES MARSHBURN, ELIZABETH CADE.

SMITH, ROBINSON W. APRIL 15, 1882. MAY 17, 1882.
          WIFE & EXECUTRIX: ANN JANE SMITH. (CHILDREN NOT
NAMED) WITNESSES: A. G. DAVIS, McK. CULBRETH. JUDGE
OF PROBATE: G. F. MELVIN.

SMITH, SAMUEL   FEBRUARY 15, 1786.
          WIFE & EXECUTRIX: SOPHIA. DAUGHTER: MARY.
SON: JOHN. BROTHER & EXECUTOR: THOMAS SMITH. WITNESSES:
DAVID RUSS, JAN'T HINE.

SMITH, STEPHEN   JULY 2, 1784.
          WIFE & EXECUTRIX: JOANNA (6 CHILDREN NOT NAMED)
(THOMAS PENNY PLANTATION ON BOGUE) BROTHER & EXECUTOR:
JOHN SMITH. EXECUTOR: RICHARD REYNOLDS. WITNESSES:
DANIEL DUPRIE, SARAH MIMS, JOANNA SMITH.

SMITH, THOMAS   NOVEMBER 27, 1836. CODICILS:
          JULY 17, 1837. MARCH 29, 1838. WIFE: MARGARET.
SON: THOMAS C. SMITH. DAUGHTERS: ANN MARIAH PURDIE &
MARY JANE McDOWELL. GRANDSONS: THOMAS McDOWELL, THOMAS
PURDIE, THOMAS E. McMILLAN & JOHN L. McMILLAN, SONS OF
JOHN IVER McMILLAN (LANDS BOUGHT OF HEIRS OF JAMES PEM-
BERTON) & JOHN McDOWELL. EXECUTORS: ALEX McDOWELL,
THOMAS C. SMITH & JOHN McDOWELL, SONS OF MY DAUGHTER MARY
JANE McDOWELL.

SMITH, THOMAS C.   AUGUST 3, 1874. DECEMBER 27, 1874.
          SISTER: A. M. PURDIE. OTHER LEGATEES: JOHN W.
PURDIE, ELIZA I. PURDIE, JAMES A. PURDIE, JOHN A. McDOWELL,
THOS. D. McDOWELL, ALEXANDER McDOWELL, JOHNY McDOWELL,
JAMES S. ROBINSON, THOMAS A. ROBINSON, IRVING ROBINSON,
NEWTON ROBINSON, MARY E. ROBINSON, CHARLES ROBINSON,

JOHN L. MCMILLAN. EXECUTORS: THOMAS D. MCDOWELL, JOHN A. MCDOWELL, J. W. PURDIE. WITNESSES: THOMAS I. NORMAN, B. T. RANDOLPH. JUDGE OF PROBATE: EVANDER SINGLETARY.

SMITH, WILLIAM   DECEMBER 4, 1798.
        DAUGHTERS: ROSE BRIGHT, ELIZABETH JOYCE (DEC'D), SARAH, (DEC'D). GRANDSONS: SIMON SMITH, WILLIAM SMITH, ALFRED MULFORD (MY FERRY AT ELIZABETHTOWN). EXECUTOR: JONATHAN SMITH. WITNESSES: JAMES PEMBERTON, ELIZABETH PEMBERTON, THOMAS SMITH.

SMITH, WINNAFRED   DECEMBER 6, 1851. FEB. TERM 1852.
        LEGATEES: JOHN MCDANIEL, WINNAFORD EDGE, ARTHUR SMITH, SYLVAY DAVIS, WILLIAM DAVIS, WILLIAM SMITH, MARY SMITH. EXECUTOR: JOHN MCDANIEL. WITNESSES: STEPHEN SMITH, ZYLPHIA BRYANT. CLERK: J. I. MCREE.

STEWART, HUGH (PLANTER)   JUNE 6, 1771.
        WIFE & EXECUTRIX: CATHERINE. BROTHER: ROBERT STEWART. NIECE: ELIZABETH STEWART, DAUGHTER OF ROBERT STEWART. WITNESSES: NEILL MCCAULSKEY, WILLIAM MCNEILL, NEILL SHAW.

STEWART, PATRICK   DECEMBER 14, 1777.
        FATHER & EXECUTOR:: WILLIAM STEWART. SISTERS: MARGARET, ANN. BROTHERS: DUNCAN, JAMES. OTHER LEGATEE: JEMIMA MATTHEWS. EXECUTORS: DAVID BAILEY, WILLIAM CROMARTIE. WITNESSES: WILLIAM CROMARTIE, ALEX'R. CARMICHAEL, JOHN DOANE.
                                        W B 4/177L

STEWART, WILLIAM   AUGUST 2, 1778.
        WIFE & EXECUTRIX: JANNETT. PLANTATIONS: BOONES-FIELD, NEWFIELD, SKIPPERS FIELD. SONS: CHARLES, DUNCAN, JAMES. DAUGHTERS: CATHERINE, JANNETT, ANN, ELIZABETH, HELEN, MARGARET SPILER. WIFE'S GRANDDAUGHTERS: JANNETTE BAILEY, JANNETTE WHITE. GRANDSON: WALTER STEWART. OTHER LEGATEES: WILLIAM STEWART BEATTY, WILLIAM STEWART WRIGHT. EXECUTORS: DUNCAN STEWART (SON), DAVID BAILEY. WITNESSES: ROBERT HENDREY, ANN STEWART, ELIZABETH STEWART.

STONE, BENJAMIN   SEPTEMBER 17, 1780.
        SON: WILLIAM STONE, WHO WAS 19 ON 1 SEPT. 1780, "LANDS IN BRUMPTON". FATHER, NOW IN JERSEY. OTHER LEGATEES: MARY CADDINGTON AND HER DAUGHTER, NANCY CADDINGTON.

EXECUTORS: WILLIAM MCKEE, ESQ., ROBERT WILLS. WITNESSES: ARABELLA WILLS, ARCH'D DARRACK, JOHN WHITE.

STORM, MARY   DECEMBER 10, 1803.

SON: JOHN STORM. DAUGHTERS: MARY SESSIONS, MARGARET PURNELL. GRANDDAUGHTERS: MARY PURNELL, DAUGHTER OF MARGARET PURNELL, MARGARET MAULTSBY, DAUGHTER OF MARY SESSIONS. GRANDSON: WINDAL PURNELL, SON OF MARGARET PURNELL. EXECUTOR: JAMES MOORE. WITNESSES: BARTRAM ROBESON, MARGARET ROBESON.

STORM, WANDAL   MARCH 5, 1770.
WIFE (NOT NAMED). SON: JOHN. DAUGHTERS: MARGARET STORM, MARY STORM. EXECUTORS: JOHN LOCK, JOHN MOORE. WITNESSES: DANIEL BEARD, THOMAS LOCK, JONES ELLIS.

STUBBS, GEORGE, SR. MARCH 7, 1845.
WIFE (NOT NAMED). SON & EXECUTOR: GEORGE STUBBS, JR. WITNESSES: JOHN MCKAY, ELIZABETH HADDOCK.

SUGGS, WILLIAM   MARCH 27, 1872. CODICIL: JULY 4,
1772. APRIL 27, 1874. WIFE: SARAH ANN. SONS: ALLIGOOD, ALLYON, RAFORD, MCKOY, (LILLY J. SUGGS, WIDOW OF MCKOY SUGGS). DAUGHTERS: CELIA CAIN, MARY EDGE. EXECUTORS: JOHN A. MCDOWELL. WITNESSES: THOS. D. MCDOWELL, JNO. MCDOWELL. CLERK: EVANDER SINGLETARY.

SUTTON, JOHN   SEPTEMBER 30, 1806.
SON: WILLIAM. GRANDSON: JOHN SUTTON. GRANDDAUGHTERS: ELIZABETH SUTTON, JANE SUTTON. BROTHER: CHRISTOPHER SUTTON. WITNESSES: JAMES SUTTON, TOM SUTTON. GRANDDAUGHTER: MARGARET SUTTON

SUTTON, MARGARET (WIDOW OF JOHN SUTTON)
JULY 27, 1822. DAUGHTER: ANN SUTTON. GRANDSON: JOHN SUTTON. GRANDDAUGHTERS: JANE SUTTON AND HER DAUGHTER CATHERINE ANN SUTTON, SARAH ANN MELVIN, ELIZABETH MELVIN, SARAH JANE SUTTON. OTHER LEGATEES: ELIZA RUSS, PATRICK KELLY. EXECUTORS: JAMES CROMARTIE, DAVID LLOYD. WITNESSES: ELIZABETH KELLY, PATRICK KELLY.

SUTTON, SARAH, SR. MARCH 12, 1823.
SISTER: FANNY SUTTON. WITNESSES: EDWARD B.

MULFORD, SALLY SUTTON, JR., ELIZABETH MELVIN, SR.

SUTTON, WILLIAM   OCTOBER 9, 1804.

        WIFE & EXECUTRIX: SUSANNAH. SONS: JAMES, WILLIAM,
ROBIN. DAUGHTERS: ANN, SARAH, CATHERINE, HOPER. EX-
ECUTOR: JAMES SUTTON (SON). WITNESSES: EVAN ANDERS,
ROBERT MURPHY.

SUTTON, WILLIAM   JANUARY 28, 1841.
        WIFE AND TWO DAUGHTERS (NOT NAMED). SON & EXECUTOR:
WILLIAM T. SUTTON. EXECUTOR: THOMAS J. CORBETT. WIT-
NESSES: G. W. BANNERMAN, SAMUEL SMITH.

SWINDAL, SAMUEL, SR. JULY 31, 1841.
        SONS: SAMUEL, DAVID. GRANDSONS: CHESTER & JOHN,
SONS OF DAVID. (GIVES LANDS FOR THE METHODIST EPISCOPAL
CHURCH "THE HOUSE LATELY ERECTED AND BUILT FOR A PLACE OF
WORSHIP NEAR ME", ALSO NOTES TO THE MISSIONARY SOCIETY
OF THE METHODIST EPISCOPAL CHURCH.) EXECUTORS: HAYES F.
SHIPMAN & SAMUEL SWINDAL (SON). J. F. BARNES, ALEX'R.
MCDOWELL.

TARBE, PETER A.   FEBRUARY 24, 1822.
        WIFE: JANE. BROTHER: S. A. TARBE, COLLECTOR OF
THE CUSTOM HOUSE IN PARISH. OTHER LEGATEES: ISABELLA
FOUNTAIN, MRS. J. FOUNTAIN, MISS JANE MILLER, WM. L.
MILLER (ALL THE LAW BOOKS). TRUSTEES: GEN'L. THOMAS
DAVIS, PARISH OF TILLINGHAST AND GEN'L. THOMAS OWEN.
FRIEND TO WORK WITH TRUSTEES: BERNARD LASPEYRE, "TRANS-
LATE MY FRENCH PAPERS". WITNESSES: ROBERT JOHNSON, ALEX.
J. BYRN.

TATOM, JOHN H.   23 MARCH 1893. CODICIL: 17 AUGUST
        1896. 7 MARCH 1899. WIFE & EXECUTRIX: A. C.
CHILDREN: A. L., R. P., L. P., E. VANCE TATOM, LULA
SHAW, WIFE OF D. M. SHAW, CHARLEY H. TATOM. (E. VANCE
TATOM WILL BE 21 YEARS OF AGE ON 28TH DAY OF JULY 1897)
EXECUTOR: A. L. TATOM (SON). WITNESSES: R. W. TATUM,
EVANDER EDGE. CLERK: A. M. MCNEILL.

TATOM, M. W.   JULY 29, 1889. AUGUST 12 1889.
        WIFE: SARAH J. SONS: G. W., J. T., MARSHAL C.,
DAVID A., JOHN W., A. G. EXECUTOR: M. N. TATOM. WIT-
NESSES: O. J. TATOM, I. J. CAIN. CLERK: G. F. MELVIN.

TATOM, THEOPHILUS   JAN. 24, 1863. MAY TERM 1863.
        WIFE: NOT NAMED. SONS: DANIEL, LENSON, JOHN
HENRY. DAUGHTER: MARY JANE DOWNING. (OTHER CHILDREN
NOT NAMED) EXECUTOR: JOHN HENRY TATOM (SON). WITNESSES:
M. MONROE, H. R. FRANCIS. CLERK: D. BLUE.

TAYLOR, DANIEL   NOVEMBER 1, 1830.
        WIFE: CATHERINE. SON: DUNCAN. DAUGHTERS:
CATHERINE, WIFE OF JAMES CROMARTIE, MARIAN, WIFE OF
DUNCAN MCKEITHAN. OTHER LEGATEES: ARCH & MARY PATTERSON
AND THEIR CHILDREN, DUNCAN, CATHERINE, EMILY AND DANIEL
PATTERSON. EXECUTORS: JAS. CROMARTIE AND DUNCAN MCK-
EITHAN. WITNESSES: JAMES I. MCKAY, K. MCLEOD. N. MCLEOD.

TAYLOR, JOHN   21 MAY 1832.
        (OF HAMMONDS CREEK, BLADEN COUNTY) SON & EXECUTOR:
ANGUS TAYLOR. DAUGHTERS: FLORA TAYLOR, CATHERINE MC-
NEILL. EXECUTOR: JOHN IVER MCMILLAN. WITNESS: HARRIET
HAILLS.

TEDDER, GEORGE (PLANTER)   SEPTEMBER 7, 1795.
        WIFE: MARY. SONS: JESSE, THOMAS, (OTHER CHILDREN
NOT NAMED) BROTHER & EXECUTORS: WILLIAM AND SAMUEL
TEDDER. WITNESSES: ELIZABETH MEREDITH, MARGARET THOMAS,
EPH'M. MULFORD.

THAGGARD, ISAAC   JULY 6, 1844. MAY TERM 1846.
        WIFE: NANCY SON & EXECUTOR: WILLIAM C.
DAUGHTERS: ELIZA JANE, LUCINDA L., SARAH ANN, MELISSA,
HAZZLETINE J. WITNESSES: CHAS. HALL, STEPHEN HAIR.

THOMAS, GEORGE   APRIL 10, 1796.
        WIFE & EXECUTRIX: MARGARET. SONS: FRANCES, JOHN.
DAUGHTERS: ANN, MARY, MARGARET. EXECUTOR: FRANCIS
THOMAS. WITNESSES: HUGH MURPHY, JOHN SUTTON, JOHN
THOMAS.

THOMAS, JOHN   DECEMBER 25, 1811.
        WIFE: MARY. MOTHER: MARGARET SUTTON. NIECE:
SARAH ANN KELLY. NEPHEWS: JOHN SUTTON, JAMES SUTTON.
OTHER LEGATEES: EDWARD HENRY, GEORGE THOMAS. EXECUTORS:
GEORGE THOMAS, PATRICK KELLY. WITNESSES: J. P. REEVES,
HUGH MAULTSBY.

THOMAS, JOSEPH   OCTOBER 11, 1780.

WIFE & EXECUTRIX: MARTHA. SONS: JESSE, THOMAS, JOSEPH, WILLIAM, JOHN, SAMUEL. DAUGHTER: MARTHA. EXECUTORS: JAMES JACKSON, JOSEPH THOMAS, WILLIAM THOMAS. WITNESSES: BENJAMIN CLARK, DAVID HOLLOWAY, JAMES JACKSON.

THOMAS, MICHAEL   MARCH 2, 1807.
WIFE: JANE. SONS: JAMES, JONATHAN. EXECUTORS: JAMES PURDIE, SANDERS SIMMONS, JONATHAN THOMAS. WITNESSES: SAMUEL JESSUP, GEORGE SIMPSON.

THOMAS, SARAH   JANUARY 7, 1839. MAY TERM 1846.
SISTER AND EXECUTRIX: PERTHENY WESTBROOK. NIECES: SOPHRONIA WESTBROOK, LUCY ANN WESTBROOK. NEPHEW: WILLIAM WESTBROOK. WITNESSES: JOHN O. DANIEL. SOPHRONIA WEST-BROOK.

THOMPSON, BENJAMIN A. JUNE 7, 1873. APRIL 13, 1874.
WIFE: MARY JANE. DAUGHTER: HENRIETTA. EXECUTOR: ZACHARIA G. THOMPSON. WITNESSES: JONATHAN CASHWELL, J. H. SMITH. CLERK:: E. SINGLETARY.

THOMPSON, LEWIS   JANUARY 5, 1864. MAY TERM 1864.
SON & EXECUTOR: WILLIAM R. (LANDS ADJOINING JON'A SINGLETARY, STORM'S, H. F. HILBURN AND AARON HESTER). GRANDCHILDREN: WILLIAM J. THOMPSON, MARY ANN THOMPSON, ELIZABETH ANN MONROE. WITNESSES: COLIN MONROE, JOHN T. BUTLER. SURETY: ARCHIBALD DOVE. CLERK: D. BLUE.

TREADWELL, RACHEL ANN   APRIL 13, 1891. JULY 27, 1891.
SONS: CHARLES, HENRY. DAUGHTER: NETTIEFIELD. SISTERS: MRS. LOUISA LEE, MISS LOTTIE TREADWELL. BROTHER" WILLIAM JOHNSON. OTHER LEGATEES: WILLIAM H. G. BEATTY, DR. W. K. ANDERS, JOHN TREADWELL. EXECUTOR: JOHN A. MURPHY. WITNESSES: L. T. BEATTY, E. S. BANNERMAN. CLERK: GEO. F. MELVIN.

TROY, ROBERT E. (OF ROBESON COUNTY) JANUARY 9, 1859.
NOV. TERM 1862. WIFE AND EXECUTRIX: MARY. SON: ALEXANDER. BROTHER: ALEXANDER J. TROY. WITNESSES: N. A. MCLEAN, J. M. HARTMAN. CLERK: D. BLUE.

TURNER, SARAH   SEPTEMBER 23, 1819.
DAUGHTER: LYDIA CAMPBELL. GRANDDAUGHTER: MARGARET CAMPBELL. FRIENDS & EXECUTORS: WILLIAM DAVIS, GRIFFITH J. WHITE, WILLIAM HENDON. WITNESSES: JOHN DUNCAN,

WILLIAM LEWIS, WILLIAM J. COWAN.

VERNON, ANNE   SEPTEMBER 23, 1760
    SONS: THOMAS LUCAS, HENRY LUCAS, JOHN LUCAS.
DAUGHTER: LILLAH JOHNSTON. EXECUTORS: JOHN LUCAS (SON),
WILLIAM BARTRAM. WITNESSES: JAMES KERR, SUSANNA GULLEY,
ELIZABETH BARTRAM.

WADDELL,HUGH   NOVEMBER 10, 1772.
    WIFE & EXECUTRIX: MARY. SONS: HAYNES, HUGH AND
JOHN BURGWIN WADDELL. (PLANTATIONS: BELLEFONT, CRANSTON
AND WINDSOR) BROTHER-IN-LAW AND EXECUTOR: JOHN BURGWIN,
ESQ. SISTER: HANNAH, IN THE COUNTY OF DOWN IN THE NORTH
OF IRELAND, ONE HUNDRED GUINEAS. WITNESSES: B. BEATTY,
RACHEL CUNNINGHAM, JAMES BAILY.

WADDELL, MARY   APRIL 20, 1766.
    SONS: HAYNES, HUGH, JOHN BURGWIN WADDELL. BROTHER:
JOHN BURGWIN, ESQ. FRIENDS: MRS. MARGARET GIBSON, MRS.
ELIZABETH BAILEY, MRS. HENRY GRAHAM, MRS. JANE HOWE,
MRS. FAITHFUL GRAHAM, MISS ANN WADDELL, LIVING IN ROWAN
COUNTY. (PLANTATIONS, "CASTLE HAYNE" AND BELLEFONT".
EXECUTORS: JOHN BURGWIN, ESQ., MR. FAITHFUL GRAHAM,
FREDERICK JONES, ESQ., WILLIAM SALTER, ESQ. WITNESSES:
JEAN THOMPSON, WALTER GIBSON, JAMES SMITH.

WATSON, WILLIAM NUNCUPATIVE WILL)
    LEGATEE: JOHN LLOYD, SON OF DAVID LLOYD. WITNESS-
ES: JOHN SIMPSON, DAVID RUSS. CLERK: WILLIAM J. COWAN.

WEATHERSBEE, CADE MAY 23, 1793.
    DAUGHTERS: MARTHA HOLLINGSWORTH, MARY SIKES, LUCY
MCLEAN, ELIZABETH, OLIVE, JANE. SONS: ABSOLOM, ISOM,
OWEN, SHADRACK. EXECUTORS: MITCHELL THOMAS, (SHADRICK
WEATHERSBEE (SON). WITNESSES: DENNIS AVERIT, WILLIAM
GRICE.

WEST, WILLIAM (PLANTER)   19 FEBRUARY 1830.
    WIFE & EXECUTRIX: HANNAH. CHILDREN: ANNAH, HANNAH
JANE, JAMES. WITNESSES: ARCH'D. CULBRETH, NEILL CUL-
BRETH, WILLIAM WILKESON, AMOS CAIN.

WESTBROOK, JAMES   NOVEMBER 19, 1832.
    WIFE & EXECUTRIX: PERTHANEY WESTBROOKS. DAUGHTERS:
SEMPHANIE WESTBROOKS, LUCY ANN WESTBROOKS. SON: WILLIAM

WESTBROOKS. WITNESSES: JOHN B. BROWN, SOPHRONIA WEST-
BROOKS.

WHITE, ANN J.   DECEMBER 18, 1819. AT PLEASANT
        RETREAT. BROTHERS: WILLIAM H. BEATTY, HAYS G.
WHITE, HAYS W. BEATTY. OTHER LEGATEES: ANNA WHITE,
DAUGHTER OF HAYES G. WHITE, JAMES AND JOSE POTTS, ANNA JANE
CALVIN, REBECCA WHITE, ANN JOSE WHITE, MARGARET A. BEATTY,
DR. WHITE. EXECUTORS: WILLIAM H. BEATTY, HAYS G. WHITE.
WITNESS: RUTH LLOYD. CLERK: W. J. COWAN.

WHITE, HENRIETTA   AUGUST 13, 1785.
        DAUGHTER AND EXECUTRIX: LUCY BROWN. SON AND
EXECUTOR: WILLIAM JONES. NEPHEW: JOHN VERNON. WITNESS-
ES: WILLIAM STREATY, LUCY STREATY.

WHITE, JOHN   MARCH 1770.
        WIFE AND EXECUTRIX: MARY. (PANTHER BRANCH, A
PLANTATION ON JONES CREEK) DAUGHTERS: JANE KEMP, ANN
HARVEY, MARY AND MARTHA WHITE. SONS: JAMES, GRIFFITH,
JOHN, WILLIAM, DAVID, MATTHEW. (LANDS KNOWN AS LITTLE
BRUMTON) EXECUTOR: JAMES WHITE (SON). WITNESSES:
RICHARD SALTER, RICHARD HARRISON, WILLIAM ELLIS.

WHITE, JOHN   AUGUST 3, 1797.
        GRANDSON: JOHN WHITE. EXECUTORS: GENERAL THOMAS
BROWN, JAMES MOOREHEAD, ESQ., MR. JOSEPH KEMP, JR.
WITNESSES: J. S. PURDIE, AMOS RICHARDSON, STEPHEN BECK.

WHITE, JOSEPH   DECEMBER 13, 1784. (EXECUTED AT
        WILMINGTON) WIFE AND EXECUTRIX: HENRIETTA. SON-
IN-LAW: WILLIAM JONES. NIECE: SARAH MCREE, DAUGHTER OF
SAMUEL MCREE. SISTER: MARY WINSLOW. EXECUTORS: EDWARD
WINSLOW, ROBERT SCOTT. WITNESSES: ROBERT BOYLE, DUNCAN
O. KELLY.

WHITE, MATTHEW ROWN SEPTEMBER 20, 1793.
        WIFE: CATHERINE. SON: DAVID JONES WHITE.
EXECUTORS: JAMES BRADLEY, JAMES MOOREHEAD. WITNESSES:
J. ELLIS, WILLIAM WHITE.

WHITE, THOMAS (PLANTER) AUGUST 3, 1768 (HOLOGRAPH WILL)
        WIFE AND EXECUTRIX: ANN. SON: JOSEPH. DAUGHTERS:
SARAH, MARY. EXECUTOR: JOHN POYNTER. WITNESS: JOSEPH
CLARK. CLERK: A. HOWE.

WHITE, WILLIAM   APRIL 2, 1783.
     WIFE AND EXECUTRIX: MARY. (CHILDREN NOT NAMED)
EXECUTOR: DUNCAN KING. WITNESSES: JOHN POWELL, SAMUEL
ROURK, JEREMIAH BIGFORD.

WHITTED, ARCHA   FEBRUARY 5, 1883.
     SONS: TIMON, LINCOLN, RUFUS. DAUGHTERS: AMELIA
ANN, CHARLOTTE, EMELETT. EXECUTOR: LYMAS ROBESON, SR.
WITNESSES: A. MCDONALD, E. W. ESTERS. JUDGE OF PROBATE:
G. F. MELVIN

WHITTED, W. N.   3 MAY 1893. 19 MAY 1893.
     SONS AND EXECUTORS: THOMAS S. AND WILLIAM WHITTED.
WITNESSES: WILLIAM WHITTED, JAMES M. WHITTED, T. S.
WHITTED, A. B. WILLIAM, A. J. MCDONALD. CLERK: G. F.
MELVIN.

WIGGINS, JESSE B.   NOVEMBER 19, 1870.
     WIFE: LUCY. DAUGHTER: MARY ELIZA. OTHER LEGATEE:
DANIEL W. MEARS. TRUSTEE: JOHN W. ELLIS. EXECUTOR:
MALCOM MCLEOD. WITNESSES: HUGH C. MCCOLLUM, JOHN D.
WOODY. JUDGE OF PROBATE: D. BLUE.

WILKESON, WILLIAM   AUGUST 29, 1795.
     WIFE AND EXECUTRIX: CHARITY. SON: CHARLES.
EXECUTORS: WILLIAM BRYAN, ISAAC POWELL. WITNESSES:
BARNABAS POWELL, EDMOND HOLMES, WILLIAM WHITE.

WILLIAMS, GEORGE MEARES   1 MAY 1819 (AT WILMINGTON)
     BROTHER AND EXECUTOR: WILLIAM B. MEARES. SISTER:
CATHERINE, WIFE OF WILLIAM B. MEARES. NIECE: CATHERINE
MEARES, DAUGHTER OF WILLIAM B. MEARES. NEPHEWS: HENRY
AND THOMAS, SONS OF WILLIAM B. MEARES. WITNESSES:
GABRIEL HOLMES, A. M. HOOPER.

WILLIAMSON, LEWIS   MARCH 3, 1795.
     WIFE: MARY. SONS: RICHARD, LEWIS, JOSHUA,
LOLAN, SETH. DAUGHTERS: REBECCAH, NANCY, PEGGY, SUS-
ANNA. EXECUTORS: RICHARD WILLIAMSON, WYNNE NANCE.
WITNESSES: STEPHEN GODWIN.

WILLIS, (BETTY) ELIZABETH   SEPTEMBER 28, 1792.
     SONS: JACOB, DANIEL, JOHN. DAUGHTERS: ANN
WILLIS, SARAH ROWLAND, DINNA STEPHENS, ELIZABETH NEWBERRY,
AMELIA CLARK. EXECUTORS: JOHN & JACOB WILLIS (SONS).
WITNESSES: DANIEL WILLIS, JOHN ROWLAND.

WILLIS, DANIEL   MARCH 10, 1784
        WIFE: ELIZABETH. SONS: DANIEL, JOHN ROBERT,
JACOB. DAUGHTERS: SARAH, ELIZABETH, DIANNA, AMELIA ANN.
EXECUTORS: THOMAS ROBESON, ESQ., JOHN & DANIEL WILLIS
(SONS). WITNESSES: JOHN NEWBURY, ROBERT WILLIS, WILLIAM
GODFREY.

WILLIS, DANIEL   JANUARY 19, 1800
        DAUGHTERS: MARTHA, MARY. EXECUTORS: JOSEPH
THAMES BARNES, JOHN ROWLAND. WITNESSES: J. WILLIS, JOHN
NEWBURY, ELIZABETH NEWBURY.

WILLIS, JOHN   JANUARY 18, 1844
        SONS: DANIEL, WILLIAM. DAUGHTERS: ELIZABETH
LEWIS, MARTHA LEWIS, ALICE WILLIS, MARGARET CAIN, SARAH
CAIN. EXECUTOR: DANIEL WILLIS (SON) WITNESSES: DURRUM
LEWIS, ELEANOR LYON.

WILLIS, ROBERT   APRIL 4, 1787
        WIFE & EXECUTRIX: ANNE. (BROTHERS AND SISTER
NOT NAMED) WITNESS: ELIZABETH LUCAS

WILSON, ABSALOM   JANUARY 13, 1863. FEBRUARY TERM 1868.
        WIFE: MARY ANN. SON: JOHN. DAUGHTERS: GANAH
WILSON, AMELIA HILBURN, WIFE OF GYRON HILBURN, CATHERINE
SINGLETARY, ELIZABETH KINLAW, WIFE OF NELSON KINLAW, MARY
JANE THOMPSON, WIFE OF T. C. THOMPSON. EXECUTORS: JOHN
WILSON, NELSON KINLAW, GYRON HILBURN. WITNESSES: C.
MONROE, BARNABAS BROWN. CLERK: D. BLUE

WILSON, JOSIAH (PLANTER) OCTOBER 6, 1772
        WIFE: (NOT NAMED) SONS: GEORGE, AMBROSE, JOHN.
(LANDS GRANTED TO CAPT. GEORGE MARTIN) DAUGHTERS: SARAH,
DEBORAH, MARY, ANN, ELIZABETH. EXECUTORS: WILLIAM
SALTER, JOHN SALTER. WITNESSES: BENJAMIN ELWELL, HANNAH
LOCK, LINARD LOCK.

WINGATE, ANN   JUNE 27, 1763.
        SON & EXECUTOR: JOHN WINGATE. DAUGHTER: MARY
SIMMONS. WITNESSES: THOMAS SESSIONS, MARGARET CHICKENE,
HANNAH WINGATE. (A TRUE COPY FROM SOUTH CAROLINA'SECRE-
TARY'S OFFICE)

WINGATE, JOHN   MAY 10, 1842. FEB. TERM 1847
        DAUGHTERS: DORCAS SHIPMAN, CAROLINE FRANCIS,WIFE

OF JOSEPH HOLLINGSWORTH. GRANDCHILDREN: HAYES F. SHIPMAN, MARIA J. SHIPMAN, CAROLINE F. HOLLINGSWORTH, LUCY A. MC-DANIEL, EMILY HELEN SHIPMAN, JOHN D. SHIPMAN, FLORILLA DORCAS SHIPMAN (INFANT), ANDREW JACKSON SHIPMAN, JAMES SHIPMAN, CHILDREN OF MY DAUGHTER DORCAS SHIPMAN. (LUCY A. MCDANIEL, WIFE OF THOMAS MCDANIEL) EXECUTOR: HAYES F. SHIPMAN (GRANDSON). WITNESSES: JAMES BROWN, JR., RIVER JORDAN. (HAYES F. SHIPMAN, THE EXECUTOR, DIED BEFORE PRO-BATE OF WILL AND HAYNES LENNON APPOINTED ADM. C.T.A. BY GIVING BOND WITH RICHARD WOOTEN AND D. J. MCCALL AS SURETIES)

WOOTEN, JOHN A. (HOLOGRAPH WILL) JUNE 14, 1853. AUGUST TERM 1859. WIFE AND EXECUTRIX: MARY. (FIVE CHILDREN, NOT NAMED) STORE HOUSE AND WAREHOUSE AND LOT AT WHITE HALL. EXECUTOR: JAMES CROMARTIE (FRIEND AND BROTHER). WITNESSES: SHADRACK WOOTEN, WILLIAM W. ANDERS. CLERK: A. K. CROMARTIE.

WOOTEN, SHADRACH   AUGUST 17, 1845. NOV. TERM 1845. WIFE AND EXECUTRIX: ELIZABETH. SONS: SHADRACH, JOHN A., ROBERT. DAUGHTERS: MARY CROMARTIE, ANN M. ASHLEY, ELIZABETH C. WOOTEN, CHARLOTTE M. WOOTEN, HENRIETTA T. WOOTEN. BROTHER AND EXECUTOR: RICHARD WOOTEN. WITNESSES: DUNC. J. MCCALL, JOHN A. WOOTEN, DUGALD BLUE. CLERK: H. H. ROBINSON.

WRIGHT, ISAAC (PLANTER)   22 DECEMBER 1806. WIFE: ANN. (CHILDREN NOT NAMED) WITNESSES: BENJ. CLARK, MERINDA WRIGHT, JOSIAH JAY.

WRIGHT, ISAAC   NOVEMBER 15, 1862. CODICILS: SEPT. 9, 1864. SONS: MOOREHEAD, CLEMENT G. (LISBURNE PLANTATION). DAUGHTERS: CATHERINE D. MURCHISON, WIFE OF DUNCAN MURCHISON, ANN ELIZA MCDIARMID, WIFE OF DAVID (DANIEL) MCDIARMID OF CUMBERLAND COUNTY, LUCY G. MONROE, WIFE OF HUGH A. MONROE (MILTON PLANTATION, WHITE PLANTATION, WALKER'S BLUFF PLANTATION). ELIZABETH R. WRIGHT, WIFE OF MOOREHEAD WRIGHT, THEIR CHILDREN, WILLIAM FULTON, ELIZABETH, IMOGENE, ISAAC, MATILDA AMELIA OF RED RIVER, ARK. ANNETTE, WIFE OF CLEMENT G. WRIGHT. CHILDREN OF CATHERINE D. & DUNCAN MURCHISON, ELIZA FRANCIS (NOW CALLED "IDA"), LUCY GILLESPIE, ISAAC ALEXANDER MURCHISON, JANE FAIRLEY. CHILD-REN OF LUCY G. AND HUGH A. MONROE, ADOLPHUS, ISAAC WRIGHT, WILLIAM CLEMENT, ELIZA JANE MONROE. EXECUTOR: CLEMENT G . WRIGHT (SON). WITNESSES: NEILL GRAHAM, A. K. CROMARTIE,

H. W. GUION, WM. T. JESSUP, JAMES W. CROMARTIE.

WRIGHT, MARCHUS   MAY 31, 1892. JUNE 20, 1892.
(SEVEN CHILDREN NOT NAMED) EXECUTORS: J. W. McKAY, J. F. FREEMAN. WITNESSES: J. W. McKAY, J. F. FREEMAN, J. A. WRIGHT, ISHAM WRIGHT, NEILL McKAY, O. E. McKAY. CLERK: GEO. F. MELVIN.

YEDDER, GEORGE, SR.   JANUARY 1796.
WIFE: SARAH. DAUGHTERS: SARAH, ELIZABETH. SONS: GEORGE, WILLIAM, SAMUEL. EXECUTOR: GEORGE YEDDER (SON). WITNESSES: JOHN THOMAS, MARGARET THOMAS.

YOUNG, MATTHEW   MARCH 11, 1856. MAY TERM 1856.
BROTHER: JOHN YOUNG (LANDS BETWEEN PHILLIPS CREEK AND HARRISONS CREEK). NEPHEW: MATTHEW YOUNG, SON OF JOHN YOUNG. NIECE: JANE YOUNG, DAUGHTER OF MY BROTHER WILLIAM YOUNG. EXECUTOR: JOHN SIKES. WITNESSES: CHAS. T. DAVIS, DAVID JONES. CLERK: F. F. CUMMING.

YOUNG, NATHAN   JANUARY 19, 1841
MOTHER: SARAH YOUNG. BROTHER & EXECUTOR: WILLIAM YOUNG. WITNESSES: SAMUEL ROBESON, JAMES ROBESON.

YOUNG, WILLIAM   AUGUST 16, 1856. NOV. TERM 1856.
WIFE & EXECUTRIX: MELVINY. SON: ROBANE O. OTHER LEGATEES: JANE YOUNG, JAMES B. YOUNG, ZEBULA YOUNG, JOHN YOUNG. WITNESSES: JOHN SIKES, EDMUND SIKES. CLERK: F. F. CUMMING.

PREFACE TO INDEX

THE SPELLING OF BOTH CHRISTIAN AND SUR-
NAMES WILL VARY IN THE PRECEDING PAGES. THE
SPELLINGS ARE AS FOUND IN THE WILL BOOKS.

IT IS ALMOST IMPOSSIBLE NOT TO MAKE SOME
MISTAKES IN A WORK OF THIS KIND. CORRECTIONS
TO THIS INDEX ARE INVITED.

CORRECTIONS AND ADDITIONS

ADDISON, MARY - ON PAGE 7 INSTEAD OF PAGE 9

ATKINSON, WILIE (WYLIE) INSTEAD OF WILLIE - P. 11 & P. 60

BARTRAM, COL. WILLIAM INSTEAD OF WOL. - P. 73

CAIN. MR. SAMUEL INSTEAD OF MRS. - P. 71

GIBBS, SARAH, ALSO NAMED IN WILL OF AMELIA DUPRER - P. 32

HENDRY INSTEAD OF HENRY (JAMES, ELIZABETH) - P. 64

HEWRY, INSTEAD OF HENRY (EDWARD) - P. 88

JESSIP INSTEAD OF JESSUP (JOHN) - P. 41

McEWEN, MATTHA INSTEAD OF MARTHA - P. 77

McFADGEN, ANGUS (WILL OF) - P..61

ROBESON, JAS. INSTEAD OF JAS. A.(WILL OF JAMES PLUMMER) P. 68

RICHARDSON, SAM'L. N. INSTEAD OF SAM'L.(WILL OF ANN McREE) P.

SCRIVIN INSTEAD OF SERIVIN (THOMAS J.) P. 9

SIKES, JOHN, RICHARD, INSTEAD OF JOHN RICHARD - P. 79

SINGLETARY, JOHN INSTEAD OF JOH - P. 81

WILLIS, AMELIA, ANN, INSTEAD OF AMELIA ANN - P. 93

WILLIS, JOHN, ROBERT, INSTEAD OF JOHN ROBERT - P. 93

WRIGHT, ISAAC, OTHER CODICILS DATED NOV. 13, 1864
                                     MAR. 12, 1865 AND
                                     PROBATED MAY TERM 1866-P.
YOUNG, ELANDER, INSTEAD OF ALANDER - P. 21

IN CHECKING THE INDEX IF YOU DO NOT FIND THE NAME LISTED ON
THE GIVEN PAGE, PLEASE CHECK THE FOLLOWING PAGE, AS SOME
NAMES LISTED ARE INDEXED BY THE PAGE NUMBER ON WHICH THE
WILL ABSTRACT COMMENCED.

INDEX

SALLY 10
SAMUEL 30
SAMUEL B.(WILL OF) 10
SARAH 20
SOPHIA (WILL OF) 10
WILLIAM 10
WILLIAM S.(WILL OF) 11
WILLIAM SAMUEL 10
WILL S. 49
W. S. 10

ANDREWS:
ANN C. 11
ELIZABETH 11
ELIZA KELLY 11
HANNAH ANN 11
HANNAH J. 11
JAMES M. (WILL OF) 11
JAMES WASHINGTON 11
JOHN (WILL OF) 11
MARY 11
PATRICK S. 11
WILLIAM W. 11

ARINTON:
MARY 6

ARMSTRONG:
EMILY 16-A
FRANK 7
MARGARET 7

ASHE:
COL. 17

ASHFORD:
ANN 11
STREET (WILL OF) 11

ASHLEY:
ANN M. 94
LUCY J. 45

ATKINSON:
SUSANNA 11
WILEY 60
WILIE ALFORD 11
WILIE 60
WILLIE (WILL OF) 11

AUTERY:
MARY MATILDA 84

AUTRY:
ALEXANDER 84

AVERETT
JOHN 43

AVERIT:
DENNIS 90

AVERITT:
DEMPSEY (SR. WILL OF) 12
DORCAS 12
JOHN 12
ROBERT A. 12
WILLIAM 12

AVERY:
ALEXANDER 69
CHLORE 69
MARY (WILL OF) 12

AYRES:
DARIUS B. 20

BACON:
EDWIN WANE (WILL OF)12
WILLIAM T. 12

BAILEY:
DAVID 85
ELIZABETH 48, 90
EZEKIEL (JR.) 47
HESTER 12
JAMES 6,35,48,60
JANNETTE 85
THOMAS (WILL OF) 12

BAILY:
JAMES 90

BAIN:
DONALD 36,49,77

BAKER:
AMOS 12
ANN 11

MARY E. 12
PENELOPE 36
SAMUEL 5
W. B. 52

BALDWIN:
A. J. 22
AMY 18
ANNA 12
BETSEY 12
CHARLES 12
DAVID 12
ELIZABETH 12
ESTHER 12
JOHN 12,(SR.WILL OF) 12,(SR)
(JR.) 76   14
JOSEPH 40
LYDIA 38
MARY 38
NANCY 12
PENELOPE 12
SARAH 12
WILLIAM 12
WILLIAM (BAULDWIN)(WILL OF)
12
W. T. 39

BALLENTINE:
CATHERINE 12
ELIZABETH 28
GEORGE W. (WILL OF) 12,62
ISABELLA 28
SARAH 28

BANKS:
HENRIETTA 17

BANNERMAN:
CATHERINE JANE 11
CHARLES 48
ELIZABETH 28,48
E. S. 89
GEORGE W. 14,48,54
G. W . 11,42,69,87
MARGARET 48- N.42 - P. W. 42

BARFIELD:
ANN 13

ELISHA 13
RICHARD (WILL OF) 13
RODERICK 13
SHADRACK 13
WILLIS 13

BARKSDALE:
GEORGE T. 40,75

BARNES:
ABSALOM 71
ELANZER 22
J. F. 87
JOSEPH THAMES 93
J. T. 87

BARNHILL:
A. J. (WILL OF) 13
CATHERINE ANN (WILL OF) 13
D. M. 16
JOHN R. 13
MARGARET 13
N. H. 13
WILLIAM H. 16

BARTRAM:
ELIZABETH (WILL OF) 1,5,90
WILLIAM 1,2,3,6
COL. 73,90

BAULDWIN:
CHARLES 12
WILLIAM 12

BAYLY:
THOMAS 3

BEARD:
CATHERINE 13
CATHERINE L.(WILL OF) 13
DANIEL 5,13,23,86
DANIEL D. 34
ELIZABETH (WILL OF) 13
JAMES 13,59
JAMES S. 13
JOHN (WILL OF) 13,56
KATHERINE 13
MARGARET 13

NEIL 5
NEILL (WILL OF) 13,68
W. F. 34

BEASLEY:
ABRAHAM 23
HENRY 14
JOHN 14
MARY 14
RICHARD 14
ROBERT (WILL OF) 14

BEATTY:
ANNABELLA 14
ANNA W. 14
B. 90
DOUGLAS 14
ELLA 14
G. H. 14
HAYS 14
HAYS W. 14,91
HAYS WHITE 14
HENRY 14
HENRY B. 14
HENRY BENBURY 14
H. W. 30
JANE 14
JANE S. H. 14
JOHN (WILL OF) 14,53
JOHN D. (WILL OF) 14,48
L. T. 89
LUCIEN 14
LUCIEN T. (WILL OF) 14
MARGARET 14
MARGARET A. 91
MARGARET HUNTER 14
MARIA 14
MARY ANNA 14
N. McL. 14
N. M. 14
POLLY 14
W. H. 16-A
W. H. G. 14
WILLIAM 14
WILLIAM G. 14
WILLIAM H. 14,61,91
WILLIAM HAYES 10
WILLIAM HENRY (WILL OF) 14

WILLIAM H. G. 89
WILLIAM STEWART 85

BECK:
STEPHEN 91

BEDSOLE:
DUNCAN 68,71
THOMAS 71
TRAVIS 71
WILLIAM 71

BELLUM:(BLOOMER)
MARY 35

BENBOW:
ANN 15
BENJAMIN 15
CHARLES 1,2, (WILL OF) 15
EVANS 1
GERSHON (WILL OF) 1,4
MARY 2,15
POWEL 1
POWELL 1
RICHARD 1
SARAH 15
SOPHIA 15
SUSANNAH 1
THOMAS 15

BENSON:
AARON 15
ANN 79
ARCHIBALD 15
CAROLINE 15
DAVID (WILL OF) 15
HELANDER ANN 15
JOHN M. 24,27,74
MARTHA 15
MARY JANE 15
NANCY 15
SARAH A. 65
THOMAS 81
WILLIAM WASHINGTON 15

BERNARD:
EDWARD J. 15, 16-A

BERRY:
  DANIEL 50
  ELIZABETH 56

BEST:
  BRYANT 68
  JOHN 68

BIDWELL:
  HARRIET V. 83

BIGFORD:
  JEREMIAH 19, 46,69,92
  WILLIAM 23

BIGGS:
  JOHN D. 39
  MARY F. 39

BINMAN:
  MARY 14

BIRD:
  WILLIAM 71

BIRK:
  N. J. 53

BIZZELL:
  A. F. (WILL OF) 15
  E. D. 50
  SALLY 15
  W. A.(DR.) 69

BLACKMAN:
  JOAN 75
  MARY 75

BLACKWELL:
  ELIZABETH (WILL OF) 15,42
  JINEY 15
  J. W. 15
  OWEN 15
  P. K. 15
  SARAH 71
  STEPHEN 15
  W. J. 15

BLAKE:
  F. 64
  SOPHIA 72

BLAND:
  DANIEL P. 25
  MARY E. 25

BLANING:
  ELIZABETH 1
  HUGH (WILL OF) 1

BLOCKER:
  CHARLES H. 52
  EDWARD DAVIS 28
  JEAN 28
  JOHN 62

BLOODWORTH:
  JAMES 30
  TIMOTHY 30

BLOOMER:(BELLUM)
  MARY 35

BLOUNT:
  JOHN 71

BLUE:
  A. L. 24
  CATHERINE (WILL OF) 15
  D. 9,12,13,15,17,21,22,26,
  30,31,33,36,42,44,45,51,54,
  55,60,61,62,68,69,73,74,77,
  78,79,80,84,88,89,92,93
  DANIEL 15
  DUGALD 41,(SR.)63,77,94
  DUGALD B. 15
  JOHN 15,(JR.)63,(SR.)63
  JOHN F. 15
  LUTHER A. 27
  MARGARET 47
  MARY J. 63

BOON:
  ISAIAH 15
  JEREMIAH 15
  JOSHUA 15

MARGARET 15
NANCY 40
NOAH 15
SAMUEL (WILL OF) 15

'OOZMAN:
  SAMUEL 64

'ORDEAUX:
  A. J. 13
  SARAH J. 43
  SYLVESTER 34

'ORDESS: (BRODESS)
  PETER (WILL OF) 15

'OSWELL:
  ANN M. 13
  CASS 16
  ELIZABETH 76
  ELLEN 13
  LEWIS C. 13
  LEWIS F. 13
  L. F. (WILL OF) 16
  NANCY 16
  PRISCILLA 13
  PRICILER 16
  WILLIAM LEWIS 16

'OWEN:
  GOODEN E. 16,46

'OWIN:
  GOODEN (WILL OF) 16
  JUDITH 16

'OWIE:
  ISABELA 65

'OX:
  JAMES 9

'OYLE:
  ROBERT 91

'RADLEY:
  ANN (WILL OF) 16
  ANNA 16

J. 49
JAMES (WILL OF) 16, (SR.WILL,
OF) 16,18, (SR.)18,31,82,91
MARGARET (WILL OF) 16
NANCY 16
PATSEY 16

BRADLY:
  JAMES 26

BRADY:
  OWEN 29

BRANCH:
  THOMAS 58

BRANTLEY:
  HELEN S. 49
  JESSE 40
  LUCY B. 46

BRIDE:
  A. H. 56

BRIDGERS:
  SARAH ANN 72

BRIGHT:
  BENJAMIN 16-A
  CHRISTIAN 16-A
  ELRICHAK 16-A
  JAMES 16-A
  JOHN 16-A
  MARY 16-A
  RICHARD 16-A
  ROBERT (WILL OF) 16-A
  ROSANNAH 30
  ROSE 85
  ROXANNA 16-A
  ROXANNE 16-A
  SIMON (WILL OF) 16-A
  WILLIAM HENRY 16-A

BRISSON:
  HELEN SOPHIA 9

BRITT:
  ELIZABETH 39

MARGARET 39
MARY 39,76

BROBSTON:
  ANN 27
  WILLIAM (REV.) 64

BRODESS:
  WILLIAM 15

BROWDER:
  THOMAS 76

BROWN:
  ALLEN 56
  ALLIE 72
  ANN 10, (MRS.) 10
  ANNA 16-A
  ASA 17
  BARNABAS 93
  BETTIE (WILL OF) 16-A
  BILL 16-A
  CAROLINE 16-A
  EDWARD A. 16-A
  ELIZA 16-A
  ELIZABETH 16-A,70
  FORMEY 16-A
  GEORGE 3,5,(WILL OF)16-A,
  30, (JR.) 30
  GEORGE L. 42
  GEORGE W. 10
  GODINA W. 17
  HANNAH M. 16-A
  HUGH 36
  JAMES 30,(JR.)78,(JR.)93
  JAMES IVER 16-A
  J. B. 54
  JOHN (WILL OF) 16-A,30,
  (CAPT.) 64,67
  JOHN B. 10,(WILL OF)16-A,
  17,35,63,90
  JOHN BRIGHT 16-A,17,30
  LUCINDA 47
  LUCY 10,16-A,17,30,42,43,91
  LUCY ANN (WILL OF) 17
  LUCY B. 16-A
  MAJOR 83
  MARGARET WHITE 17,30

MARY 16-A,30
MARY E. (WILL OF) 17
MARY J. 56
MARY JANE 55
MARY LYMAN 17
MATTNA 17
MORTIMER 17
PEGGY WHITE 16-A
PENNY 16-A
REBECCA 16-A
RICHARD 16-A,30
SAMUEL 16-A
SARAH 1
THOMAS 1,15,16-A,(WILL OF)
17,30,(SR.)30,35,54,(GEN.)
56,(MAJ.)61,67,70,(GEN.) 91
THOMAS O. 16-A,17,63,79
W. H. 17,54
WILLIAM 30
WILLIAM H. 16-A
W. M. 51
Y. J. 71

BROWNING:
  MARGARET 58

BRUCE:
  MARGERY 21

BRYAN:
  AMY BALDWIN 18
  ANN 18
  ANN JANE 48
  CAROLINE (WILL OF) 17
  EDW. 6
  EDWARD 18
  ELIZABETH O. 18
  GEORGE W. (WILL OF) 18
  HENRY 18
  J. 75
  JAMES 18,53,68
  JAMES H. 17
  JANE 9,14,18
  JOHN 13,(WILL OF) 18
  JONATHAN 12
  JOSEPH M. 18
  KORENHOFER 18
  LEVI 82

LLOYD 18
MARGARET 9,18
MARTHA J. 39
MARY ANN 18
NATHAN 9,(WILL OF)18,23,56
NEEDHAM (WILL OF)18
PHILEMON 18
PHILMORE 18
R. H. 18
ROBERT L. 41
SARAH 75,76
SARAH SIMSON 18
STEPHEN 18
THOMAS (WILL OF) 18
W. 38
WILLIAM 18,23,24,40,66,92
WILLIAM H. 18,39

BRYANT:
  CREESE 14
  DAVID 18
  ELIZA 18
  ELIZABETH ANN 18
  J. J. 18
  LEVI 18
  LUCY 18
  REBECCA JANE 18
  ROBERT H. 18
  WILLIAM (WILL OF) 18
  ZELPHIA 18
  ZYLPHIA 85

BUIE:
  ALBERT 19
  ARCHIBALD 77
  CATHERIN 77
  CATHERINE 23
  CELIA 19
  DANIEL 19
  DAN'L. N. 21
  D. M. 18
  ELIZABETH S. 46
  FLORA 19,21
  FRANCES 19
  MONROE 19
  NEIL (WILL OF) 19

BULLARD:
  BENILLA 9
  CATHERAN 52
  CATHERINE 53

BURDOX:
  SARAH 21

BURGOIN:
  JOHN 28,35

BURGWIN:
  C. 2
  HANNAH 90
  J. 3,6,7,8
  JOHN 5,90

BURNEY:
  ANDREW F. 19
  ARTHUR 19
  CHARLES H. 77
  CHARLES I. 19
  DANIEL J. 19
  DAVID T. 19
  D. T. 24
  ELENORE 78
  ELIZABETH 19,78
  ELIZABETH HART 19
  FRANCIS F. 19
  FRANKLIN 12
  JAMES 12,19
  JANE ESTHER 19
  JOHN A. 12
  JOHN N. (WILL OF) 19
  JOHN R. 19
  JOSEPH S. 12
  LUCY 19
  MASTON 12
  M. R. J. 19
  SALLIE 18
  SAMUEL 19
  SARAH 19
  SIMON 19
  WILLIAM (WILL OF) 19
  WILLIAM C. 58

BURRUS:
  ELIAS 84

BUSH:
 ISAAC 7
 MARY 19
 NEILL G. 19
 CHARLES L. 19
 OLIVER 19
 OSBORNE B. 19
 THOMAS S. 19
 WILLIAM J. C. (WILL OF) 19

BUTLER:
 CHARLES T. 19
 DAVID 4
 ELIZABETH G. 19
 FANNY 66
 GEORGE E. 19
 ISABEL 19
 JAMES A. 19
 JOHN (WILL OF) 19,66
 JOHN T. 19,89
 JOSEPH 37
 MARTHA ANN 19
 MARY 4
 ROBERT Q. 19
 SALLIE F. 19
 THOMAS V. 19
 T. V. 50

BYRN:
 ALEX J. 87

BYRNE:
 A. J. 19,20,68,72
 ALEXANDER (WILL OF) 19,20
 ALEX J. 20,54
 JAMES 20
 JAMES A. 20,54,72
 JANE D. 54
 JOHN M. (WILL OF) 19,20
 LAWRENCE 6,54,70
 MARY (WILL OF) 20,59
 MARY J. 20
 MATTHEW 7,19,(WILL OF) 20
 MOLSEY M. 20
 PETER 59
 RICHARD 20
 RICHARD L. 20
 THOMAS 20,59

THOMAS H. 10,20

BYRON:
 PETER 54

CADDINGTON:
 MARY 85
 NANCY 85

CADE:
 ELIZABETH 84
 ELIZABETH HOLESON 9
 JAMES 9
 STEPHEN 9
 WASHINGTON 9

CAIN:
 AMOS 21,90
 AMOS S. 20
 ANN 73
 ANN JANE 20
 CELIA 86
 C. M. 43
 EDWARD J. (SR.WILL OF) 20
 ELIZABETH 20,21
 ELLEN E. 20
 FLORA H. B. 20
 GEORGE 60,69
 HARRIETT M. 20
 I. J. 87
 ISAAC J. 20,28
 J. 79,82
 JAMES 20,(SR.WILL OF) 20,
 21,66
 JAMES H. (WILL OF) 20
 JAMES K. P. 20
 JOHN 20,21,82,83
 JOHN R. 20
 JONATHAN 20
 JOSEPH (WILL OF) 20,21,38,
 55,56,66,73,82,83
 LUCY 21
 MAG 20
 MALSEY 21
 MARGARET 93
 MARY 20
 MARY E. 20
 NANCY 21

CARTER:
ALMIRA 78
HAUSE J. 22
PATIENCE 47
SARAH HAUSE (WILL OF) 22

CARTHEY:
DAVID 30
JOHN HASLER 30
SARAH 30

CARTLIDGE:
E. 6

CARVER:
ANN 2
ARCADIA 2
ELIZABETH 2
JAMES (WILL OF) 2,(WILL OF)
22
JOB 2,22
JOHN 76
MARY 2
SAMUEL (WILL OF) 2
SARAH 2
SOPHIA 20

CARY:
WILLIAM 3

CASHWELL:
CHARLOTTE M. 43
JAMES 22,32,39
JOHN 22, (SR. WILL OF) 22
JOHN W. 39
JONATHAN 89
MARGARET 22
NEVEL (JR.) 22,32
THOMAS 22
THOMAS LEE 22

CATES:
PETER 6

CAUDELL:
ABSALOM 49

CAWTHOM:
A. T. 53
J. D. 53
W. M. D. 53

CHAMPION:
WILLIAM 49

CHANCY:
CHARLES 22
DEMPSEY 69
ELIZABETH 22
FANEY 22
JANE 22
JOHN 69
NEILL (WILL OF) 22
PENELOPY 22
W. H. 22

CHAVIS:
ABIGÀL 54

CHESHIRE:
BRYAN 23
CATHERINE 23
NICHOLAS 23
PURDIENCE 23
RICHARD (WILL OF) 23,37
ROBERT 66
WILLIAM 37,66

CHICKENE:
MARGARET 93

CHICKENS:
JOHN 40
REBECAH 40

CHILD:
JAMES (WILL OF) 23,34

CHIN:
EDWARD 35

CHRISTIAN:
A. C. 17
THOMAS 17

CLARDY:
James 23

CLARK:
Amelia 92
Angus 23
Ann 61
Arch'd. B. 15
Benjamin (will of) 23,24,
88,94
Catherine Amelia 24
Catherin Ann 24
Christian 23
Daniel (will of) 23
Daniel James 61
David (will of) 23,24,54
D. C. 19
D. J. 12,60,65,68
Dugald (will of) 23,47
Duncan 23,(will of) 24
Duncan N. 23
Elizabeth 23
Emeline 23
Eric C. 24
Euphamy 23
Flora 23,58
Isabel 23
James 24
James (Sr. will of) 2
James H. 24
Janie Washington 24
Jerome B. 24
J. Marvin 24
John 24,40
John H 24
John K. 61,65
John Washington (will of)24
Joseph 1,3,8,91
Luke 23
Margaret 15
Mary 23,24
Mary M. 44
Moley 24
Nancy 23
Neill 23
Penelope 24
Stephen B. 44
Thomas 23,47

William 23
Willie A. 24

CLARKE:
D. J. 74

CLAYTON:
Benone 15
Elizabeth 15
John 2,8
Richard 50

COCHRAN:
Robert 17

COHOON:
Darby 24
Debora 24
Elizabeth 24
Jean 24
John (will of) 24
Micajah 24
Rowland 24
William 24

COLE:
Eliza 42

COLEMAN:
Amos 24
Charity 24
Dempsey 24
Henry 24
John 24
Luraine 24
Lucretia 24
Moses (will of) 24
Phillip 24
Polly 24
Theophilus 24

COLINS:
Eleanor (Ellen) Jane 54

COLLUM:
Archibald 24
Dennis (will of) 24
Elizabeth 24

FRANCIS 24
MARGARET 24
MARY JANE 24
RICHARD (WILL OF) 24
SION (WILL OF) 24
SION JAMES 24

COLVILL:
ALEXANDER (REV.) 24
HENRY 24
MATURIN 1,3,18,(WILL OF)24,
29,35,38,81

COLVIN:
CHARLES (WILL OF) 25

CONKEY:
ROBERT 51

COOK:
DANIEL 66
ELIZABETH 66

COOPER:
AGNES 25
BENJAMIN (WILL OF) 25,49
ELIZABETH 25
JOSEPH (WILL OF) 25
MARY 25
TOBITHA 25
WILLIAM 25

CORBETT:
G. W. 25
JAMES R. (WILL OF) 25
THOMAS J. 87

COUNCIL:
A. McA. 72
ALEX 26
ALEX McA. 22
ARTHUR (WILL OF) 25
ARTHUR L. 25
CAROLINE 26
CATHARINE ANN 25
CATHERINE ANN 11
CATY 25
CECIL K. 25

CHARLES R. 11
C. R. 10
ELIZABETH 26
JAMES 25,42,52,55,70,73,82
JOHN G. 25
JOHN P. 25
KINCHIN B. 25
KINCHIN K. 11,(WILL OF) 25,
43
K. K. 23,61
LILLIAN 26
LOU 25
LOUISA 26
MARGARET JANE 25
MARY (WILL OF) 25,42
MARY JANE 25
ROBERT 23
SABRY 25
SALLY BRINKLEY 25
SHEPHERD 26
TYMAN (WILL OF) 26,(JR.)26
WILLIS 54,73

COVINGTON:
ANN 59

COWAN:
AMELIA 26
ANN ELIZABETH 16
ELIZABETH 76
JOHN (WILL OF) 26,75,76,82
JOHN BRADLEY 16,26
MARGARET 16
WILLIAM J. 16,(WILL OF)26,
48,62,89,90
WILLIAM JAMES 16,26,76
WILLIAM JAMES SALTER 76
W. J. 34,91

CRAWFORD:
ARCH'D. 54
MARGARET (WILL OF) 26
MARY 26

CRECH:
RICHARD 43

CREE:
WILLIAM 3

CROMARTIE:
  A. (WILL OF) 26
  A. A. 67
  A. K. 19,22,27,50,56,58,94
  ALEXANDER 26,27
  ANN 27
  CALVIN (WILL OF) 26,27
  CATHERINE 27,88
  CHARLEY D. 27
  D. 21,37
  DANIEL W. 27
  DANIEL WASHINGTON 26
  DELLA 62
  DELLA MAY 27
  DUNCAN 26,37,62
  D. W. 38
  ELEANOR J. 27
  ELIZA 62
  ELIZABETH 26,27,62
  ELLEN 27
  EMMELINE 62
  FRANKLIN TAYLOR 26,27
  GEORGE 26,(WILL OF)27,33,37
  GEO. S. 27
  HANNAH 27
  HENRY A. 27
  HOWARD 27
  IDA 62
  ISABELLA 62
  JAMES 26,(WILL OF)27,86,88,
  94
  JAMES W. 38,75,94
  JAMES WILLIAM 26,27
  JAMES WILLIAMS 26
  JEAN 27
  JOHN 26,(WILL OF) 27,38
  JOHN Q. 26
  JOHN QUINCY 26,27
  J. W. 29
  LLOYD McKAY 62
  LUTHER 14,26,27
  MAGGIE F. 27
  MARGARET 27
  MARIAN 62
  MARIAM N. 26
  MARY F. 27,94
  MARY ANN 62
  PATRICK L. 14

  PATRICK LAFAYETTE 26,(WILL
  OF) 27
  PETER 27
  P. SIDNEY 27
  R. B. 60
  RHENNY (RUHAMAK) (WILL OF)
  27
  R. S. 27
  SARAH A. 27
  STELLA 27
  THANKFUL 27
  WILLIAM 26, (WILL OF) 27,85
  WILLIAM J. 26,61
  W. J. 27

CROOM:
  J. F. 25

CROSS:
  JOHN 38

CROWELL:
  H. P. 25

CROWSON:
  MARY 75

CULBRAITH:
  ARCHIBALD (WILL OF) 27
  HARRIET 27
  JANNETTA 27
  JOB 27
  MARY 27

CULBRETH:
  ARCH'D. 90
  CATHERINE 28
  JOHN J.(WILL OF) 28
  McK. 28,84
  M. K. 32
  NEILL 90
  RACHEL 32

CUMMING:
  ANN O. 28
  ANN OLIVIA 28
  F. F. 11,18,21,23,(WILL OF)
  28,36,45,48,65,82,95

FRANCIS E. (WILL OF) 28
J. J. 29,33,47
WILLIAM ANDRES 11

CUMMINGS:
ANN J. 11

CUNNINGHAM:
JAMES 78
RACHEL 82,90
WILLIAM SINGLETARY 82

CURRIE:
ANGUS 23
DANIEL (WILL OF) 28
DAVID 44
D. M. 28
DUNCAN 44
EMILY JANE 11
F. ANN 28
JOHN 44
JOHN D. 51
NEILL 55
NOVELA D. 28

CURRY:
ANGUS 21
MARY 21
SAMUEL 14

DAFFERN
JEREMIAH 22

DANIEL:
ANNA 28
ARTHUR 3
JOHN 28
JOHN C. 46
JOHN O. 49,89
OVERTON (WILL OF) 28,46

DARRAH:
ARCHIBALD 62
JOHN 62

DARRACK:
ARCH'D. 85

DARROCH:
JOHN 21

DAVIS:
ABRAHAM 49
A. G. 84
ANN 2,29
ANNA MARIA 29
ANNIE JANE 29
CHARLES T. 12,25,29,95
CHARLES THOMAS 44
DAVID (WILL OF) 2
EDMOND (WILL OF) 28
EDWARD 16-A,(WILL OF) 28
EDWARD GREENWOOD 28
E. L. 45
ELIAS 28
ELIZA 29
ELIZA L. 45
ELIZABETH 16-A,28,29
FRANCIS 64
GABRIEL 28
G. W. 29
H. 29
HENRY (WILL OF) 28
HESAKIAH 29
HEXAH 29
ISAAC A. 41,71
ISABELLA (WILL OF) 28,29
JAMES (WILL OF) 29
JAMES MCKAY 29
JOHN 29,54
JOHN BURGWIN 28
JOHN RICHARDSON 29
JOSEPH 41
JOSHUA 29
JUDITH 7
J. W. 45
KATHARINE 21
LUCY JANE 30
MARGARET 28
MARGARET HARRIS 29
MARY 28,29
MARY JANE 29
MICAJAH 29,(SR. WILL OF)29
MOLLY 29
NANCY 29
PETER 28

110

PHOEBE ELIZABETH 29
RACHEL 2, 47
ROGER 54
SARAH 29
SARAH ELVIRA 29
SARAH JANE 29
SUSANNAH 29
SUSY 29
SYLVAY 85
THOMAS (WILL OF)2, 28, 29
(GEN.) 87
TURNER (WILL OF) 29
W. E. 45
WILLIAM 2,28,(WILL OF) 29
(SR.)WILL OF) 29,31,44,81,
82,85,89
ZILPHIA 28

DEACON:
    MARY (WILL OF) 29

DEAL:
    DURTIS 38

DEESE:
    R. E. 22

DEEZE:
    R. E. 42

DENNARD:
    JOHN 53

DERRY:
    BEN 30
    LONDON (WILL OF) 30
    MILLY 30

DEVANE:
    ANN 30
    GEORGE 30
    JAMES 30
    J. D. 10
    JOHN (WILL OF)30,(JR.) 64
    J. S. 10, 19
    LIZZIE S. 10
    MARGARET 30
    REBECCA 30

TOBITHA 30
THOMAS 30, (SR.) 30
W. F. 9
WILLIAM 30

DEWEY:
    EUPHEMIA (WILL OF) 30
    ROBERT 50, 81

DICKSON:
    DALVIN J. 14,(WILL OF) 30
    CATHERINE 30
    CATHERINE F.30
    JAMES W. 30
    JOHN 30, 79
    JOSEPH 30
    J. W. 30
    PICKETT 30
    ROBERT 30
    S. F. (WILL OF) 31
    SUSAN E. 30

DOANE:
    JOHN 85

DOBBS:
    ARTHUR 6, 7

DORTCH:
    SARAH B. 12

DOUGLAS:
    A. 71

DOVE:
    ARCHIBALD 89
    ESTHER (WILL OF) 31
    JOHN 78
    MARGARET 32
    MARY 22

DOWAY:
    CATHERINE 3
    ELIZABETH 3
    JAMES 3
    ROBERT (WILL OF) 3

DOWEY:
 ELIZABETH ANN 31
 JAMES (WILL OF) 31
 MARY 31
 ROBERT 31

DOWIE:
 ROBERT 1

DOWLESS:
 ANNA 21
 MARGARET 21
 WILLIAM 48

DOWNIE:
 A. 10

DOWNING:
 EVAN 31
 GEORGE (WILL OF) 31,70
 GEORGE W. 31
 JOHN J. 31
 JOSEPH 31
 MARY ANN 31
 MARY JANE 31,88
 SARAH 31
 SOPHIA 68
 STEPHEN 57
 VALENTINE 31

DRANTON:
 JOHN 26

DRAUGHAN:
 ANN 16
 CHARLES 16
 JAMES H. 16
 JANE 16
 MARGARET 16
 MILLER 16
 NANCY 16
 ROBERT 16

DRAUGHON:
 JAMES H. 16
 MARGARET 16
 MARY 16

DRY:
 GRADY 51
 WILL (JR.) 54

DUBOSE:
 JOHN 33

DUDLEY:
 EDWARD B. 17

DUE:
 SETH 16

DUN:
 JOHN D. 38
 PHOEBY 38

DUNCAN:
 ALEXANDER 35
 JANNETT 64
 JOHN 89
 PEYTON 57,62
 SARAH NEILL 57

DUNHAM:
 ALLICE 31
 ELIZA J. 69
 ELIZABETH 31
 G. B. 31
 JAMES A. 31
 JAMES S. (WILL OF) 31
 JAMES SNOWDEN 81
 JOHN S. 31
 JONATHAN S. 31
 J. R. 31
 SAMUEL 31
 SARAH 20,31
 SILVIAH 31
 THOMAS 31
 W. C. 29,31
 WILLIAM H. 31
 WILLIAM J. (WILL OF) 31,72
 WILLIAM R. (WILL OF) 31
 W. R. 81

DUNN:
 JOSEPH S. (JR.) 31
 PRISCILLA 7

DUPRER:
  AMELIA (WILL OF) 32

DUPRIE:
  DANIEL 84

EAGAN:
  JAMES (WILL OF) 3

EAGER:
  CHARLES 17
  LAURA (MRS.) 17
  LAURA E. 17

EDGE:
  ALEXANDER MATTHEW 32
  ALLEN (WILL OF) 32
  CHARLES L. 32
  DRUSILLA J. 32
  ELIZA M. (WILL OF) 32
  EVANDER 87
  JOHN 37
  JOHN W. 32
  LUCY A. 32
  MARGARET A. 32
  MARY 86
  MARY M. 28
  SOPHIA 32
  WINNAFORD 85

EDWARDS:
  ALFRED 32
  ALLEN (WILL OF) 32
  ANNA F. 32
  APPA 32
  BETSY 32
  CALVIN 32
  CATHERINE (WILL OF) 3
  ELIA F. 32
  CHARLES (WILL OF) 32
  C. S. 41
  ELIZABETH 32
  ELLA J. 32
  GILLMORE 39
  GILMORE 18,32
  HARRIETT B. 32
  HAYNES 32,42
  J. A. 68
  JAMES 32

JOHN 32
JOHN A. 19,65
LIZZIE 32
LYDIA 32
MARTHA ELIZABETH 42
MARY 32
RALSEY 32
RHODA ANN 32
ROBERT 3,59
ROBERT J. (WILL OF) 32
SALLIE C. 32
SALLIE L. 32
SARAH E. 39
SOPHIA 32
STEPHEN (WILL OF) 32
SUSANNAH 32
SUSY 32
TRAVIS 32
UNITY 13
WRIGHT 32

ELISS:
  JOHN 3

ELKINS:
  AGNES 30
  JAMES A. 77
  JOHN Q. 58

ELLICE:
  EVEN 5
  PHILLIS 5

ELLIS:
  ANN 40
  ELIZABETH 33,76
  EVAN 4,(WILL OF) 33
  G. W. 17
  J. 47,75,91
  JAMES 47
  JAMES SAMUEL 33
  JANNETT 33
  JOHN (WILL OF) 33,35,43,46,
  66
  JOHN W. 51,92
  JONES 86
  LUCY 33
  MARY 46
  PENELOPE ANN MARIAH 51

PHILLIS 33
REYE "RUSS" 33
WILLIAM 33,91

ELLISS:
  EVAN 68

ELWELL:
  BENJAMIN 40,49,93
  ELIZABETH 49
  HANNAH 49
  SARAH 49
  WILLIAM 11

ENECKS:
  ANN 4
  ISAAC 4
  JANE 4
  WILLIAM 4

ESTERS:
  E. W. 92

EUSTACE:
  MITCHELL 80

EVANS:
  BENJAMIN 51
  DANIEL 36
  ELLEN 12
  HELEN 25
  JACOB 53
  JACOB A. 79
  JAMES 12,31
  JONATHAN 2,4,7,68
  JOSIAH 7,22
  MARY ANN 79
  PETER 43
  THOMAS S. 46

EVENS:
  JONATHAN 4
  WILLIAM 30

EVERS:
  AARON 9
  DAVID 33
  JAMES (WILL OF) 33

NANCY 9
WILLIAM JAMES 33
ZYLPHIA 33

FAIRCLOTH:
  ANNA M. 28
  EDNEY 34
  F. 71
  SOLOMON 34

FAISON:
  J. W. (REV.) 13

FARFAX:
  NEDON 41

FAULK:
  GRACE 36
  RICHARD 24

FENNEL:
  MARY C. 27

FENNELL:
  GEORGE 30

FISHER:
  ELIJAH 22,34
  HAYWOOD 33
  JEMINA 34
  JOHN 33
  M. W. 33
  RAIFORD 12,(WILL OF) 33
  REUBEN 22
  SIVIL 22
  WILLIAM T. 18

FITZRANDOLPH:
  B. 25,37
  BENJAMIN 4,5,6,(WILL OF)33,
  (JR.) 33,37,38,43,73,81,93
  EDWARD 33
  GAINOR 33
  RUTH 33
  SARAH 33

FLINN:
  CATHERINE 33

CHARITY 35
DANIEL (WILL OF) 33,(JR.)33,
 (SR.) 33
ELIZABETH 33
JAMES 33,40
JOHN 33
MARY 33

FLOWERS:
 ALICE 34
 DAVID F. (WILL OF) 34
 EMMA 34
 FRED J. 34
 GOOLSBURY 34
 IGNATIOUS (WILL OF) 34,41
 JAMES G. 34
 MARY 13
 MILLY 34
 MORGAN 34
 NANCY 34
 RICHARD 34
 SARAH 34
 SARAH E. 34
 SUSANNAH 34
 THOMAS 77
 URIAH 34

FLOYD:
 ELIZABETH 43
 ELIZABETH ANN 48
 JOHN 7

FOGARTIE:
 EDWARD 77

FOGARTY:
 EDMUND 7

FOKES:
 JOHN 76
 WILLIAM 76

FOLEY:
 FLOOD 57

FORDS:
 JOSEPH 12

FORMEE (FORMEDUVAL)
 A. J. 77

FORMYDUVAL:
 CHARLES 78
 DEMOSTHAIN 78
 JOHN PAUL 78

FORSHA:
 ROBERT 6

FORT:
 ARTHUR 53
 GRAY 34
 JOHN (WILL OF) 34
 JOSEPH 12
 JULIA ANN 34
 THOMAS 34
 THOMAS M. 34

FOUNTAIN:
 ISABELLA 87
 J. (MRS.) 87

FOWLER:
 JOHN 59
 WILLIAM 59

FRANCES:
 HUBERT R. (WILL OF) 34
 NANCY E. 34

FRANCIS:
 H. R. 29,88
 HUBERT R. 42

FRAYSHER:
 SILAS CLARK 23

FREEMAN:
 ABRAHAM 54
 A. J. 71
 JAMES H. 46
 J. F. 95
 LYDIA 59
 MOSES 21
 S. (D) T. 47

115

FRINK:
 AMANDA 47

FURMIDGE:
 ROBERT 22

GARDNER:
 O. J. 21

GARSON:
 JOHN 83

GARVAN:
 ANN (WILL OF) 34
 CHARLES LEE 34
 RICHARD (WILL OF) 34,57

GARVIN:
 NANCY 48
 RICHARD 26,48

GATES:
 EDWARD 35
 ELIZA 42
 ELIZABETH 35
 JANE (WILL OF) 35
 JEAN 13
 JOHN 35
 MARGARET 35
 MARY 35
 PETER (WILL OF) 35

GAUSE:
 ANN 25
 ELIZABETH 35
 EMILY R. 54
 HANY 25
 J. I. 54
 JOHN 35
 J. W. 25
 MARY 25,67
 MARY JANE 83
 MAY 67
 NEEDHAM (WILL OF) 35
 PHILZO E. 40
 SAMUEL 25,35
 SAMUEL C. 83

WILLIAM 35 JAMES 25

GAUTIER:
 ANN 30
 JOSEPH R. (JR.) 35
 J. R. (WILL OF) 35
 PETER WILLIAM 36
 P. W. 35
 T. N. 35

GIBBS:
 AMELIA 35
 GEORGE 3,(WILL OF) 35
 JOHN 32,(WILL OF) 35,66
 JOSEPH 35
 MARGARET 35
 ROBERT 32,35
 SARAH 32,66
 SOPHIA 32

GIBSON:
 AGNES 9
 JOHN 9
 MARGARET 4, (MRS.) 90
 WALTER 4,90

GILLESPIE:
 ALBERT 48
 DAVID 16-A
 DAVIS (WILL OF) 35
 D. B. 31,46
 ELIZABETH 36
 J. 17
 JAMES (WILL OF) 36
 JAMES F. 18,63
 JOSEPH 36,44
 RICHARD 36
 RICHARD T. (WILL OF) 36
 R. S. 63
 SARAH 35
 SUSAN 36
 THARVEY 10

GILMORE:
 JOHN T. 62
 WILLIAM L. 54

GLASS:
BECKY 36
LEVY (WILL OF) 36
LITTLETON 36
MARY 36
RITTA 36
SOLOMON 36
THOMAS 36

GLISSON:
ANN SOPHIA 13

GLOVER:
WILLIAM 35

GODFREY:
WILLIAM 35,40,93

GODWIN:
PAUL 92
STEPHEN 92

GONTIER:
PETER W. 28

GOODEN:
B. 64
CATHERINE 22
CHRISTOPHER 77
DANIEL 22,50,77
DRUCILLA 21

GRAHAM:
ANDREW 13
CORA J. 27
ELIZA A. 27
FAITHFUL 90,(MRS.)90
GEORGE A. 27
HENRY 24,(MRS.) 90
NEILL 11,36,(DR.) 58,61,62,
94

GRANGE:
JAMES 3
JOHN 7
JOHN P. 77

GRANT:
LEONARD 39

GRAY:
ABRAM (WILL OF) 36
CORNELIUS 36
JESSE 36
JOHN 4

GREADY:
KATHERINE 2
MARY 2

GREEN:
A. 3
ANN 57
CALEB 33
JAMES 3,36
JOHN 1,(WILL OF) 3
LUCY 1
MARY 3, (WILL OF) 36,45
ROBERT 3
SARAH 3
SILENCE 57
WILLIAM 33

GRICE:
WILLIAM 90

GRIMES:
COLUMBIA 36
DANIEL J. 36
DAVID 36
DAVID J. 36
ELIZABETH 36
FRANKLIN 36
JAMES (WILL OF) 36
JAMES C. 36
JOHN 36
MOSES W. 36
SARAH ANN 36
VICTORIA 36

GUTHRIE:
JEAN 66
WILLIAM 66

GUTRIER:
J. R. 56

GUION:
ELLEN 17

ELLEN P. (WILL OF) 37
H. W. 94

GULLEY:
  SUSANNA 90

GUYTON:
  MOLCY 18

HADDOCK:
  ELIZABETH 86

HAILES:
  JOHN 37
  SAMUEL 37

HAILLS:
  HARRIET 88

  HAILS:
  WILLIAM 68

HAIR:
  JOHN 68,(SR.) 79
  STEPHEN 79,88

HALL:
  CHAS. 88
  ELIZABETH 1,3
  ENOCH 59
  JAMES 18,37
  JOHN 77
  JONATHAN (WILL OF) 37
  L. J. 9,50,58
  LUCY 7
  MAURICE 33
  NANCY 71
  PACHYAUE 37
  PEGGY 50
  RAFORD 27
  S. J. S. 17
  THOS. 1,2,7
  THOMAS G. 17
  WILEY 28
  WILLIAM 1,(WILL OF) 3

HALLS:
  FLORA 14

HAMILTON:
  ESABEL 3
  ESTHER 3
  JAMES 3
  JOHN (WILL OF) 3

HAMMONDS:
  PHOEBE 79

HANCOCK:
  MARGARET 18

HARDWICK:
  LOUVILL 76

HARDY:
  REBECCA 39

HARGRAVES:
  BRITTON 69

HARGROVE:
  BRITIAN 23
  DAVID J. 65
  DAVID JAMES 65

HARGROVES:
  JOHN 21

HARNETT:
  CORNELIUS 6

HARRELL:
  URIDIA 13

HARRIS:
  MARY M. C. 74

HARRISON:
  ANN 37
  EDWARD 37
  ELIZABETH 37
  JOHN 24,(WILL OF) 37,(SR.)
  40,68
  MARGARET 37

RICHARD 40, 75, 91
SUSAN 37
SUSANNA 40
WILLIAM 6

HARRISS:
EDWARD 58
N. T. 74

HART:
ANN (MRS.) 35
THOMAS 1

HARTMAN:
J. M. 89

HARVEY:
A. L. 38
ALEX'R. 68
ALEXANDER L. 37
ANN 91
ANNA JANE 37
ELIZA ANN 37
JOEL Y. 42
JOHN TRAVERS 37
MARGARET 37
MARY 42, 75
MARY E. 42
PRISCILLA 37
R. 33
ROBERT (WILL OF) 37, 42, 62
SARAH 37
TRAVIS W. (WILL OF) 37
T. W. 75
WILLIAM W. (WILL OF) 37
WILLIAM WHITE 37

HAWES:
EDWARD A. 48
ENOCH 48

HAWTHORNE:
WILLIAM 66

HAYNES:
ANN 38
ELIZABETH (WILL OF) 38, 83
JOHN 38

JOSHUA (WILL OF) 38
MARY 38
MR. 38

HAYS:
JOHN 38
SOUTHY (WILL OF) 38
WILLIAM 38

HEGGONS:
JEPTETH (WILL OF) 38
MARTHAR 38
ANNA 38

HELLIER:
ANN 2
RICHARD 2

HENDERSON:
JAMES 3

HENDON:
ELIZABETH ANN 38
JAMES 3
JOSIAH 28, (WILL OF) 38, 43, 59
LYDIA 38, 59
MARGARET ANN 38
SARAH ANN 28
WILLIAM (WILL OF) 38, 89

HENDRY:
ELIZABETH 64
JAMES 64
JOHN 82
ROBERT 85

HENRY:
EDWARD 88

HERRING:
ELIZABETH 38
ENOCH 69
JOHN 30
LUKE 38
MARY (WILL OF) 38
MARY ANN 38
RICHARD 20
SARAH 20

HERRINGTON:
  ANN 52
  ELIZABETH (WILL OF) 38
  JOHN B. 38

HESTER:
  AARON (WILL OF) 38,89
  A. KILLIS 39
  ALEFAIR F. (WILL OF) 39
  AMMY 66
  COMFORT 39
  DANIEL (WILL OF) 39,48
  DANIEL EDMOND 39
  DAVID (WILL OF) 39
  DAVID ASBERRY 39
  D. M. 39
  EDWARD T. 39
  E. J. 39
  ELIZABETH 42,43
  EMILINE S. 39
  EPHRIAM 48,82
  E. T. 18
  F. E. 39
  H. F. 39
  JAMES 39
  JOE 19
  JOHN 28,82
  J. W. 39
  KESIAH 81
  KILLIS 42
  LEONARD GRANT 39
  MARGARET 39
  MARY 39
  MONROE 32
  N. E. 39
  PATIENCE 39
  RACHEL 39
  REBECCA 39
  SARAH 39
  SNOWDEN 56
  STEPHEN 39
  THOMAS (WILL OF) 39
  W. F. 39
  WILLIAM 39

HETIER:
  RICHARD 3

HIGH:
  AMOS 19
  ELIZABETH G. 19
  ESAW 78
  JACOB 68
  JULIA 43
  LUKE 44
  MARTHA JANE 44

HIGHSMITH:
  ROBERT 51

HILBURN:
  AMELIA 93
  GYRON 93
  H. F. 89

HILL:
  AMEY 49
  ISAAC (WILL OF) 39
  JOHN 54
  WILLIAM 54
  WILLIAM BARTRAM 39

HILLYARD:
  ROBERT 5

HINE:
  JAN'T. 84

HINES:
  C. V. 17,61
  MARY ANN 24
  MARY E. 61

HODGE:
  ROBERT (WILL OF) 39,43

HOG:
  ELIZABETH 3
  RICHARD (WILL OF) 3

HOGG:
  JOHN 3
  ROBERT 3

HOLLINGSWORTH:
  ALEXANDREA 40
  AUGUSTUS 40
  CAROLINE 78
  CAROLINE F. 93
  CAROLINE FRANCIS 93
  ISAAC 3
  ISABELLA 40
  JENATY 34
  JOHN 3
  JOSEPH 93
  MARTHA 90
  MARY 40
  MARY JANE 34
  MARY MARGARET 40
  REBECCA J. 40
  SAMUEL 3
  STEPHEN (WILL OF) 40
  SUSAN T. 40
  VALENTINE 3

HOLLOWAY:
  DAVID 88

HOLMES:
  ANN 40
  EDMOND 92
  EDWARD (WILL OF) 40
  GABRIEL 40,92
  H. L. 74
  JAMES 46
  JOHN 40
  JOHN H. 46
  LUCIEN 14
  MARGARET 14
  MARGARET ANN 14
  MARY 40
  MOSES (WILL OF) 40
  RICHARD 33,38,40,71

HOLTON:
  JAMES 11
  JANE 11

HOOPER:
  A. M. 92

HOUGHTON:
  ELIZABETH 4
  JOSHUA 4
  MARY 4
  WILLIAM 4
  THOMAS (WILL OF) 4

HOUSTON:
  ANNA 43
  GRIFFITH 43
  WILLIAM 43

HOWARD:
  CALVIN 72
  EMELINE (AMELIA) 40
  GEORGE W. 70
  HEZEKIAH 40
  H. S. V. 71
  JAMES 40
  JOHN (WILL OF) 40
  JOS. 7
  MARY 40
  PRIMUS 40
  SARAH 40
  THOMAS 60
  WILLIAM 40

HOWE:
  A. 91
  ARTHUR 2
  JANE (MRS.) 90

HOWEL:
  CALEB 6

HOWELL:
  LOUISA 50
  MARY 50

HUFFMAN:
  ELER 16

HUFHAM:
  ANN 40
  FRANCIS 40
  SOLOMON (WILL OF) 40

HUFMAN:
HUDNEL (WILL OF) 40
JAMES 40
MARTHA 40
MARY 40
SOLOMON 40

HUGHES:
WILLIS 5

HUMPHREY:
BENJ. 16-A,43,51,82
JEAN 43
JOSEPH (WILL OF) 4

HUMPHREYS:
BENJAMIN 82
GAINOR 82
JOSEPH 82

HUNT:
GASTON 56
JANE 56
JOHN 56
ROBERT 56

IKNER:
DOROTHY 40
GEORGE (WILL OF) 40
PHILLIP 40
SOLOMON 40

INMAN:
HARDY 47
JAMES 13

INNES:
JAMES 1

ISHAM:
JAMES 24,(WILL OF) 40

IVEY:
CHARLES (WILL OF) 41
JOHN (WILL OF) 41

JACKSON:
JAMES 74,76,88

JACOBS:
ARTHUR 41
CAROLINE 21
MARY 41
PEGGY 41
SHADRACH (WILL OF) 41

JAMES:
HINTON 55
SARAH 55

JAY:
JOSIAH 94

JEFFRIES:
TAMMESIA 42

JERNIGAN:
ELY 41
FREDERICK 41
JESSE 13
RICHARD 41
WHITMEL (WILL OF) 41

JESSIP:
JOHN (WILL OF) 41

JESSUP:
AMOS 53
ELIZABETH 53
ELIZABETH ANN 41
HARRIET N. 41
ISAAC (WILL OF) 41,44
JAMES M. 28,41
JAMES McD. 41
JOSHUA 41
ROBERT M. 53
SAMUEL 89
THOMAS A. 29
WILLIAM S. 41
WILLIAM T. 53,94

JOHNSON:
ANN 42
DANIEL (WILL OF) 41,42

DAVID 27
ELIAS D. 19
ELIZABETH 42
EVAN 42
HELEN 42
HUGH 45
JAMES 22,41
JEAN 27
JOEL 37,(WILL OF) 42
J. M. 19
JOSHUA 41
KINION 42
LUCINDA 43
MARGARET 41
MARY ANN BUTLER 19
MARY E. 11
OWEN 42
RICHARD (WILL OF) 42
ROBERT 19,87
R. W. 42
SALLIE 42
SALTER 80
SAMUEL 48
SARAH A. 11
SOLOMON (WILL OF) 42
TAYLOR 41
T. J. 12
WILLIAM 16,(WILL OF) 42,
(CAPE FEAR) 48,55,81,89
WILLIAM S. 42,49
W. J. 51

JOHNSTON:
ALEXANDER 9
GAB 2,5
GABRIEL 1
JOHN 42,65
JOHN M. 56
LELAH (WILL OF) 42
LILLAH 3,90
PRUDENCE 42
ROBERT 3,42,34
WM. 34
WILLIAM S. 56

JONES:
AMOS L. 43
ANDREW J. 44

ANN 4,43
ANN MARIA 74
ARTHUR (WILL OF) 4
BRITIAN 24
CALVIN 21,(WILL OF) 42,43
CHARITY (WILL OF) 42,43
DAVID 30,44,95
EDWARD (WILL OF) 4,43
E. S. 10
FRANKLIN 43
FREDERICK 90
GEORGE W. 19,32,39,42,43,45,
80
G. R. 22
GRIFFITH 4,6,(WILL OF) 43
HENRIETTA 1
HENRY B. 43
ISAAC 4,(WILL OF) 43
J. 53
JAMES 3
JESSE 43,44
JINNEY 43
JOHN 1,6,36
JOHN F. 43
JONATHAN (WILL OF) 43
JONES 48
JOSEPH 43
LEVI 14,42,(WILL OF) 43
LEWIS 4
LOVE 43
MARY J. 80
MOSES 42,(SR.) 42, (JR.) 43,
(WILL OF) 43
MUSGROVE 37,43,(WILL OF) 44,
68
NANCY 48
NATHAN 9,18
NATHAN HENRY 43
OLIVER 43
PENELOPE 43
REUBEN 42
RHODA A. 42
RUEBEN 43
SARAH 43
SARAH J. 42,(WILL OF) 44
SIPHRES 4
SNOWDEN SINGLETARY 43
SUSANNA 4

EMILIA McKAY 59
EMILY S. 62
FANNY 46
FLORA C. 46
ISAAC N. 46
J. 46
JAMES I. 46
JANE 91
JOHN 46
JOSEPH (WILL OF) 46,(JR.)
91
JOSEPH R. 28,(WILL OF) 46,
54,75
JOSEPH RICHARD 46
LUCY 79
STRANGE 59
SUSAN 45
TENA H. 46
WILLIAM 46,79
WILLIAM J. (WILL OF) 46,59

KENNEDY:
ADELINE 46

KENNEY:
JOHN 3

KEPER:
MARY S. 47

KERR:
JAMES 90

KING:
A. J. 46
ALEXANDER 36,40,(WILL OF)
46,(SR.WILL OF) 46
CATHERINE ELIZABETH 46
DAVID D. 46
DUNCAN 19,32,(WILL OF) 46,
92
E. B. 46
EVANDER D. 46
FRANKLIN 46
FRANCENIA W. 46
GEORGE 11
HARY 72
JAMES 32

JAMES A. 46
JOHN 10,46
LENORA 11
LYDIA 46
MARGARET 60
MARGARET ANN 49
MARGARET R. 60
MARSDEN 46
MARTHA L. 46
MAETHA W. 60
MARY 17,46
MICHAEL 60
PETER W. 72
S. B. 54
S. M. 61
SOLOMON 32
WILLIAM 46
WILLIAM A. 46
WILLIAM ARTHUR 60
WILLIAM M. (WILL OF) 46

KINLAW:
ALEX W. 12
ELIZABETH 93
NELSON 93

KIRBY:
ELIZABETH 27

KNOWLES:
ESTHER 31
GEORGE 33

KNOWLS:
ROBERT 1

KNOX:
ELIJAH 26

LACEWELL:
DELPHA 12

LAMB:
ABSALOM 47
ISAAC 47
JACOB 47
JOSHUA 47
MARY (WILL OF) 47

NEEDHAM 47
THOMAS 47

LAMBERTSON:
BENJAMINE 35

LAMMON:
MARY 67

LAMMOND:
ALEXANDER 47
ANGUS (WILL OF) 47
ELIZABETH 47

LAMON:
ALEXANDER (WILL OF) 47
ANGUS (JR.) 77
MALCOM 29
MARION 47

LAMONT:
ANGUISH 47
CHRISTIAN 47
D. A. 34
DANIEL 47
DUNCAN (WILL OF) 47
ELIZABETH 47
FLORA 47
MARGARET 47
NANCY 47

LAND:
SUSAN J. 70

LANNELL:
BENJAMIN 25

LANSDELL:
BENJAMIN 35

LARKINS:
BETTY 35
ELIZABETH L. 13

LASPEYRE:
BERNARD 87

LAURENCY:
ANN D. 3

LAWSON:
FRANCES 36

LEACH:
J. T. 11

LEARY:
JOHN 1

LEE:
LOUISA (MRS.) 89

LEGETT:
JOHN 40

LENNON:
ANN 5
DENIS' 5
DENNIS 47
EPHRAIM 5
FRANCIS M. 47
GEORGE (WILL OF) 47
HAYNES 78,93
JANE ROSELINE 78
JOHN (WILL OF) 5,33,43,53
JOHN E. 43
JOHN M. 42,(WILL OF) 47,81
JOSEPH E. 47
MARIAH 78
MARY M. 47
O. 47
WILLIAM 78

LEONARD:
JOHN 83
SOPHIA 83

LESESNE:
JAMES W. 26,50
J. W. 33
LUCY ANN 48

LeSHAW:
ISABELLA 60

WILLIAM 74

LONDON:
  JOHN R. 17

LONG:
  DELILAH 84
  JAMES 82
  JOHN 70
  SUSANNA 82

LOOPS:
  KATE N. 27

LORD:
  PETER 7,70
  WILLIAM 73

LOVE:
  EMMA S. 72
  JOHN B. 46
  T. D. (SR.) 79

LOVEL:
  JAMES 35

LOWE:
  DANIEL 49
  JOHN 49
  THOMAS (WILL OF) 49
  WINIFRED 49

LUCAS:
  A. B. 50
  AMELIA B. 49
  ANNELIN B. 49
  ELIZA 42
  ELIZABETH 49,93
  ELIZABETH R. 49
  FRANCES (WILL OF) 49
  FRANCIS 22
  GEORGE 22,49,50,(DR.) 74
  HENRY 28,(WILL OF) 49,90
  HENRY L. 49,(WILL OF) 50
  J. J. D. (WILL OF) 50
  JOHN 2,49,50,79,90
  JOHN D. A. 50
  JOHN J. D. 49

LENORA 50
LIZZIE 63
MARY 50
MARY JANE 49
OWEN M. 50
PRESCILLA 50
PRISCILLA 50
SARAH 50
SUSAN 50
THOMAS 22,(WILL OF) 50,90
THOMAS A. E. M. 50
VIRGINIA T. 50
WILLIAM 49,50
WILLIAM B. 49,50
WILLIAM H. G. 50

LUNIES:
  ELIZABETH 78

LUTTERLOH:
  T. S. 57

LYON:
  ANN 5
  CASSIUS WADE 31
  C. C. 17,28,45,50,70
  C. W. 50
  ELEANOR 23,33,(WILL OF) 50,
  93
  ELIZABETH 5
  GEORGE 5,42
  HENRY 50
  J. A. (REV.) 17
  JAMES (WILL OF) 5
  JOHN 5
  KARL 50
  MARY 1,5
  R. H. 36
  R. HENRY 50
  ROBERT H. (WILL OF) 50
  ROY 50
  SALLIE 50
  ZILLAH 5

LYTLE:
  JOHN P. 18,23,42
  R. A. 28

ROBERT 29,46
SARAH K. 46

MAHONEY:
  HELEN 72
  JAMES 72

MALLETT:
  CHARLES B. 14
  CHARLES P. 71
  PETER 14
  SOPHIA S. 14

MALLINGTON:
  RICHARD 2

MANLEY:
  BAZIL 50
  . LYDIA (WILL OF) 50

MANLY:
  KITRAH 38
  REBECCA 38

MACKKEY:
  MARY 5

MARKS:
  JAMES MCKAY 62

MARSH:
  JOHN MCKAY 77

MARSHALL:
  ELIZA N. 72
  JAMES 16-A

MARSHBURN:
  DANIEL H. (WILL OF) 51
  EMMA 51
  FRANKLIN M. 51
  JACOB W. 51
  JAMES M. 51
  JAMES W. 51
  LAURA 51
  MARIAN 51
  MARION L. 51

MATILDA 51
ROBERT M. 51
SARAH E. 51
SUSAN 51

MARSTELLA:
  L. H. 24

MARTIN:
  C. 12
  GEORGE (CAPT.) 93
  JOHN A. 15
  SALLIE 12

MASON:
  F. M. 16-A

MASSINGAE:
  JOSEPH (WILL OF) 51
  MARY 51

MATTHEWS:
  JEMIMA 85

MATTOCKS:
  PHILLIP PAUL 81

MAULTSBY:
  ANTHONY (WILL OF) 51
  DEALA 51
  HUGH 88
  J. A. 10
  JAMES 51
  JOHN (WILL OF) 6
  JOSIAH 10,51
  MARGARET 86
  MARY 6
  SAMUEL (WILL OF) 51
  SARAH 6,51
  THOMAS (WILL OF) 51
  WILLIAM 2,6,51

MAXFIELD:
  MARY (WILL OF) 51

MAY:
  RICHARD 1

MAYNARD:
  MARY 16

MEARES:
  CATHERINE 92
  HENRY 92
  LEVI 45
  THOMAS 92
  WILLIAM B. 83,92

MEARS:
  CHARLOTTE 51
  DANIEL W. 92
  ELIHUE (WILL OF) 51
  FRANCES 51
  JACK 51
  JOHN 51
  WM. J. 65

MEEK:
  GEORGE (WILL OF) 52
  MARY 52

MELDEAN:
  THOMAS 41

MELVIN:
  ADA D. 50
  ANDREW 53
  ANN JANE 12,52
  ARTHUR 40,41,52
  ARTHUR W. 53
  BARBARA A. (WILL OF) 52
  BARBARA ANN 58
  B. SPURGEON 52
  C. T. 31
  DAMARIS 53
  DANIEL 52,(SR. WILL OF) 52
  DANIEL M. 52
  DANIEL MARSHALL 53
  DANIEL MILES 52
  DAVID B. 12,53
  DAVID MILES 13
  DAVID T. 29,53
  D. B. 25,69
  DEMARIS & ROSANNA J. (WILL
    OF) 52
  DEMARUS 53

D. M. 13
D. R. 53
DUNCAN 53
EDWARD 53
ELIZA ANN 53
ELIZABETH 53,86,(SR.) 86
ELIZA 13
ELIZA J. 52
ELIZA JANE 53
ELIZA S. 13
GEORGE 32,53
GEO. F. 9,10,12,15,16,18,19,
  24,25,27,28,41,45,51,53,58,
  59,67,70,72,79,89,95
GEORGE W. (WILL OF) 52,53
G. F. 9,13,16-A,18,19,22,25,
  26,29,32,34,39,42,45,46,50,
  52,54,56,57,58,61,63,69,70,
  80,84,87,92,95
G. W. 52
HANNAH JANE 52
HENRY 52
ISAAC C. 41
JAMES 13,(SR.) 28,(WILL OF)
  52,53,65
JAMES B. 27
JAMES H. 53
JAMES KELLY 52
JAMES S. 75
JANNET 34
J. B. 52
JOHN (WILL OF) 52,(WILL OF)
  53,60
JOHN BEATTY 52
JOHN J. 11
JOHN S. 53
JONATHAN 52,(WILL OF) 53
JOSEPH 53
JOSEPH M. 53
JOSHUA (WILL OF) 53
MARGARET ANN 52
MARGARET E. 56
MARGARET M. 13
MARIAM 52
MARSHALL 58
MARY A. 50
MARY E. 50
MARY ELIZA 11

R. A. 13,53
RENA G. 50
ROBERT 18,21,40,52,53,
(SR. WILL OF) 53,60,(SR.)69
ROBERT P. 15,53
ROSANA 53
ROSANNA JANE 53
SALLIE 63
SAMUEL 53
SARAH 53
SARAH ANN 52,86
URA M. 50
WASHINGTON A. 52
W. F. 52
WILLIAM 34,53
WILLIAM H. 41
WILLIAM S. 13,53
W. S. 52

MEMORY:
  CELIA 53
  GEORGE (WILL OF) 53
  SARAH 53
  THOMAS 53

MENZIES:
  JAMES 1

MERCER:
  SALLY 66

MEREDITH:
  ELIZABETH 88
  JAMES 48,(WILL OF) 54
  JAMES H. 54
  SARAH 54

MERGE:
  ELISHA 30

MERIDETH:
  MARGARET ELIZABETH 11

MERRITT:
  M. 51

MESHAW:
  ANJREW J. 74
  JOEL 24

ME
  JACOB 6

MILHOUS:
  SAML. 2

MILLER:
  ALEXANDER C. 17
  AUGUSTIE S. (WILL OF) 54
  F. 35
  FREDERICK (WILL OF) 54,73
  HANNAH 54
  JAMES T. 24
  JANE 87
  LEOPOLD 54
  MARY 16-A,17,54
  MARY E. 54
  RALPH 2,29,57
  THOMAS C. 16-A,67
  WILLIAM L. 54,87
  W. L. 25

MIMS:
  DAVID 24
  SARAH 84

MITCHELL:
  JOHN 2,6
  NANCY 21
  THOMAS 23

MONLEY:
  DAVID 3

MONROE:
  ADOLPHUS 94
  ANGUS 55
  ANN E. 56
  ARCHIBALD 44,(WILL OF) 55
  C. 9,39,42,81,93
  CATHERINE 55
  COLIN 42,43,(WILL OF) 55,56,
  63,73,76,78,80,81,89
  DANIEL 55,56
  DAVID 55
  DUGOLD 55,56
  DUNCAN (WILL OF) 55
  ELIZABETH ANN 89

ELIZABETH SILLER 55
ELIZABETH JANE 94
GEORGE W. 56
HARRIET J. 56
HUGH A. 94
ISAAC WRIGHT 94
JAMES 55,56
*JANE 52,56
JOHN W. 55
LUCY G. 94
M. 52,88
MALCOM 55,56,71,84
MARY 55
MARY ANN 44
MARY G. 55,56
NANCY 55, (WILL OF) 56
NANCY C. 56
PETER 55,56
SARAH 42,52
SARAH E. 56
SARAH I. 55
SARAH J. (WILL OF) 56
WM. 54
WILLIAM CLEMENT 94
*JOHN 55,(WILL OF) 56
MOOR:
BENJA 5

MOORE:
ALFRED 55
ALMIRA THERESIA 37
ANN 7
ARTHUR 54
BENINJR 7
BENJAMIN 41
BERENGER (WILL OF) 54
CATHERINE 13
DANIEL 20
EARDICE 54
ELISHA 78
HANNAH 54
HARIET 17
JAMES 49,(WILL OF) 54,55,86
JOHN 49,54,55,86
LEVI 3
LYDIA 54
MARY 49,54
MATTHEW 55,78

MAURICE (WILL OF) 54
NANCY 44
NATHAN 54
ROBERT 54
SKENKINE 54
SUSANNAH 32
THOS. C. 37
WALTER R. 11
WILLIAM (WILL OF) 54,(WILL OF)
55,71

MOOREHEAD:
JAMES (WILL OF) 55,36,67,78,
91
MARY (WILL OF) 55
SARAH 55

MOORHEAD:
JAMES (WILL OF) 6,36,59
JANE 6
SARAH 6
WILLIAM 6,20

MOREHEAD:
JAMES 20,46,59

MORHEAD:
JAMES 66

MORGAN:
JOHN BRADLEY 16
MARGARET ANN 16
PATSEY 16
WILLIAM (WILL OF) 56

MORLEY:
DAVID 7

MORRISON:
DUNCAN 76
FLORA 56
JOHN (WILL OF) 56
KENNETH 56
MARION 56
MR. 32
NEILL 56

MORSE:
ELISHA 28,38

MOSICK:
JACOB (WILL OF) 56

MOSLY:
AMILI 76

MOSS:
JESSE 55

MOTE:
DAVID 23
JAMES 83
POLLY JANE 83

MULFORD:
ABIGAIL 30
ABIGAL 56
ALFRED 85
DAVID 56
EDWARD B 86
ELIZABETH (WILL OF) 56
EPHM 4,15,56,(WILL OF)57,
(JR.) 57,82,88
JOHN 56
REBECCA ANN 57
SARAH 34,(WILL OF) 57
THOMAS 56

MULLINGTON:
RICHARD 5,(WILL OF) 57

MUMPHREY:
JOSEPH 24

MUN:
CHRISTIAN 47
JOHN 59

MUNCE:
MATTHEW 76,81

MUNN:
A. 56
ANGUS 19
D. 56,57,70

DANIEL 67
FRANK P. 57
MARY (WILL OF) 57
W. A. 57

MUNTS:
JACOB 18
MATTHEW 18

MURCHISON:
ISAAC ALEXANDER 94
CATHERINE D. 94
DUNCAN 94
ELIZA (IDA) FRANCIS 94
IDA F. (WILL OF) 57
JANE FARLEY 94
LUCY G. 57
LUCY GILLESPIE 94

MURPHY:
ANN E. 58
ARCH'D 38,54,57
CATHERINE 15,57
ELIZABETH 57
ELIZABETH ANN 15
HANSON F. 57
HUGH 48
HUGH (WILL OF) 57,88
JANE 27,57
JOHN 57
JOHN A. (WILL OF) 58,89
MARGARET 57
MARY JANE 57
MARY LOU 58
PATRICK 30,57
P. H. 58
R. J. 58
ROBERT 57,87
TIBBY 10
W. B. 58
WM. B. 79
WORTHLY 57

MURRAY:
JAMES 1

MURRELL:
JOHN 58

MATTHEW 58
MOLSEY 58
REBECCAH 58
REBEKAH 58
SAMUEL 58
ZACHARIAH 58
ZACKARIAH (SR.WILLL OF) 58

MUSTLEWHITE:
ALEXANDER 58
AMELIA 58
AMEY 58
BRIDGET 58
ELIZABETH 58
ELLEN 58
JESSE 58
MARY 58
MILBAY 58
NATHAN 58
PATIENCE 58
SARAH 58
THOMAS (WILL OF) 58
WINNEY 58

MYRILD:
JOSE 15

MacCOULASKIE:
DUNCAN 6
NEILL 6

MacDONALD:
ARCHIBALD 6

MacFEE:
DUNCAN 6

MacLEARAN:
ARCHIBALD (WILL OF) 6
FLORANCE 6
JOHN 6

MacNAUGHTEN:
CHARLES 6
ISBELL 6
MARY 6
NEILL 6
RANALD (WILL OF) 6

McALESTER:
ALEXR. 5

McALISTER:
D. J. 72

McALLISTER:
EMILY 60
HECTOR 64
JANE 16
MARGARET 16

McBEAN:
JAMES 16
WILLIAM FORBES 16

McBRIDE:
CATHARINE ELIZABETH 58
ELLA FRANCES 58
MATTHEW (WILL OF) 58
SARAH 58
WILLIAM RICHARDSON 58

McBRYDE:
JOHN A. 15
M. H. 15

McCALEB:
NANCY 81

McCALL:
ANN 58
ARCH'D 47,70
CATHERINE 58
D. 59
D. J. 93
DUNCAN 47,(WILL OF) 58,59,
63,77
DUNC. J. 94
HARRIET (WILL OF) 58
ISABELLA ANN 58
JANE N. 46
JOHN 43,52,(WILL OF) 58
JOHN NEILL 58
NEILL 47,58
RANDALL 58

McCALLUM"
HAYES C. 62
HUGH C. 12

McCAULSKEY;
NEILL 85

McCAULSKY:
DUNCAN 47
NEIL 47

McCLALLAND:
ANDREW (WILL OF) 5
JAMES 5
JANE 5
THOMAS 5

McCLURE:
RICHARD 4

McCOALSKEY:
ANN 58
DUNCAN 58
NEIL 58
NEILL 58

McCOLLUM:
DONALD 55
H. C. 77
HUGH C. 12,46,92

McCONKEY:
ALEXANDER 4,6,8
PATRICK 2
ROBERT (WILL OF) 59
RUTH 59

McCONLSKEY;
JAMES 77
MARGARET 77

McCOULSKEY:
DUNCAN 63

McCOULSKY:
ANN 59
DANIEL 59
DUNCAN (WILL OF) 59

MARY 59
NEILL 59
SARAH 59

McCOY:
HENRY 7

McCULLOCH:
DUNCAN 77
ROBERT MAXFIELD (WILL OF) 59

McCULLOCK:
NANCY 75

McDANIEL:
ABSALOM 59
AGNES 59
ANNA 67
DANIEL 59
ELIZABETH 63
JAMES 25,59
JAS. I. (WILL OF) 59
JOHN (WILL OF) 59,85
LUCY 78
LUCY A. 93
LOVE 37
MARGARET 59
MARY 59
SOULE 65
TAMER 34
THOMAS 93
WILLIAM 25
WILLIAM GRAY 59

McDIARMID:
ANN ELIZA 94
DAVID (DANIEL) 94

McDONALD:
A. 15,92
A. J. 92
ALEX 26
DONALD 19
MARY A. 46,(MRS.WILL OF) 59
MARY ANN 46
W. F. 15

McDOUGAL:
  ALEXANDER 60
  ALLEN (WILL OF) 60
  HERR 60
  MARY 60
  RANDAL 60

McDOUGALD:
  A. G. 44
  ALEX'R. 26
  HUGH 60
  JOHN C. 23
  MARGARET A. 58
  NEILL 64

McDOWELL:
  A. 83
  ALEX 33,61,83,84
  ALEXANDER 28,37,38,(WILL OF)
  60,65,70,74,84,87
  J. A. 45,63
  JOHN A 60,84,86,
  JOHN A 23,33,73,84,86
  JOHN ALEXANDER 60
  JOHNY 84
  MARY JANE 60,84
  T. D. 63
  THOMAS 84
  THOMAS D. 55,(WILL OF) 60,
  62,69,70,73,84,86
  THOMAS DAVID 60
  THOMAS S. D. 36

McDUFFIE:
  DANIEL (JR.) 29,53,60,
  (SR.WILL OF) 60,71,83
  DUGAL 60
  ELIZA ANN 60
  J. 42
  JAMES 60
  JOHN (WILL OF) 60
  MARGARET 42
  MARY 60
  WORTHELY 57
  ROBERT 60

McDUGALD:
  ALEX'R. 31

ANN (WILL OF) 60
CALL 60
COLL 80
DUGALD 60
EMILY 60
EMILY J. 60
HUGH 23,60
JAMES 57,60
JAMES I. 60
J. G. 65
JOHN G. 18,23,60
MARGARET (WILL OF) 60,70
MARGARET ANN 60
MARGARET ELENOR 60
MARGARET G. 60
NEILL 60
RAY (WILL OF) 70
WILLIAM J. 60

McEWEN:
  ANN 61
  ARCHIBALD 61
  CATHERIN 77
  DANIEL 61
  GEORGE 45,61
  JAMES 61
  JANE 45,53,61
  JEAN 77
  JOHN (WILL OF) 61
  M. 61
  MARGARET 61
  MARY 61
  MATTHA 77
  MATHEW 77
  MATTHEW 53,61
  PATRICK NEILL 61
  R. J. 45
  ROBERT (WILL OF) 61
  WILLIAM 61,77

McFADGEN:(McFAYDEN)
  ANGUS (WILL OF) 61
  A. W. 61
  E. G. 61
  H. B. 61
  JOHN B. 61
  MARGARET 61
  THOMAS B. 61

McFAYDEN:
  ANGUS 17
  ARCHIBALD 27

McFATTER:
  ANNA JANE 51
  ISABELLA 51
  JOHN 83
  JOHN SAVAGE 51
  MARGARET 63
  MARY 48
  MARY ANN 51
  SAMUEL CARVER 51
  WILLIAM ALEXANDER 51

McFEE:
  JOHN 48

McGEE:
  JOHN 28

McGHEE:
  _ DANIEL 79
  EMILY 79
  JOHN 27

McGILL:
  ANN 11
  ASHFORD BRYAN 11
  JOHN 11
  NEILL 22
  NEILL A. 22

McINNIS:
  ALEXANDER 61
  ANN 61,64
  CATHERINE 61
  CATHERINE ANN 61
  CHRISTIAN 61
  DUNCAN (WILL OF) 61,64
  MALCOM (WILL OF) 61
  MARY 61
  THOMAS 61

McKAY:
  A. A. 63
  A. E. 71,83
  ALEXANDER 62

ANN 50,(WILL OF) 61,62,77
ANN ELIZA (WILL OF) 62
ARCHIBALD 62
A. S. 63
CHARLES 58
DANIEL 62
DUGAL 62
EFFIE 62
ELIZA ANN 62
ELIZABETH 62
EMELINE 83
FLORA 62
GADY 63
ISABEL 62
IVER (WILL OF) 62
J. 27,51
JAMES I. (GEN'L.) 37,(WILL
  OF) 62,64,72,88
*JAMES L. 62
JOBEY 61
JOHN 33,61,(WILL OF) 62,75,
  76,77,86
JOHN L.34,62,83
*J. L. 63
J. W. 95
L. J. 52
MARGARET 62
MARY 62
MATILDA 63
MINERVA 58
NANCY 31,62
NEILL 62,95
O. E. 95
RALPH (WILL OF) 62
SANDY 63
VANCE 63
WILLIAM J. 62
WILLIAM JAMES 76
W. J. 63
ZEBAN 62

McKEE:
  CATHERINE 55
  GEORGE 45
  WILLIAM 85

McKEITHAN:
  ANN 65

137

ARCHIBALD 21
CHRISTIAN 58
DANIEL 47,58,61,64
DANIEL T. (WILL OF) 62
D. F. 62
DONALD 5
DOUGAL 47
DUGALD (WILL OF) 5,38,59
DUNCAN 51,(WILL OF) 63,88
ELIZA 58
ELIZABETH 63
JAMES 5
JOHN 5
M. A. 62
MARIAN 88
MARY 5,58
SARAH 5
WILLIAM JAMES (WILL OF) 63

McKENZIE:
  CAROLINE 80
  ELIAS 80

McKINNON:
  DR. 45
  ELCY KELSEY 44

McKISSACK:
  ARCH'D. 9

McKOY:
  IVER 63

McLAIN:
  ARCH'D. 49
  JOHN 13
  THO. 49

McLARRON:
  JOHN 41

McLAUCHLIN:
  NANCY 5

McLAURIN:
  HELLEN J. 52

McLEAN:
  COLIN 56
  DUNCAN 56
  LUCY 90
  MARAN 36
  N. A. 56,89
  PETER 53

McLEANEN:
  MALCOM 77

McLEARAN:
  DUNCAN 6

McLEARN:
  JOHN (WILL OF) 63
  MALCOM 63
*
McLELLAND:
  *ANDREW 47,(WILL OF) 63,
  MARY 47
  SAM'L. 33,(WILL OF) 63,72
  THOMAS 63
  ANGUS 63
*McLEAUD:
  MORAN 36

McLEMORE:
  ELIAS 53
  JOHN R. 79

McLEOD:
  E. J. 51
  EVANDER J. 63
  EVANDER JAMES 63
  JOHN WILLIAM 63
  K. 88
  KENNETH 52,53,65
  LAUCHLIN (WILL OF) 63
  MALCOM (SR.) 12,51,(WILL OF)
  63,92
  MALCOM G. 63
  MALCOM GIFFORD 63
  N. 88
  SALLIE ANN 63
  SARAH 63

McMASTER:
  CAROLINE 64
  CATHRON 64
  FELIX (WILL OF) 64

McMILLAN:
  ARCHEY 64
  BETSEY 64
  D. A. 69
  DANIEL 47
  DANIEL N. 26,27,38,64
  DELILA ANN 60
  DOUGAL 48
  DUGAL 64
  DUGALD (WILL OF) 64,80
  DUNCAN 48(WILL OF) 64
  EDWARD (WILL OF) 64
  EFFE 64
  ELIZABETH 20,27,64
  ESEBET 64
  G. I. 52
  HUGH W. 60
  I. (SR.) 64
  IVER 60,64
  JACK 64
  JANNETT (WILL OF) 64
  JENNETT 27
  JOHN (WILL OF) 64,77
  JOHN I. 31
  JOHN IVER 60,64,65,84,88
  JOHN L. 84
  MAG 20
  MARGARET 64
  MARGARET ANN 60
  MARGARET ELIZABETH 64
  MARIAN 47
  MARRION 77
  MARTHA 20
  MARY 20,64
  MARY ANN 60
  MILLY 64
  NANCY 64
  NEILL 48,64
  ROBERT 27
  RANALD 64
  THOMAS E. 84
  WORTHILY 48

McNAUGHTON:
  JOHN (WILL OF) 65
  LEWIS 65
  NEILL 16-A,65

McNEILL:
  A. M. 9,14,17,18,28,34,87
  ARCHIE 44
  CATHERINE 88
  DUNCAN 65
  HECTOR 5,(WILL OF) 65
  JOHN (WILL OF) 65
  JOHN KENNETH 65
  MALCOLM 33
  MARGARET 65
  MARY (WILL OF) 65,72
  W. D. 45,64
  WILLIAM 60,85
  WILLIAM D. 65,78

McNORTEN:
  A. 52

McNORTON:
  CHAS. 63,77
  HARRIET C. 65
  JOHN (WILL OP) 65
  MARY 77
  MARY E. 65
  S. 46

McPHERSON:
  JOHN 57

McRACKEN:
  EMILY 78
  ROBERT 78

McREE:
  ALACE 66
  ALEX 66
  ANN (WILL OF) 65,72
  CHRISTIAN 66
  EDWARD LAWRENCE 33
  ELIZABETH 66
  G. J. 33
  GRIFFITH JOHN 66
  HELEN 66

J. A. 75
JAMES 33,66
JAMES IVER (WILL OF) 65
JAMES P. 64,70
JANE 66
J. I. 14,20,34,41,44,53,65,
67,72,75,85
JOHN 66
JULIA WRIGHT FLOWERS 65
MARGARET 28,43,64,66,83
MARY 48,66
ROBERT (WILL OF) 66
SAMUEL (WILL OF) 66,91
SARAH 66,91
SARAH CHRISTIAN 66
SUSANNAH 66
WILLIAM 5,7,24,28,43,(WILL
OF) 66,68,85

McTYER:
ADAIR 9
SARANNA 9
WILLIAM 9

NANCE:
DANIEL (WILL OF) 66
DANIEL M. 39,66
DAVID T. 66
DOROTHY 66
ELIZABETH 66
JOSEPH (WILL OF) 66
JOSEPH I. 66
JOSHUA L. 50,66
MARY 66
MARY W. 66
PATIENCE 66
WYNNE 66,92

NAYLOR:
ABRAHAM 75

NEAL:
WALTER H. 15

NEALE:
SAMUEL 1
WILLIAM 1

NEELEY:
NETTIE 17
P. P. (REV.) 17

NEILL:
BLUFF JOHN 65

NELSON:
JOHN (WILL OF) 66

NESSFEILD:
ANN 6
JOHN (WILL OF) 6

NEWBERRY:
ELIZABETH 92

NEWBURY:
ELIZABETH 93
JOHN 93

NEWELL:
HARRIET 37

NEWTON:
JANE 6
JOHN 6
MARY 6
THOS. 2,(WILL OF) 6

NICHOLSON:
DAVID F. 34
JAMES L. 34
MARGARET JANE 61,64

NIXON:
SARAH 22

NORMAN:
CAROLINE 72
CAROLINE EMILY 66
HENRETTA 50
J. 76
*JEREMIAH 61,(WILL OF) 66,72
SARAH 72
SARAH B. 17
SARAH BAILEY 66
SIMEON 37
*MARY 66

THOMAS 72
THOMAS I. 84
THOMAS J. 33,37,63
THOMAS JAMES 66

NORRIS:
  AMANDA 67
  GUILFORD 82
  MOLSEY 82

NORTHROP:
  ISAAC 39

NORTON:
  DANIEL 6
  ELIZABETH 6
  JACOB 6
  THOMAS 6
  WILLIAM (WILL OF) 6

NUGENT:
  EDWARD 3

NUNERY:
  M. E. 71

NURTONS:
  MARY 29

NYE:
  J. Q. 46
  RACHEL E. 25

OLDHAM:
  ELIZABETH (WILL OF) 67

OLIPHANT:
  EUPHAMY 16-A
  EUPHEMIA 30
  SARAH 75
  UPHEMIA 16-A
  WILLIAM 39

OPTAN:
  JOHN 6

O'QUINN:
  FARLOW 68

OWEN:
  CATHERINE 14
  ELEANOR 67
  ELLEN PORTERFIELD 67
  JAMES 20,35,67
  JOHN (GOVERNOR) 10,16-A,17,
  18,20,33,35,54,(WILL OF) 67,
  74
  LUCY ANN 17,67
  THOMAS 2,18,20,(WILL OF) 67,
  73,81,(GEN'L.) 87

OWENS:
  CATHERINE 29
  JOHN 29
  MARY 29
  THOMAS 29

PAGE:
  ABRAM (WILL OF) 67
  EMMA 67
  SARAH 67
  W. C. 67

PAIT:
  A. E. 32
  ANN 41
  JINNIE (JINNY) ANN 41
  JOHN 32

PARKER:
  AARON 67,71
  CHARLES P. 67
  C. P. 70
  ELIZABETH E. 27
  GEO. O. 34
  HENRY 67,71
  JOHN 67
  MARY 67
  MARY ELIZABETH 36
  MARY G. 36
  RHODA 71
  ROBERT HUMPHREY 36
  SALLIE JANE 36
  WILLIAM (WILL OF) 67
  W. J. 58,63,67
  WILLIAM J. 42,54

PATE:
  DAVID 78

PATRICK:
  JOHN 18,35

PATTERSON:
  ALEX 55
  ALEXANDER 67
  ARCH. 88
  CATHERINE 88
  DANIEL (WILL OF) 67,88
  DUNCAN 88
  EMILY 88
  JOHN 54,67
  MARY 88
  NANCY 67
  NEILL 62,67

PEARSON:
  ANNABELLA 14
  ELIZA 14
  JOHN 14
  JOHN S. 14
  JOHN STOKES 13
  WILLIAM 14

PEMBERTON:
  ABIGAL 67
  ANN 67
  ELIZABETH 56,(WILL OF) 67,85
  JAMES 57,84,85
  JOHN 82
  NANCY 67
  SOPHIA 67
  THOMAS 67

PENNY:
  THOMAS 84
  WILLIAM 51

PEPPER:
  REBECCA ELIZABETH 36

PERRY:
  A. H. 23
  ANDREW H. 24
  DANIEL 59

DAVID M. 61
D. T. 50
ELIJAH M. 68
G. D. 34
HARRIET REBECCA 68
JAMES HARRISON 68
JAMES W. 68
JOHN (WILL OF) 68
MARGARET 68
REBECCA 68

PETERSON:
  JEREMIAH MELDON 22
  LAURA 67
  MARY M. 22
  MARY NEILL 22
  MARY P. 51
  M. P. 69
  WILLIAM 22

PHARES:
  ELIZABETH 68
  SAMUEL (WILL OF) 68

PHILLIPS:
  LUCY 76
  SARAH 39

PHOEBUS:
  ELIZABETH 48

PIERCE:
  ANN 20
  BENJAMIN F. 78
  JAMES C. 78
  JOHN J. 78
  JONATHAN 67
  SARAH ANN 78

PIKE:
  SAMUEL 4

PINKINGTON:
  ELIZABETH 43

PITMAN:
  BOTHANY 68
  HANNAH 68

JACOB (WILL OF) 68
SAMPSON 68
STEPHEN 47

PITTMAN:
  JESSE 47
  MOSES 23
  *JACOB 12
PLATT:
  NATHL. 7
  THOMAS 8

PLUMMER:
  ANN (WILL OF) 68
  JAMES (WILL OF) 68
  JOHN 44
  LUCY 68
  MARY ELIZABETH 44
  MORRIS 82
  ROBERT 65
  SKINKIN M. 68
  SUSAN 44
  WILLIAM 49,54

POINTER:
  AGATHEY 38
  FRANCIS 68
  JOHN (WILL OF) 68
  MARGARET 68

POLLOCK:
  MARY J. 42

POPE:
  AMEY (WILL OF) 68
  ELIZABETH 68
  MARY 68
  URITY 71

PORD:
  PHILLIP 36

PORTER:
  ANN 33
  HUGH 7,68
  JAMES 7
  J. B. 19
  J. H. 61
  JOHN 7,(WILL OF) 68
  JOHN C. (WILL OF) 69
  MARGARET ANN 69
  MARY ANN 63
  SAMUEL (WILL OF) 7,33,84
  (SANDY) 68
  SUSANNAH 33
  WILLIAM H. 63

PORTERVINE:
  JOHN 30
  SAMUEL 30

POTTS:
  JAMES 91
  JOSE 91
  JOSHUA 16

POWELL:
  BARNABAS 69,92
  BETSY 80
  EASTER 69
  EDE 69
  ELIZABETH 69
  ESTHER 32
  ISAAC 69,92
  JOHN (WILL OF) 69,92
  LARKEN 80
  MARY 32,69
  ZYLPHIA 32,(WILL OF) 69

POWERS:
  JOSEPH 4
  WINNEY 66

POYNTER:
  ELIZABETH 52
  JOHN 57,81,91
  MARY 75,81

PRICE: (OR RICE)
  JOHN 12

PRIDGEN:
  ANNA 69
  CATHERINE 69
  ELIZABETH 69
  EVAN 69
  HANNAH 48,69
  HENRY (WILL OF) 69
  JANNET 57,69
  MATTHEW (WILL OF) 69
  P. H. 69
  STEPHEN 48,69
  TIMOTHY 11,48,69
  WILLIAM G. 69
  WILLIAM H. (WILL OF) 69

PRIEST:
  MARGARET 24

PROTHRO:
  JAMES 3
  JEREMIAH 3

PRUSH:
  ARCH'D. 23

PURDIE:
  A. M. (MRS.) 17,84
  ANN M. (WILL OF) 69
  ANNA MARIAH 70
  ANN MARIAH 84
  ELIZA I. 84
  ELIZA JANE 69,70
  FRANCIS 74
  JAMES 69,89
  JAMES A. 70,74,84
  *JAMES B. 65,(WILL OF) 70
  JAMES S. 38,59,(WILL OF) 70, 73
  JOHN W. 69,(WILL OF) 70,84
  JOHN WESLEY 70
  J. S. 23,30,55,91
  J. W. 74,79,84
  MARIA 25
  MARY JANE 70
  SALLIE 70
  SARAH ANN 70
  THOMAS 70,84
  THOS. J. (COL.) 69
  *JAMES BAILEY 70

PURDY:
  ELIZA 17
  WESLY 17

PURNELL:
  ELIZABETH 75
  MARGARET 86
  MARY 86
  MARY J. 75
  WINDAL 86

QUINCE:
  RICHARD 35

RANDOLPH:
  B. T. 84

RABURN:
  ELIZABETH 41
  GEORGE 41

RAY:
  DUGALD (WILL OF) 70
  DUNCAN 44,77
  ISAAC (WILL OF) 70
  JEAN 44
  MARGARET 70
  MARY 44
  MELIA 70

RAYFORD:
  ANNE 7
  DRUSILLA 7
  GRACE 7
  MARY 7
  MATTHEW (WILL OF) 7
  MOURNING 7
  PHILIP 7
  REBECKAH 7
  ROBERT 7
  WILLIAM 7

REED:
  DAVID 65
  ELIZA ANN 65
  MARY 65

REEVES:
  ELIZA 70
  EVAN (WILL OF) 70
  JAMES 70,(SR.) 70,
  JANE 53
  JOHN M. (WILL OF) 70
  J. P. 57,88
  MARY 32
  NANCY 53
  SARAH 32

REGAN:
  ALFORD (WILL OF) 70
  ANNA 71
  HARRIET 70
  JOHN 71
  JOSEPH (WILL OF) 71
  MARIAN 70
  RALPH 71
  RICHARD 71

REGISTER:
  A. A. 20
  ANN 71
  DANIEL (WILL OF) 71
  D. J. 71
  ELIZABETH 71
  JANE 71
  JOHN 71
  JOSIAH 71
  MARY (WILL OF) 71
  OWAN 20
  OWEN 28
  RUFUS 46
  THOMAS 71
  WILLIAM (WILL OF) 71
  W. O. 71
REID:
  DAVID 14
  JOHN BEATTY 14

RESGOW:
  RICHARD 55

REYNOLDS :
  MARY 71
  RICHARD (JR.WILL OF) 71,84

RIAL:
  DANIEL 71
  HARDY 71
  NOAH 71
  OWEN 71

RIALLS:
  BETSY 71
  STEPHEN (WILL OF) 71

RIALS:
  ELIZABETH (WILL OF) 71

RICE (OR PRICE)
  JOHN 12

RICHARD:
  MOSES 48

RICHARDSON:
  AMOS 91
  EDWARD B. 29
  EDMUND B. 31,72
  GREEN 72
  HAYNES 65,72
  J. A. 36
  JAMES 72
  JOHN A. 18,23,65,72
  JOHN L. 72
  JOHN S. 29,53,72,(DR.) 67
  LUCY G. 72
  MOSES 12,72
  NATHANIEL (WILL OF) 71
  PURDIE 56,72
  RANSOM (WILL OF) 72
  RICHARD 81
  SAMUEL 65,71
  SAMUEL A. 56,73
  SAMUEL N. 31,65,(WILL OF)
  72
  SAMUEL NEAL (WILL OF) 72
  S. N. (SR.) 72
  STEPHEN ARCHIE 72
  WILLIAM 35

RIGGAN:
  ASBERY 26

RILLEY:
  WILLIAM 29
  WILLIAM DAVIS 40

ROBERTS:
  B. M. 50
  JOHN 81
  MOLEY 9
  PRUDENCE 81
  SARAH 4

ROBESON:
  ALEXANDER (WILL OF) 72
  ANN 20,74
  ANN MARIA (MRS.) 19
  ANN MARIAH 20
  ANNA MARIE 20
  B. 20,54
  BARTRAM 19,37,39,55,67,
  (WILL OF) 72,73,81,86
  CAD 72
  CATHERINE 74
  DAVID G. 44
  ELIZA 72,73
  ELIZA A. (WILL OF) 72
  ELIZABETH 23,55,73,74
  ELIZABETH E. (MRS.) 67
  E. M. 9
  E. N. 72
  FRED 72
  G. D. 9
  GEORGE 23
  HESSIC L. 72
  HESSICK L. 72
  J. 75
  J. A. 25,70   54,(JR.)60
  JAMES 19, (JR.) 50/67,(JR.)
  67,68,72,(WILL OF) 73,74,95
  J. D. 72
  J. McK. 72
  JOHN 6,23
  JOHN A. 44,74
  JOHN LORD 73
  JONATHAN 19,20,37,55,73
  LYDIA 72
  LYMAS (SR.) 92
  MARGARET 72,(WILL OF) 73,74,
  86
  MARY 1,55,73,74,80

MARY ELIZABETH 67
PETER 42,52,70,(WILL OF) 73
RACHELL 72
RAIFORD 72
ROBERT RAIFORD 73
SAMUEL 20,30,(WILL OF) 73,76,
81,95
SARAH 54,55,72,73
S. E. 31
T. A. 25
THOMAS 1,2,3,4,5,6,55,70,72,
(WILL OF) 73,(SR.WILL OF) 73,
(COL. WILL OF) 73,74,(JR.)
80,93
THOS. J. 20,67,73
T. J. 25
TYMAN 26
W. I. 72
WILL 31
WILLIAM 37,46,55,73,(WILL OF)
74,82
WILLIAM P. 74

ROBERTS:
  B. M. 50
  JOHN 81
  MOLEY 9
  PRUDENCE 81
  SARAH 4

ROBINSON:
  CHARLES 84
  CHARLIE 17
  DAVID G. 74
  ELEANOR 26
  ELIZA S. 74
  ELIZABETH B. 74
  GEORGE 26
  H. (DR.) 17
  HELEN JANE 69
  HEMAN H. 33,37,52,(DR.)65
  H. H. 11,12,14,16-A,20,21,
  26,36,38,43,50,52,53,55,60,
  63,69,70,71,77,78,94
  IRVING 84
  JULIA 26
  JAS. S. (DR.) 69,84
  JANE W. 74

JOHN A. (WILL OF) 74
MARY 17
MARY E. 84
NEWTON 84
SARAH ANN 74
THOMAS A. 84
THOS. F. 74

ROE:
  JAS. 35

"ROGER" (NEGRO)
  20

ROGIER:
  JANE 15

ROOT:
  JOHN 2

ROOTS:
  HANNAH 6

ROSE:
  MARGARET 15

ROTHWELL:
  EVAN 50
  MARY 46

ROURK:
  DOROTHY 7
  EDMOND (WILL OF) 7
  SAMUEL 7, 92

ROWAN:
  MATT. 5
  MATTHEW 1

ROWELL:
  ELIZA 36

ROWLAND:
  DAVID 74
  ELIZABETH 74
  JAMES (WILL OF) 74
  JOHN 74,92,93
  MARY 74

SAMUEL 74
SARAH 74,92
THOMAS 74

RUSS:
  ALEAZER 75
  ANN 75
  ANNAH 56
  ANNA S. 59
  ANN ELIZA 75
  ARGLUS P. 74
  DAVID 16-A,24,31,84,90
  ELIZA 86
  HANNAH 75
  JAMES 29,56,57,75,(SR.) 75
  JAMES P. 74
  JANE 75
  J. D. 25
  JOHN 4,15,51,(WILL OF) 74,
    75,79
  JOHN A. 74
  JOHN D. (WILL OF) 74
  JOHN JONES 16-A
  JOHN SINGLETARY 75
  JONADAB 75
  JOSEPH (WILL OF) 75
  JOSIAH 75
  JOSIAH T. 71
  J. W. 79
  LYDIA 74
  MARGARET ANN 80
  MARY 16-A,(WILL OF) 75
  MARY ANNAH 75
  MARY POYNTER 75
  RACHEL 75
  SARAH 75
  SARAH OLIPHANT 75
  SHEPHARD 74
  SION 74
  SUSAN 75
  SUSANNAH 75
  THOMAS (WILL OF) 75
  WILLIAM H. 51
  WILLIAM 75
RUSSELL:
  SAMUEL 36
  TOM 50

SALKELD:
  ISAAC (WILL OF) 75
  RUTH 75

SALTER:
  ANN 75,76
  ELIZABETH 46,75,76
  JAMES 37,75,76
  JANE 75
  J. D. 37
  JOHN 75,93
  JOHN D. (WILL OF) 75,76
  JOSEPH 46,68
  JOSEPH R. 76
  MARGARET 76
  MARY 75
  RICHARD 29,50,66,68,(WILL OF)
  75,(SR.) 75,76,91
  SARAH (WILL OF) 75,76
  WILLIAM 39,43,46,68,73,75,
  (WILL OF) 76,82,90,93
  WILLIAM JAMES 75,76
SANDFORD:
  J. 58
SANDERS:
  ABRAM 1
  AMELIA 76
  CHRISTOPHER (WILL OF) 76
  ELCY 76
  ELENORE 78
  ELIZABETH 76
  ELVIRA 76
  EMILIA 76
  SARAH 76,78
  SUALLA 29
  THOMAS (WILL OF) 76

SAUCER:
  POLLY 44

SAVAGE:
  LUCY ANN 71
  W. A. 60
  WILLIAM A. 60

SAWREY:
  ANN 76
  EDWARD 76

*HENRY 76,(SR. WILL OF) 76
  MILDRED 76
*JOHN 76
SCOTT:
  CATHERINE 10
  ROBERT 38,91

SCRIVEN:
  HELLEN 18
  JAMES 76
  JEAN 20,35
  JOHN (WILL OF) 76
  THOMAS 20,76

SCRIVIN:
  THOMAS J. 9,20

SELLERS:
  ELIZABETH ANN 26

SESSIONS:
  MARY 86
  THOMAS 93
  W. I. 21

·SESSOMS:
  ROBERT M. 19,80
  THEO. 79

SEYMORE:
  SARAH (WILL OF) 77

SHADRACH:
  DANIEL 83

SHAFFER:
  GEORGE (REV.) 17

SHAW:
  ALEXANDER 22,60,77,78
  ANGUISH 6
  ANGUS 5,77
  ANN 77,78
  ARCHIBALD 22,60,(WILL OF)
  77,78
  CATHERINE 26,63,(WILL OF)
  77
  CHRISTIAN 22,78

148

COLIN 11,47,77
DANIEL (WILL OF) 77,(SR.WILL
OF) 77,(SR.WILL OF) 77,
(SR.) 78
D. F. 77
D. M. 87
DUNCAN 26,77,78
DUSHEE 6
JANE 50,64,77   77
JOHN 16-A,22,(JR.)/77,78,
(SR.WILL OF) 78
LULA 87
MALCOM 50,77
MARGARET 64,78
MARIAN 47
MARION 77
MARY 22,26
MARY ANN 78
MARY JANE CAROLINE 78
MOLSEY 50
NED 26
NEILL 26,77,85
PENELOPE 23,(WILL OF) 78
RANDALL 77
REBECCA 50
SANDERS 26
W. I. 14
WILLIAM 22,77,78,79
W. IRVING 79

SHERIDAN:
  LOUIS 35
  MARTHA 78
  NANCY 35
  THOMAS 30,(WILL OF) 78

SHERMAN:
  MARGARET 13
  WILLIE 13

SHIPHERD:
  CYPRIAN 4

SHIPMAN:
  ABNER 78
  ANDREW J. 78
  ANDREW JACKSON 93
  ANN 78

DANIEL 33 (WILL OF) 78
DORCAS 93
DOREAS 78
ELENORE 78
ELIZA ANN 78
EMILY HELEN 93
FLORILLA DORCAS 93
FLORINA D. 78
FRANCES ELENOR 78
HAYES F. (WILL OF) 78,87,93
HAYES MCNEILL 78
JAMES 23,76,78,93
JAMES W. 78
JOHN D. 78,93
MARIA J. 93
MARY ELIZA 78
REBECCA 78
SAMUEL 23
SARAH DORCAS 78
SARAH JANE 65,78

SHOARD:
  JAMES 13

SIBBLY:
  WILLIAM 4

SIBET:
  MARY 16-A
  WILLIAM 16-A

SIKES:
  ALEXANDER J. (WILL OF) 79
  AMOS 17,79
  ANN 11
  CALEB 79
  CATHERINE 79
  COLIN 79
  DAVID (WILL OF) 79
  DAVID R . 79
  EDMON 79
  EDMUND 95
  ELIZABETH 79
  EMILIA 79
  EMELIA ALLIS 79
  GILES 79
  HENRY MITCHELL 11
  ISAACK 75

ISABELLA 79
ISIAH 79
JAMES 79
JOEL 79
JOHN (WILL OF) 79,95
JONAH 79
JONATHAN (WILL OF) 79
JOSEPH 79
JOSHUA 79,82
JOSIAH (JR.) 79,(WILL OF)79
JOSIAH PRIDGEN 11
JULIA ANN 15
LUCIUS 17
LUKE 11,79
MALLETT 17
MARIAH 79
MARY 11,28,79,90
MARY E. 20
MARY F. 25
RICHARD 13,79,82
RUSION 17
SAMUEL 79
SARAH 79
SARAH E. 17
THEODORE M. 42,79
THOMAS 69
T. M. 42
W. J. 65

SILLER:
ELIZABETH 55

SIMMOND:
HENRY 4

SIMMONDS:
GRACE 22
HENRY (WILL OF) 7
MARY 22
WILLIAM 7

SIMMONS:
ANN MARIAH 79
. BLUFORD 71
MARY 93
SANDERS 52,(WILL OF) 79,89

SIMONDS:
WILLIAM 7

SIMPSON:
A. 54
ARTHUR 68
ELIZABETH 34
EMELINE 80
FREDERICK 80
GEORGE 89
JACOB 76
JAMES 7,31
JAMES B. 80
JOHN 51,(WILL OF) 80,90
JOSEPH 80
MARY 16,80
ROBERT 16-A
RICHARD M. 80
SEGMORE 76
SIMON 76
WILLIAM 31,48,80

SIMS:
WILLIAM 25

SIMSON:
SARAH 18

SINGLETARY:
ABAGAIL 80
ALACE 73
ALICE 23
AMELIA 82
ANNA JANE 81
BENJAMIN 68,(WILL OF) 80,82
BRATON 75
BRAYTON 68,81
BREYTON (WILL OF) 80
BRISTER (WILL OF) 80
CALVIN 80
CAROLINE 58,81
CATHERINE 93
COLIN 55
COUNCIL 82
DANIEL M. 82
DAVID 44,48,(WILL OF) 80,81
DAVID M. 80
DEBORAH 74,80,81

DEBROAH 4
DENNIA 81
DENNIS L. 47
D. L. 42
E. 12,24,36,42,56,89
ED 80
EDWARD (WILL OF) 80,81
ELIZA 32
ELIZABETH 80,81,82
ELIZABETH CAROLINE 41
EPHRIAM 82
EVAN 50
EVANDER 13,19,22,32,33,41,
43,47,51,53,58,62,63,65,69,
74,82,84,86
FITZRANDOLPH 50
GENERAL 80
GEORGE S. 80
GOODMAN 80
G. S. 60
HANNAH 82
HARRIET B. 80
HOKE 39
ITHAMA 58
ITHAMAR 4,7,(WILL OF) 81
ITHAMORE 50
JAMES 80,(SR.) 73,81,(SR.WILL
OF) 81
JAMES B. 50
JAMES E. 80
JAMES F. 80
JANE 82
JOHN 4,16,74,75,80,(WILL OF)
81,82
JOHN DUNHAM 81
JOHN H. 82
JON'A. 89
JONATHAN 66,80,(SR.)80,(JR.)
81
JOSEPH 38,43,66,80,(WILL OF)
81
JOSHUA 80,(WILL OF) 81
JOSIAH (WILL OF) 81
JOSIAH W. 80
JOYCE 82
LENNON P. 32
LENON P. 80
MARTHA 80

MARY 80(WILL OF) 81,82
MARY ANN 80
MARY F. 80
MONROE 41
NANCY 81
NANCY J. 32
NATHAN 80
NEPAY 80
NEPSEY 82
OWEN 50
PETER 82
RICHARD 21,73,(SR.) 73,80,
(WILL OF) 82,(SR.) 82
R. L. 39
ROLAND 55
ROWLAND 63,80
SALLIE D. 31
SAMUEL 81
SARAH 74,81,82
SARAH ANN 18
SARAH E. 80
SARAH ROBESON 74
SIDNEY 82
SNOWDEN 43,63,80
SOPHIA 82
THOMAS 29,66,81,(WILL OF)
82
W. B. 72
WILLIAM 37,43,66,68,75,
(WILL OF) 82
WILLIAM M. 74
WILLIS 28,81
WINNIE 80
WRIGHT 80

SLOAN:
HARRIET A. 27

SLUYTER:
BENJAMIN 8

SMITH:
ALICE HENRYETTA 82
ALLEN 83
AMOS 21,82
ANN 25
ANN JANE 84
ARTHUR 85

BENJAMIN 71
CATHERINE 52
C. L. 71
DANIEL 42,(WILL OF) 82,83
DAVID J. (WILL OF) 82
D. L. 63
EDWARD 70
ELIZA 84
ELIZABETH 84
ELIZABETH ANN 82
ELIZABETH J. 84
ELIZABETH JOYCE 85
ELLEN 67
HENRY E. 70,84
ISHAM 59
JAMES 67,73,74,82,(WILL OF) 83,90
JANE (MRS.) 36,83
JESSE 40
J H. 89
J. J. 84
JOANNA 84
JOHN 3,4,17.18,20,40,48,63,(DR.)65,68,70,72,82,(WILL OF) 83,(SR.) WILL OF 83,84,
JOHN B. 82,84
JONATHAN 38,57,(WILL OF) 83,85
KINION A. 82
LEE 10
L. M. 28
LONIMAS 16
LUCY 37;(WILL OF) 83,84
LUCY ANN 48
MACOM 84
MALCOM 83
MARGARET 67,75,82,84
MARGARET ANN 84
MARGARET C. (WILL OF) 83
MARIAN 83
MARTHA 82
MARY 7,25,37,63,(WILL OF) 84,85
MARY ANN 72
MARY B. 67
MASSEY 84
NANCY 23
NOBLE 83,84

OWEN 13,21,29,32,52,53,79
RICHARD 37,(WILL OF) 84
ROBERT 82
ROBINSON W. (WILL OF) 84
S. A. 42
SAMUEL 63,67,71,82,83,(WILL OF) 84,87
SARAH (MRS.) 36,53,84,85
SARAH R. 67,73
SHADRACH 83
SIMON 16-A,85
SOPHIA 84
STEPHEN (WILL OF) 84,85
SUSAN 16,84
TERCEY 82
THOMAS 7,16,25,29,38,56,59,67,71,81,83,(WILL OF) 84,85
THOMAS C. 34,60,69,70,72,83,(WILL OF) 84
THOMAS CYRUS COUNCIL 25
THOMAS F. 83
TOBITHA 84
TRYON 84
W. DOUGLAS 70
WILLIAM 48,82,(SR.) 82,83,(WILL OF) 85
WILLIAM B. 16
WINNAFRED (WILL OF) 85

SPAULDING:
  A. 21
  RHODA 21

SPEIRS:
  THOMAS 4

SPENDLOVES:
  JENNET 40

SPILER:
  MARGARET 85

SPRUNT:
  W. H. 14

SQUIRES:
  JOHN H. 69
  SUSAN C. 69

STACK:
 JOHN 2,3

STANFORD:
 WILLIAM 35

STAR:
 SARAH 1

STARLING:
 G. W. 50

STEDMAN:
 ELISHA 67
 J. O. (REV.) 17
 MARY 20,67
 N. A. (JR.) 22,(JR.)32,
 (JR.) 42, (JR.) 52,(JR.) 72

STEPHEN:
 HANNAH 80
 JACOB 80

STEPHENS:
 DINNA 92
 MARGARET WHITE 16-A

STEWART:
 ANN 95
 CATHERINE 85
 CHARLES 85
 DUNCAN 85
 ELIZABETH 85
 HELEN 85
 HENRY 51
 HUGH (WILL OF) 85
 JAMES 85
 JANNETT 85
 JOHN (JR.) 65, (SR.) 65
 MARGARET 85
 PATRICK (WILL OF) 85
 ROBERT 7,85
 WALTER 85
 WILLIAM (WILL OF) 85

STINTON:
 STEPH'N. 35

STITH:
 ANNA GUION 10,37

STONE:
 BENJ'M. 28,(WILL OF) 85
 WILLIAM 85

STORM:
 JOHN 49,86
 MARGARET 86
 MARY (WILL OF) 86
 WANDAL (WILL OF) 86

STRAHAN:
 NOAH 40

STREATY:
 J. 33
 LUCY 56,80,91
 WILLIAM 56,80,91

STREETY:
 LUCY 22

STRONG:
 RETERON 34
 RETURN 41

STUART:
 HENRY MCK. 52

STUBBS:
 GEORGE (JR.) 86,(SR.WILL OF)
 86
 JOHN 3
 MARY 65
 RICHARD 54

SUGGS:
 ALLIGOOD 86
 ALLYON 86
 EZEKIEL 53
 LEWIS 53
 LILLY J. 86
 MCKOY 86

RAFORD 86
SARAH ANN 86
WILLIAM (WILL OF) 86

SUTTON:
ADDA 25
ANN 3,11,86,87
BAILEY 10
CATHERINE 87
CATHERINE ANN 86
CHRISTOPHER 86
ELIZABETH 48,86
FANNY 86
HOPER 87
JAMES 86,87,88
JANE 86
JOHN (WILL OF) 86,88
JOHN G. 42,84
LARRY 10
MARGARET (WILL OF) 86,88
M. G. 28
ROBIN 87
ROLEN 48
SALLY (JR.) 86
SARAH (SR.) WILL OF) 86,87
SARAH JANE 86
SUGAR 26
SUSANNAH 87
TOM 86
W. 48
WILLIAM 86,(WILL OF)87
WILLIAM T. 87
W. J. 10,20,27,31,32,37,39,
44,50,57,60,61

SWAIN:
JOHN 38

SWENDAL
SAMUEL 36

SWINDAL
CHESTER 87
DAVID 87
JOHN 87
OWEN 22
SAMUEL 87,(SR.) WILL OF 87

SWINDALL:
DAVID 45
ELIZA JANE 22
MARY 45

SWINDEL:
SAMUEL 87

SWINDELL:
HENRY 14

SYKES:
W. H. 25,45

TAIT:
GEORGE 12
GEORGE W. 56
ROBERT 56

TARBE:
JANE 87
PETER A. (WILL OF) 87
S. A. 87
TATOM: A. C. 87
A. G. 87
A. L. 34,87
CATHARINE 61
CHARLEY H. 87
DANIEL 88
DAVID A. 87
ELIZABETH 52,53
E. VANCE 87
G. W. 87
JESSE 64
J. H. 34
JOHN H. (WILL OF) 87
JOHN HENRY 88
JOHN W. 87
JOSHUA 52
J. L. 61
J. L. 61
J. S. 61
J. T. 87
LENSON 88
L. P. 87
M. N. 87
MARSHAL C. 87
N. McI. 61

M. W. (WILL OF) 87
N. McI. 69
O. J. 87
OLLEN 61
RICHARD W. 61
R. P. 87
SARAH J. 87
THEOPHILUS 38,(WILL OF) 88

TATUM:
R. W. 87

TAYLOR:
A. 22,58
ANGUS 88
CATHERINE 44,88
DANIEL 44,47,(WILL OF) 88
DAVID 43
DUNCAN 88
FLORA 88
FRANKLIN 26
JOHN (JR.) 44,64,(WILL OF) 88
LUCY ANN 43
MARY 19
MARY 75
SARAH 75

TEDDER:
GEORGE (WILL OF) 88
JESSE 88
MARY 88
SAMUEL 88
THOMAS 88
WILLIAM 88

THA ARD:
JAMES 40

THAGGARD:
A. J. 15
ELIZA JANE 88
HAZZLETINE J. 88
ISAAC (WILL OF) 88
LUCINDA L. 88
MELISSA 88
NANCY 88
SARAH ANN 88

SUSAN A. 33
WILLIAM C. 12,88

THAMES:
JOSEPH 68

THEMS:
THOMAS 5

THOMAS:
AMOS 7
ANN 88
CORNELIUS 7
DAVID 60
DAVID LLOYD 34
ELIZABETH 7
ELIZABETH ANN 34
ELIZABETH MARY 34
FRANCES 83,88
FRANCIS (WILL OF) 88
GEORGE 7,34,74,75,83(WILL OF) 88
JAMES 89
JAMES C. 15
JANE 89
JANE FLOYD 34
JESSE 88
JOAN 7
JOHN 7,39,57,75,(WILL OF) 88,95
JOHN D. 22,42,44
JON 75
JONATHAN 75,83,89
JOSEPH 7,59,(WILL OF) 88
MARGARET 39,74,75,83,88,95
MARTHA 7,88
MARY 57,88
MICHAEL (WILL OF) 89
MITCHELL 90
PHEBE 7
PRUDENCE 7
RICHARD 58
SAMUEL 7,88
SARAH (WILL OF) 89
SARAH I. 75
THOMAS (WILL OF) 7,88
WILLIAM 75,88

THOMPSON:
  BENJAMIN A. (WILL OF) 89
  CAROLINE 25
  FREDERICK 13
  HENRIETTA 89
  JEAN 90
  LEWIS (WILL OF) 89
  MARY ANN 89
  MARY JANE 89,93
  T. C. 93
  WILLIAM J. 89
  WILLIAM R. 89
  ZACHARIA G. 89

TOLAR:
  ISAIAH 20
  JAMES 72
  JULIA 72

TOMKINS:
  JONATHAN 41

TOOMER:
  ANTHONY 29
  HENRY 29
  JOHN 29
  JOHN D. 17

TOON:
  PRINCESS ANN 83
  WILLIAM 83

TOURNER:
  HENRY 35
  JOHN 35

TOWNSEND:
  LITTICE 51
  THOMAS 51

TREADWELL:
  CHARLES 89
  HENRY 89
  JOHN 89
  LOTTIE 89
  NETTIEFIELD 89
  RACHEL ANN (WILL OF) 89

TROY:
  A. A. 10
  ALEXANDER 89
  ALEXANDER A. 10
  ALEXANDER J. 89
  MARY 10,89
  MARY A. 34
  ROBT. E. 11,(WILL OF) 89
  SALLIE F. 34

TRYON:
  WM. 3,4,7

TURNER:
  AMEY (MRS.) 36
  ANNA 36
  BENJAMIN 79
  ELIZABETH 79
  JNO. 2,3
  SARAH 36,(WILL OF) 89
  THOMAS 36

TUCKER:
  ROBERT 54

TYLER:
  CHRISTIAN 7
  ELISABETH 7
  JOHN 64
  LUCRETIA 7
  MOSES (WILL OF) 7
  NEEDHAM 7
  OWEN 7
  PENELEBY 7
  SARAH 7

VAUGHN:
  S. G. 63

VERNON:
  ANNE (WILL OF) 90
  E. 8
  JOHN 91

VICKERS:
  JAMES J. 53

WADDELL:
  Ann 90
  H. 16
  Hannah 90
  Haynes 90
  Hu. 6
  Hugh (Sr.) 14,(will of)90
  Hugh Y. 14
  John 78
  John Burgwin 90
  Mary (will of) 90

WALKER:
  James 20
  Thos. 2

WALLACE:
  Jacob 15

WALLSON:
  Peter 5

WALTERS:
  Sam'l. 17

WAMAN:
  Thomas 8

WARD:
  Ellender 53
  James 18
  John 79
  John B. 42,78
  Ruth 42,43
  Tom 79

WASHBURN:
  James 84

WATSON:
  Ann 38
  Eliza 24
  Margaret 40
  William (will of) 90
  William J. 36
  William James 24

WATTERS:
  Sam'l. 7

WAYNE:
  Gabriel 2

WEATHERSBEE:
  Absolom 90
  Cade (will of) 53,90
  Elizabeth 90
  Isom 90
  Jane 90
  Olive 90
  Owen 90
  Shadrack 90

WEIR:
  George 26
  Margaret 26
  Robert 26

WELCH:
  Fannie Annis 24

WESSON:
  Henry 40

WEST:
  Annah 90
  Ann C. 13
  Catherine 41
  Hannah 90
  Hannah Jane 90
  James 90
  Molcy 42
  William (will of) 90

WESTBROOK:
  Lucy Ann 89
  Pertheny 89
  Sophronia 89
  W. 63
  William 89

WESTBROOKS:
  James (will of) 90
  Lucy Ann 90
  Perthaney 90

SEMPHANIE 90
SOPHRONIA 90
WILLIAM 90

WHITE:
  A. 66
  ANN 6,91
  ANNA 22,91
  ANN J. (WILL OF) 91
  ANN JOSE 91
  A. S. 66
  ARCHIBALD 32
  BENJAMIN RANDOLPH 33
  CAROLINE 36
  CATHERINE 91
  DANIEL 19
  DAVID 42,51,91
  DAVID L. 70
  DAVID JONES 91
  DAVID SINGLETARY 36
  DR. 91
  EDITH 69
  ELIZABETH 30
  G. J. 28
  GRIFFITH 91
  GRIFFITH J. 89
  GRIFFITH JONES 43
  HAYES GRAHAM 10
  HAYS G. 91
  HENRIETTA (WILL OF) 91
  JAMES 3,30,69,91
  JAMES B. 55
  JAMES BENBURY 10
  JANE 31
  JANNETTE 85
  JOHN 18,24,(SR.) 24,26,31,37,
  42,43,76,83,85,(WILL OF) 91
  JOSEPH (WILL OF) 91
  KEZIAH 32
  MARTHA 91
  MARY 19,30,38,42,43,46,91,92
  MATTHEW 91
  MATTHEW ROWN (WILL OF) 91
  NEPSEY W. 19
  REBECCA 91
  SARAH 91
  THOMAS 6,33,(WILL OF) 91
  W. H. 62,63

WILLIAM 24,30,46,91,(WILL OF)
92
WILLIAM H. 36

WHITEHEAD:
  HELEN M. 34

WHITTED:"
  AMELIA ANN 92
  ARCHA (WILL OF) 92
  CHARLOTTE 92
  EMELINE 62
  EMELETT 92
  EMELITT 70
  JAMES M. 92
  LINCOLN 92
  LIZZIE M. 59
  RUFUS 70,92
  THOMAS S. 92
  TIMON 92
  T. S.' 59,92
  WILLIAM 92
  W. N. (WILL OF) 92

WIER:
  THOMAS 5

WIGGINS:
  JESSE B. (WILL OF) 92
  LUCY 92
  MARY ELIZA 92

WILES:
  MARY 28

WILKESON:
  CHARITY 92
  CHARLES 92
  WILLIAM 90,(WILL OF) 92

WILKINGS:
  MARY 19
  WILLIAM 19

WILKINSON:
  ANN 70
  CHARITY 69
  H. K. 25

RICHARD 59
WILLIAM 69

WILKISON:
  ELIZABETH 8
  JOHN WILLIAM 8
  MARTHA 8
  MARY 8
  PHILLIP (WILL OF) 8
  RICHARD 8
  THOMAS 8

WILLIAM:
  A. B. 92

WILLIAMS:
  A. B. 57
  A. H. 59
  ALEXANDER 38
  C. W. 45,80
  DAVID JACKSON 38
  GEORGE MEARES (WILL OF) 92
  JAMES 40
  JULIA 51
  MARGARET 8,38,42,56
  OWEN W. 51
  RICHARD 38
  SARAH 24
  WILL 38
  WILLIAM 27,34,48

WILLIAMSON:
  ANN 11
  JOHN 8
  JOSHUA 92
  LEWIS (WILL OF) 92
  LOLAN 92
  MARY 75,92
  NANCY 92
  PEGGY 92
  RECECCAH 92
  RICHARD 92
  SETH 92
  SUSANNA 92

WILLIS:
  ALICE 93

AMELIA 93
ANN 92,93
ANNE 93
BENJAMIN 56
DANIEL 9,23,92,(WILL OF) 93
DAVID 31
DIANNA 93
ELIZABETH (BETTY) (WILL OF)
92,93
F. M. 50
GEORGE 2,(SR.) 20,21
J. 93
JACOB 92,93
J. D. 32
JEREMIAH 56
JOHN 84,92,(WILL OF) 93
JOHN S. 56
MARGARET A. 43
MARTHA 93
MARY 93
ROBERT (WILL OF) 93
SARAH 48,93
WILLIAM 55,56,93

WILLS:
  ARABELLA 85
  ROBERT 85

WILSON:
  ABSALOM (WILL OF) 93
  AMBROSE 93
  ANN 93
  DEBORAH 93
  ELIZABETH 93
  GANAH 93
  GEORGE 81,93
  J. 25
  JANE 82
  J. D. 32
  JOHN 75,93
  JOHN S. 81
  JOSEPH 12,(WILL OF) 93
  JOSIAH (WILL OF) 93
  MARY 93
  MARY ANN 93
  MARY COMFORT 32
  ROBERT 5

SARAH 93
WILLIAM 50

WINGATE:
  ANN (WILL OF) 93
  HANNAH 93
  JOHN 40,78,(WILL OF) 93
  SARAH 45

WINSLOW:
  EDWARD 91
  MARY 91

WINSOR:
  JOHN 74

WOOD:
  AMELIA 81
  JOSEPH 80,81
  LUCY 83
  SUSAN 81
  WILLIAM 81

WOODBURY:
  JOHN 66
  R. 66

WOODWARD:
  SAMUEL 1

WOODY:
  JOHN D. 92

WOOSTER:
  JOHN 17

WOOTEN:
  CHARLOTTE M. 94
  ELIZABETH 94
  ELIZABETH C. 94
  F. M. 51
  HENRIETTA T. 94
  JOHN A. (WILL OF) 94
  MARY 94
  RICHARD 78,93,94
  ROBERT 94
  SHADRACH (WILL OF) 94
  SHADRACK 94

WORTH:
  B. G. 50
  ELIZABETH 8
  JOHN (WILL OF) 8
  JOHN (OF N. J.) 8

WRIGHT:
  ANN 94
  ANNETTE 94
  C. G. 36
  CLEMENT G. 94
  ELIZABETH 55,94
  ELIZABETH R. 94
  IMOGENE 94
  ISHAM 95
  ISAAC 10,35,38,55,61,(WILL
    OF) 94
  I. W. 67
  J. A. 95
  JOHN 51
  JOSHUA GRANGER 30
  MARCHUS (WILL OF) 95
  MARGARET 70
  MATILDA AMELIA 94
  MERINDA 94
  SUSANNAH (MRS.) 30
  WILLIAM A. 14
  WILLIAM FULTON 94
  WILLIAM STEWART 85

YATES:
  JOHN 24

YEDDER:
  ELIZABETH 95
  GEORGE (SR. WILL OF) 95,95
  SAMUEL 95
  SARAH 95
  WILLIAM 95

YOUNG:
  ELANDER 21
  ELIZABETH 52
  JAMES B. 12,95
  JANE 95
  JOHN 33,95
  MATTHEW (WILL OF) 95

MELVINY 95
NATHAN (WILL OF) 95
ROBANE O. 95
ROBERT 52
SARAH 95
WILLIAM (WILL OF) 95
ZEBULA 95

YOUNGER:
  JOHN 16

(handwritten, top right) NEW FIELD Plantation IS 27 miles from Willington or CAPD FEAR RIVER. Sold to Waddell

(handwritten, bottom right) Boonesfield Possibly From Boone (DAN) NEWFIELD sold to Hugh Waddell

Possibly

Boonesfield Plantation - at Swamp Lakes
New Field Plantation - on Stewart Creek
Land Reigned Above Harriers, NC Towards Wallace

Skipper's Field - Fayetteville - on Stewart Creek

HELEN PENELOPE STEWART
B. March 4, 1771 NC
D. JAN 13, 1845 NC
D. WILLIAM & JANNETT. (McDOUGAS)
WIFE ENS Thomas Bell DEVANE III
MOTHER STEWARD DEVANE
STRETON DEVANE
MARY TORD DEVANE
Thomas DEVANE IV
WILLIAM KING DEVANE   6 OTHER

SISTER
        CATHERINE STEWART
        CHARLES STEWART
        JAMES McDOUGAS) STEWART
        COLS JUPERN STEWARD STEWART
            JARNETY S

        HALF SISTER
            ALEXANDER STEWART
            HUGH STEWART
            ROBERT STEWART
            CAPT PATRIC STEWART

FROM SPEED
        DUNCAN ADD
        WILLIAM, CATHERINE
        TIGRAL ADD
            ELIZA
            JAMES
            CHARLES

Stewart Key   79078B

Patrick Laird of Ledrick
with wife children + brother William
+ 5 other gentlemen from Argyll
+ over 300 immigrants came over 1739
+ settled at Browns Marsh Bladen Cty

Patrick was supporter of Prince
Charlie Stuart
Land sold estate to yoger Brother
about 1766 moved to Cheraws S.C.
+ died in 1779
      Patrick was son Alexander

Pat - Andrew Duncan John no Turner
who married Helen Campbell daughter
of Sir John Campbell.

Settled NC. Then moved to Dorchester
in 1723   And then to Liberty Co GA   SC
in 1752   Jenoshe died 1766
      John died 1785

John Stewart 1698 - Hanna
in 1730 John Stewart got land in GA
of 40 acres

James McDougal Stewart
1763 Bladen Co
1818 Woodville
Son William Stewart + Jannet McDougal
Husband Catherine Knowlan
Jane

Father
Nolan Stewart
William Stewart
James McDougal Stewart
Robin Stewart
2 other

Brother
Catherine Stewart
Charles
Duean
Jannette
Ann Carraway
Half Brother
Alexander
William
Hugh
Robert
Capt Pat Stewart

P. 85
Firmly established
William as
Father of Patrick
and other Brothers

Son of D
William T
Unknown Wife

Stewards of
York D SC
Came from
William
ca 1740
Also S. of
York Co SC
Co 1820 AC
1758

Balquidder Stewart arrived
from Albany Family

An Archibald Steward of Liberty Co GA
came to US ca 1740

William Stewart Edward Co St
                    m Elizabeth
was Planter Rowan Co
made will Apr. 2, 1781
        Salisbury
    Had William + Thomas

Mathew St Bose Co 1745 married Eliz

1682 · La Salle   Passed
    St. Francisville

PEE DEE River SKIPPER MOTTOWAY NELSHID

WACCAMAW

NW DROWNING CREEK

NW - BADEN LAKES SWAMP

WACA

Myrtle Beach. -WACCAM

IN 1830
LEROY
SARA~COUPER DUNCAN'S HOME FROM
KIAPEIS
ST FRANCISVILLE
1804 350 WENT
WAS PROMINENT

DUNCAN'S HOME
Holly Grove
WILKINSON Co MISS
Still There 2022

BAYOU SARA
Charles Stewart
got 1361
ACRES IP
1713 British
NUOE
Religious CHARLES STEWART
MAD MAGNOLIA PLANTATION
W. FLATCHOJANA
OVERSEER~CLAINED
SPANISH CONTROL CHARLES~DBQUINCY & DAVIS
1779

CPSIA information can be obtained
at www.ICGtesting.com
Printed in the USA
BVHW07s0255181018
530448BV00002B/438/P

9 780893 089405